D1756866

teach yourself...
Visual Basic 5

John Socha
Dan Rahmel
Devra Hall

teach yourself…
Visual Basic 5

John Socha
Dan Rahmel
Devra Hall

MIS:
PRESS

Henry Holt & Co., Inc. ■ New York

MIS:Press
A Subsidiary of Henry Holt and Company, Inc.
115 West 18th Street
New York, New York 10011
http://www.mispress.com

First Edition—1997

Library of Congress Cataloging-in-Publication Data

```
Socha, Jphn
      Teach tourself... Visual Basic 5 / John Socha, Dan Rahmel.
         p.   cm.
      ISBN 1-55828-547-4
      1. Microsoft Visual Basic.  2. BASIC (Computer program language).
I. Rahmel, Dan. II. Title.
QA76.73.B3S6352 1997
005.35'8--dc21                                            97-2629
                                                         CIP
```

MIS:Press and M&T Books are available at special discounts for bulk purchases for sales promotions, premiums, and fundraising. Special editions or book excerpts can also be created to specification.

For details contact: Special Sales Director
                         MIS:Press and M&T Books
                         Subsidiaries of Henry Holt and Company, Inc.
                         115 West 18th Street
                         New York, New York 10011

10 9 8 7 6 5 4 3 2 1

Associate Publisher: *Paul Farrell*

Managing Editor: *Shari Chappell*
Editor: *Michael Sprague*
Copy Editor: *Betsy Hardinger*

Production Editor: *Anthony Washington*
Copy Edit Manager: *Karen Tongish*

Contents-in-Brief

CHAPTER 1: STARTING WITH BASIC 1

CHAPTER 2: CREATING A SIMPLE PROGRAM 23

CHAPTER 3: LEARNING ABOUT VARIABLES, VALUES, AND
PROCEDURES 39

CHAPTER 4: LEARNING ABOUT OBJECTS 63

CHAPTER 5: BUILDING PROGRAMS 81

CHAPTER 6: ADDING A MENU BAR 105

CHAPTER 7: USING ARRAY VARIABLES TO SAVE LINES 125

CHAPTER 8: BUILDING A CLOCK CONTROL 159

CHAPTER 9: DESIGNING AND BUILDING PROGRAMS 199

CHAPTER 10: ACCESSING DATA: VISUAL DATA MANAGER 217

CHAPTER 11: BUILDING THE ADDRESS BOOK INTERFACE 233

CHAPTER 12: SEARCHING, PRINTING, AND SORTING 257

CHAPTER 13: ADDING THE CLOCK USER CONTROL 275

CHAPTER 14: USING COMMON CONTROLS 287

CHAPTER 15: OVERVIEW OF ADVANCED TECHNIQUES 309

CHAPTER 16: BUILDING AN ACTIVEX CONTROL 323

APPENDIX A: USING COMMERCIAL COMPONENTS 341

APPENDIX B: USING THE DEBUGGER .347

GLOSSARY 353

INDEX 365

Contents

CHAPTER 1: Starting with Basic 1

Starting Visual Basic 2

Exiting Visual Basic 3

What Is Programming? 4

    Using the Immediate (or Debug) Window 4

    Visual Basic's Modes 9

    The Print Command 9

    How Print Got Its Name 10

The Making of a Basic Command 11

    Arguments and Delimiters 12

    Why We Don't Program in English .13

    Language Syntax 14

    Doing Arithmetic 16

    Matching Parentheses 20

Related Tools 21

Summary 22

CHAPTER 2: CREATING A SIMPLE PROGRAM 23

Working with the Form Window 24
Visual Basic Programming Environment 24
Adding Four Command Buttons 26
Adding Event Code to the Buttons 32
Related Tools 37
Summary 38

**CHAPTER 3: LEARNING ABOUT VARIABLES, VALUES, AND
PROCEDURES** 39

What Are Variables? 40
   Equal is Not Equal—It's Assignment 42
   Where Are Variables Stored? 42
   Naming Variables 43
   Naming Variables 44
Values and Types 44
   Variables and Types 46
   More about Types and Numbers 49
   Floating-Point Numbers 49
   Bytes and Numbers 51
   Exploring the Limits on Numbers 51
   How Visual Basic Rounds Numbers 52
   Scientific Notation 54
Procedures: Subroutines and Functions 55
Related Tools 58
Summary 60

CHAPTER 4: LEARNING ABOUT OBJECTS 63

What Is an Object? 64
Methods and Properties 66
Understanding Class and Instances 68
   Creating an Instance 70
   Collections of Objects 73
Building a Program Using Objects 74

Information Hiding 75
Related Tools 77
Summary 78

CHAPTER 5: BUILDING PROGRAMS 81

Anatomy of an Event Handler 82
    A Look at Event-Driven Programs 84
Building a Sketch Program 85
    Create a New Project 86
    Choosing the Event 87
    Writing Event Code 88
    Clicking to Draw 90
    Saving Sketch 91
    Opening Your Sketch Project 95
The If..Then Command 95
    Boolean Expressions (Conditions) 96
Boolean Expressions 97
    The Else Part of If..Then 98
    Boolean Operators 99
    Finishing Sketch 101
Related Tools 103
Summary 103

CHAPTER 6: ADDING A MENU BAR 105

Building a Menu Bar 106
    Creating the Menu Title 107
How to Choose Mnemonic Characters 108
    Controls and Control Names 109
    Creating the Exit Item 109
    Adding Code to a Menu Item 111
    Adding the Erase Menu Item 112
Completing the Menu Bar 113
    Inserting Lines in Menus 113
    Adding Control Arrays 114

Changing the Line Width 115
Anatomy of an Argument 116
Checking Menu Items 117
Pop-Up Menus 120
Summary 123

CHAPTER 7: USING ARRAY VARIABLES TO SAVE LINES **125**

Designing a New Sketch 126
A Word About Variable Names 127
Array Variables 127
The As Keyword versus Type Characters 130
Defining Form Variables 130
A Word on Scope and Location of Variables 132
Saving Points in Sketch 133
Redrawing Forms 135
Redrawing Sketch's Lines 137
The For..Next Command 139
Why We Use the Variable i 140
Remembering Separate Lines 142
Remembering Line Widths 146
Printing a Drawing 147
Creating an EXE Program 150
The Final Sketch Program 151
Related Tools 154
Summary 156

CHAPTER 8: BUILDING A CLOCK CONTROL **159**

Designing Icon Clock 160
Working with Icons 167
Setting the Caption 168
Reading the Clock 168
Using Timers 169
Creating a Timer 169
Using the Toolbox to Create Objects 170
Setting the Timer 171

The Timer Interval 173
Showing the Time 174
   Using Time Functions 174
   Getting Information from Dates 177
Drawing the Clock Face 179
   Setting the Icon 179
Drawing the Clock Hands 180
   Showing One Second Hand 183
   Drawing with Color 184
   Using Xor to Erase a Line 185
Pseudocode: The Tool of Pros 191
   Drawing the Hour and Minute Hands 193
Related Tools 196
Summary 197

CHAPTER 9: DESIGNING AND BUILDING PROGRAMS **199**

How to Design Programs 200
   Detailed Specifications 201
   Programming as Evolution 201
   In-Between Approaches 202
   The Approach We'll Use 202
Designing the User Interface 202
   Copy Other Programs 203
   Be Consistent 204
   Keep the User Informed 205
   Consider Process Flow 205
   The Initial Design 207
   Writing a Feature List 207
   Drawing the Screens 210
Building Programs 211
   Alpha Testing and Beta Testing 211
The Origin of the Term Bug 212
   Add, Test, Redesign 213
   What Is Good Design? 213
Summary 215

CHAPTER 10: ACCESSING DATA: VISUAL DATA MANAGER 217

What is a Database 218
   Indexes 222
Planning Your Database 223
Using the Visual Data Manager 224
Adding an Index 228
Using the Visual Data Manager to Enter Data 229
Summary. 231

CHAPTER 11: BUILDING THE ADDRESS BOOK INTERFACE 233

Using the Data Form Designer 234
   How the Data Control Works 237
   What Are Data-Aware Controls? 239
   Modifying the Form 240
Bringing Address Book to Life 242
   Controlling the Tab Order 243
   Setting Up the Combo Boxes 244
   Initializing the cboType Combo Boxes 246
Creating the Menu Bar 249
   Adding Code to Menu Items 250
Cut, Copy, Paste, and Undo Code 252
Related Tools 253
Summary 254

CHAPTER 12: SEARCHING, PRINTING, AND SORTING 257

Searching 258
Sorting the Database 267
Printing Addresses 269
Summary 273

CHAPTER 13: ADDING THE CLOCK USER CONTROL 275

Set Up a Controls Folder 276
Modification of the Clock Control 277
Add Drag Support to the Clock Object 280
DragMode Property 281
Add Drop Support to the Notes Field 282
DragIcon Property 283
Summary 284

CHAPTER 14: USING COMMON CONTROLS 287

Using Intrinsic Controls 288
    Frames and Option Buttons 288
    DriveListBox, FileListBox, PathListBox and PictureBox Controls 290
Using the Common Dialog Control 291
Creating Bar Charts with the Chart Control 294
Accessing a Modem with the Comm Control 297
Using the Data Bound Grid Control 299
Using the FlexGrid Control 300
RichTextBox Control 302
Tabbed Dialog Control 303
Windows Common Controls 304
    Progress Bar 305
    TreeView Control 306
Summary 308

CHAPTER 15: OVERVIEW OF ADVANCED TECHNIQUES 309

Creating Installation Disks 310
Using OLE Automation 312
Custom Controls 316
DLLs and Windows Functions 316
    The Declare Statement 317
    Translating between Types in C and Visual Basic 318
Summary 320

CHAPTER 16: BUILDING AN ACTIVEX CONTROL 323

ActiveX and OLE Controls 324
Building an ActiveX Control 325
Using Microsoft Excel as a Container 328
  Placing the Control on the Sheet 328
  Using the Control from Code 331
ActiveX Controls and the Internet 335
ActiveX Support in Browsers 336
  Creating a CAB File 337
Related Tools 339
Summary 340

APPENDIX A: USING COMMERCIAL COMPONENTS 341

APPENDIX B: USING THE DEBUGGER .347

GLOSSARY 353

INDEX 365

CHAPTER 1

Starting with Basic

- Introducing Visual Basic
- Using the Immediate window
- Learning simple Basic commands: Beep, End, and Print
- The basics of command syntax
- Computer arithmetic and precedence

In this chapter, we'll get off to a quick start. After we cover some introductory material to make sure we're all starting in the same place, we'll get straight to the business of learning about programming.

Our first journey into programming will be relatively easy, and you won't need to learn very much before you write some short Basic programs. Each program will be one line long, and you'll be able to run these programs directly from within Visual Basic to see what they do. You'll be surprised at how much fun learning Basic can be.

1

First, though, we need to cover a few preliminaries.

STARTING VISUAL BASIC

The first step is to make sure that you've installed Visual Basic. If you haven't already done so you'll find help and installation instructions in Microsoft's Visual Basic manual. Return here when you're finished.

At this point you should have a program group called Microsoft Visual Basic, which is created by the Setup program. If you open the Start menu to the Visual Basic 5.0 program group, it should look something like the one in Figure 1.1.

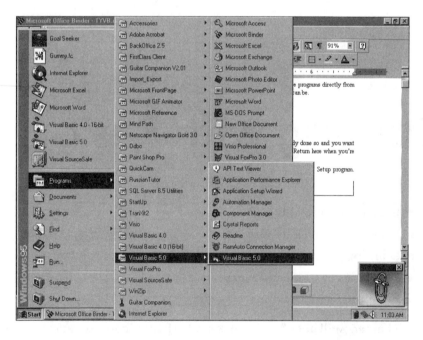

Figure 1.1 *After installing Visual Basic, you should have a program group that contains the Visual Basic icon.*

Notice the small clock icon at the lower right of the screen. This small program displays the current time. You'll learn how to write your own clock program completely in Visual Basic, and you'll find the entire program later in this book.

N O T E

Click on the **Visual Basic 5.0** icon to run the development environment. Once Visual Basic has loaded, a window will be displayed. This window, shown in Figure 1.2, allows you to open an existing programming project or begin a new one. Visual Basic automatically selects the option **Standard EXE** (which is the option we want). Simply click the **Open** button to accept this selection.

Now the screen will show a small window labeled **Form1**. Several types of windows are available in Visual Basic, but the most common type you'll use is known as a *form*. In Chapter 2, you will draw buttons and other items on this form for use in a program. For now, we'll use Visual Basic to type in simple commands.

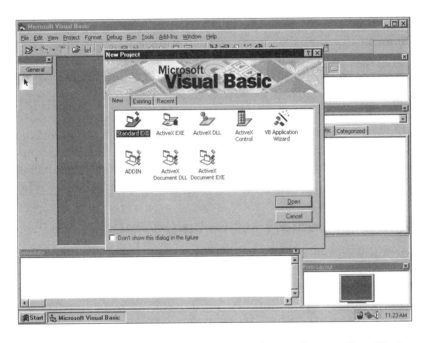

Figure 1.2 You should see a screen like this one when you first start Visual Basic.

Exiting Visual Basic

If you've used other Windows programs, you probably already know how to exit from Visual Basic. In case you're new to Windows, here's how: pull down the File menu (or press **Alt+F**) and select the **Exit** item (or press the **X** key).

What Is Programming?

In the next few chapters, you'll learn that programming in Visual Basic consists of writing instructions that tell Visual Basic the steps you want it to perform. Programmers tend to use several terms for such instructions: *statements*, *instructions*, *commands*, and *code* are the most common. In this chapter, we'll usually refer to them as *commands*.

You'll also see the term *programming language*. There are a number of programming languages, including Basic, C, Pascal, and Assembly Language—that you can use to write programs. In a sense, these languages are like different spoken languages, because each one has its own grammar and set of words. Each language has its strengths and weaknesses. Many professional programmers (including the ones at Microsoft) write their programs using the C language because of its power and flexibility. C, however, tends to be difficult to learn, and writing Windows programs in C takes a lot of work. Of all the programming languages we've worked with, Visual Basic is the easiest to learn and use.

In this chapter, you'll learn about three commands in the Basic language by using the Immediate window in Visual Basic. This window lets you enter commands and run them right away. *Running* a command simply means that you tell Visual Basic to actually perform the steps you've asked it to follow.

Using the Immediate (or Debug) Window

The window we'll use for the rest of this chapter is the Immediate window (also known as the Debug window). Within this window you'll write one-line programs. It's called the Immediate window because it allows you to type in commands (parts of a program) that Visual Basic will run immediately. If this doesn't make sense, don't worry; it will become clear after a couple of examples.

Showing the Debug Window

Let's first learn how to access the Immediate window. Follow these steps:

1. The Immediate window is available for use whenever a project is open. Because you have already clicked the **Open** button when Visual Basic first executed, the Immediate window should be showing at the bottom of your screen.

2. You can also access the Immediate window while Visual Basic is running your program. Press **F5**, or pull down the Run menu and select **Start**. This action tells Visual Basic to switch from Design mode, which you'll use later to design programs, to run mode, which you use to run programs.

3. Press **Ctrl+Break** or pull down the Run menu and select **Break**. This tells Visual Basic to switch to Break mode, brings the Debug window to the front, and makes it the active window.

You should now see an Immediate window like the one shown in Figure 1.3.

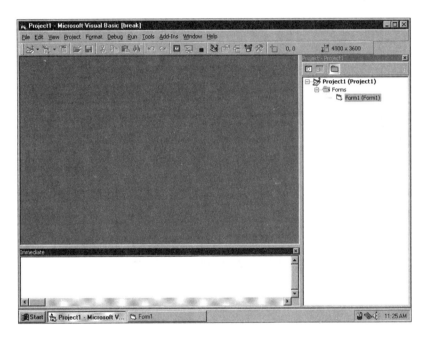

Figure 1.3 *The Debug window. The blinking insertion point in the upper-left corner shows where text will appear as you type.*

You can also select the **Immediate window** option from the View menu or press **Ctrl+G**. The difference between this method and pressing **F5** or selecting **Start** from the Run menu is that this way you remain in Design mode. When you want to set breakpoints to test code in the **Immediate window** or to view output that you directed to the Immediate window after your program finishes executing, you'll find the View menu option approach useful.

Typing in the Immediate Window

The Immediate window is like a text editor; characters appear as you type, and you can use the mouse to select and edit what you've typed. But the Immediate window differs from a text editor in one important way: when you press **Enter**, the Immediate window does more than just move the insertion point to the next line; it also tries to run what you've typed.

To understand this more clearly, let's enter a simple Basic command called **Beep**, which emits a sound from your computer. Try entering this command now. Simply type **beep** and press **Enter** (see Figure 1.4). The insertion point moves to the next line, and your computer makes a sound.

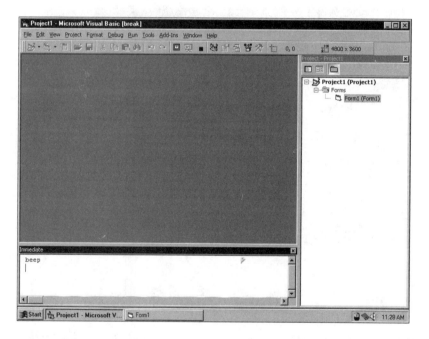

Figure 1.4 *The Immediate window after entering the Beep command, which tells Visual Basic to generate a beep sound.*

It was a number of years ago, but we can recall being excited the first time we were able to enter a command like this. There's something electrifying about typing a word on your computer and having it respond with an action. Programming, after you get the hang of it, can be addictive.

Beep Command
The Beep command tells Visual Basic to emit a sound from its speaker.

REFERENCE

You'll be use the Immediate window often to test new commands, so let's spend a few minutes exploring other aspects of it. First, press the **Backspace** key. This action causes the insertion point to move back to the previous line. If you press **Backspace** again, you'll delete the letter **p** at the end of **beep**. Type **p** again and then press **Enter**. Visual Basic beeps again.

You could also enter the letter **p** as a capital **P** without any change in the results. Commands can be typed in either uppercase or lowercase, as can variables, function names, and other content. The Visual Basic ignores the case of typed commands and is therefore known as a *case-insensitive* programming language.

Now let's explore further. Click the left mouse button between the two **e**'s so that the insertion point looks like the following:

be | ep

Press **Enter**. Instead of moving **ep** to the next line as you might expect, Visual Basic again emits a beep sound. In other words, pressing **Enter** in the Immediate window tells Visual Basic to run the command on the line that contains the insertion point.

You can also edit previous commands. Let's say you made a mistake when typing the **Beep** command, typing **Beaep** instead of **Beep**. When you press **Enter**, Visual Basic displays an alert box, as shown in Figure 1.5. At this point, the message probably seems mysterious, but it isn't. In essence, it means that Visual Basic couldn't find a command having the name you typed.

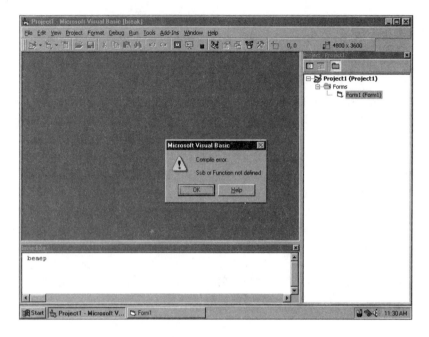

*Figure 1.5 You'll see this alert box if you mistype a command, such as typing **Beaep** instead of **Beep**. Basically, it means, "Huh?"*

You can press **Enter** or click **OK** to dismiss this alert box. Then you can edit the flawed command using the mouse or the keyboard. When you're finished making corrections, press **Enter** to run the corrected command.

Leaving Run Mode

The next command you'll learn, **End**, tells Visual Basic to stop running a program. In other words, **End** tells Visual Basic to switch from Run mode to Design mode.

End Command
The **End** command tells Visual Basic that you're finished running your program. Visual Basic returns to Design mode when it executes this command.

REFERENCE

Try entering this command now. Type **End** in the Immediate window and press **Enter**. Visual Basic will return to Design mode. By the way, you can tell which mode you're currently in by looking at the top of the screen. When you're in Design mode, the top line will look like this:

```
Project1 - Microsoft Visual Basic [design] - [Project1 -
Form1(Form)]
```

The word in square brackets—[design] in this case—indicates which mode is currently active. If you enter Run mode again (press **F5**), you'll notice that the mode changes to [run]; and when you press **Ctrl+Break** to access the Immediate window, it switches to [break]. We'll discuss these three modes when you graduate from the Immediate window.

Visual Basic's Modes

Visual Basic has three modes, and you'll work with all three in this book. You can tell which mode is active by looking at the word in square brackets at the top of the screen: Microsoft Visual Basic [design].

Visual Basic's Modes

MODE	WHEN IT'S USED
[design]	When you're designing programs
[run]	When Visual Basic runs the current program
[break]	While the program is stopped, allowing you to use the Immediate window.

You can use the pull-down menus, rather than the **End** command, to exit from programs: pull down the Run menu and select **End**.

You've now learned almost everything there is to know about two simple Basic commands: **Beep** and **End**. In the next section, we'll discuss an interesting command that can do a number of things. You'll use it quite a bit in your explorations of the Basic language as well as in programs that you write.

The Print Command

In this section, you'll learn about the **Print** command, which you'll use to explore how Basic handles arithmetic.

How Print Got Its Name

The name **Print** is a little misleading. Most people think of printing as the act of sending output to a printer. The **Print** command, on the other hand, sends output to the screen. Why is it called **Print** and not **Display**? The reasons lie in the history of the Basic language.

Basic was created by two professors—John G. Kemeny and Thomas E. Kurtz—at Dartmouth College between 1963 and 1964. At that time, people worked with large mainframe computers; personal computers had not yet been invented. Mainframe computers filled large, air-conditioned rooms with very expensive equipment. To communicate with such computers, you used a teletype. Whenever a program sent output to the user, it was printed on paper, rather than displayed on a screen. That's why Kemeny and Kurtz chose the name **Print** for this command.

The name Basic is an acronym (it stands for Beginner's All-purpose Symbolic Instruction Code) and usually is written in all uppercase letters: BASIC. In Visual Basic, however, Microsoft chose to change the spelling to mixed case.

Let's begin by using **Print** to display a number. If you type **Print 10** and then press Enter, you'll see the following:

```
print 10
  10
|
```

Notice that 10 appears after you press **Enter**, and then the insertion point moves down another line.

Now try something a little more involved: adding two numbers. Type **Print 11+23** and press **Enter**. Notice that **Print** does the arithmetic for you and "prints" the answer:

```
print 11+23
  34
|
```

THE MAKING OF A BASIC COMMAND

So far, you've been working with simple Basic commands. **Beep** and **End** are the simplest commands you can type: they're only one word long. In a sense, these commands are like one-word sentences in the English language—for example, "Run!"

But one-word sentences don't convey much meaning. To communicate effectively with your computer, you need to build longer sentences, and you need rules telling you how to combine words. For programming languages, such rules make up what is called *syntax* and describe how to combine various elements to form a command.

Any command you write must have at least one word, which is called the *keyword*. Keywords are the names given to commands, such as **Beep**, **End**, and **Print** (you'll learn other keywords as well). The commands tell the computer to perform an action and are roughly equivalent to a verb in a natural language.

Commands can also include additional information, such as the equations you asked **Print** to calculate and display. These equations are one type of *argument*. The syntax rules spell out how to combine keywords and arguments. For **Print**, there is a syntax rule that says the keyword must appear first, followed by arguments. The following is correct:

```
print 10+2
```

The following is incorrect:

```
10+2 print
```

Another syntax rule says that you can display the results of several equations using one **Print** command. You do this by typing a space between each of the arguments (equations) as follows:

```
print 10+2 3
   12 3
|
```

Arguments and Delimiters

Whenever you have more than one argument (as in the preceding example), you need to separate the arguments so that Visual Basic will know where one argument ends and the next one begins.

Visual Basic has definite rules about which characters you can use to separate arguments. In the **Print** example, we used a space, but you can also use a comma or a semicolon in a **Print** command. Characters that are used to separate arguments, have a special name: *delimiters*. They delimit, or set the boundaries, between arguments next to each other.

The following is a list of the delimiters that you can use in the Print command (other commands use other delimiters):

DELIMITER	WHAT IT DOES IN PRINT
Semicolon (;)	Displays one value after the other, with no gap between them. **Print** always puts a space in front of positive numbers and a minus sign (without a space) in front of negative numbers.
Space	Same as a semicolon. Actually, Visual Basic converts a space internally to a semicolon.
Comma (,)	Moves to the next tab stop before displaying the next value.

You can also place a comma between the 10+2 and the 3 to tell **Print** to move over to the next tab stop after it displays the first result:

```
print 10+2, 3
  12       3
|
```

There is one major difference between English grammar and Basic syntax: unlike English, the meanings expressed in a Basic statement are severely limited. A given Basic command has one, and only one, meaning. (A single English sentence can have many meanings. That allows us to write poetry but would make it difficult for a computer to interpret what we want.) In addition, each Basic command has its own syntax rules.

Why We Don't Program in English

Have you ever wondered why you have to learn a programming language such as Basic rather than write your programs in English? It's because computers are stupid, and they can't understand the subtleties of English. Computers can perform amazing feats of computation, but they have no idea what they're doing or what it means.

The English language is often ambiguous, and some sentences can have a number of meanings. Even we humans don't always understand a sentence correctly. So computer scientists created programming languages in which each "sentence" has one, and only one, meaning. You might not understand Basic's rules and you may write the wrong sentence, but that is another issue.

Let's use the **Print** command again to make this clear. Like an English textbook, the Visual Basic manuals contain syntax examples of how a command is used. The syntax for **Print** command looks like this:

Print *expression* [{;|,| } *expression*] ...

This means that you can display the results of one or more equations, which are called *expressions* in computer jargon. When you have more than one expression, you separate them with a semicolon, a comma, or a space. You saw how this worked in the previous two examples.

Now let's look at how to read the syntax examples in this book. First, you'll notice that the **Print** command appears in boldface type. Anything you see in boldface, such as **Print**, is a keyword. You type it in as you see it.

Words that appear in italics, such as *expression*, are placeholders for other pieces of information. In this case, you supply an expression, which can be a number, an equation, or a string of characters that you want **Print** to display. (We haven't covered this yet.)

Notice that syntax descriptions often include special characters. The square brackets—[and], for example—indicate the parts of the arguments that are optional. So the second expression here is optional. The braces—{ and }—and vertical bar—|—are used to show choices. When you see something like {;|,| }, it means that you must choose one of the options separated by the vertical bars. So in the {;|,| } notation, your options are a semicolon, a comma, or a space. In other words, you must use one of these three characters between expressions in the **Print** command. Finally, the ellipsis,—…—indicates that you can repeat this process; in other words, you can have one, two, three, or more expressions in one **Print** command.

Language Syntax

Let's summarize our conventions for displaying Basic syntax expressions:

```
print expression [{;|,| } expression] ...
```

The following table lists the different parts of a syntax description.

Elements of Syntax

ELEMENT	MEANING
Command	Words in bold are words that you type as you see them. These are the keywords that exist in the language, such as **Print**.
Expression	Italic type indicates additional information you need to supply to the command. For example, you might substitute 3+4 for *expression* in the **Print** command.
[something]	Anything you see in square brackets is optional. You don't type the brackets; they indicate only that what appears inside them is optional.
{a|b}	The braces indicate that you must choose from one of the options separated by the vertical bar, I. You must choose only one of these options. In this example, you must choose either a or b. In the **Print** command, the braces indicate that you must choose a semicolon, a comma, or a space.
…	An ellipsis indicates that you can repeat an element. In the **Print** command, this means that you can combine any number of expressions in one **Print** command.

What's the difference between an argument and an expression? The answer is subtle. An expression is a value or equation by itself. In other words, 10+2 and 3 are both expressions. An argument, on the other hand, is a value used in a command to supply information to that command (see Figure 1.6). This means that an expression used in a **Print** command is also an argument to the **Print** command. It's a little confusing now, but you'll get the hang of it after a few more chapters.

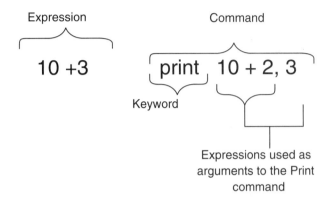

Figure 1.6 An example of an expression, showing the parts of a Basic command.

REFERENCE

Print Command

The **Print** command displays numbers and strings of characters (more on this later) on the screen. In this chapter, you're using **Print** only within the Immediate window, but you'll use it in other windows later in the book. **Print** can display multiple expressions. If you have more than one expression, separate them with spaces, semicolons, or commas. (Commas tell **Print** to move to the next column before printing the next expression; spaces or semicolons tell Print not to move before printing the next expression.) Without any parameters, Print displays a blank line.

```
print
```

Here the Print command is usually followed by an expression.

```
print expression
```

Doing Arithmetic

In addition to adding numbers, you can subtract, multiply, and divide them. Table 1.1 shows a list of *arithmetic operators*, which are symbols, such as + that you use between numbers.

Table 1.1 Visual Basic's Arithmetic Operators

SYMBOL	MEANING	EXAMPLE	RESULT
+	Addition	10+3	13
–	Subtraction	10–3	7
*	Multiplication	10*3	30
/	Division	10/3	3.333333
\	Integer Division	10\3	3
^	Exponentiation	10^3	1000
Mod	Remainder (modulo)	10 mod 3	1

You can also put a minus sign in front of a number to type a negative number, for example, –23.

Some of the operators in Table 1.1 may be new to you or a little different from what you're used to. As you learn to write software applications, you'll find that arithmetic is an important aspect of programming. Let's spend a few minutes going through each of these operators so that you understand what they do and how to use them.

The Calculator Functions

Most simple electronic calculators provide four functions—addition, subtraction, multiplication, and division—so you're probably used to the +, –, *, and / symbols. The only difference from what you might be used to is the multiplication symbol. People (especially scientists) use one of the following forms to indicate multiplication:

```
2 x 3

2 · 3

2 3
```

None of these forms works in Basic; you must use the form 2*3. And the same thing applies for division. You can't use 2 ÷ 3; instead, you must type **2 / 3**.

Quotient and Remainder

Two of the operators,—\ and Mod—provide functions that you may not have thought about since grade school, so we'll review them. When you first learned division, you learned that 7 / 3 = 2 with a remainder of 1. In other words, you can divide 3 into 7 evenly only two times, with 1 left over. Expressed to a higher degree of precision, 7 / 3 = 2.333333, which is the result **Print** display:

```
print 7/3
  2.333333
|
```

But what if you want to get only the whole part of this division? Or what if you want only the remainder? Basic has two operators designed to return exactly these two parts.

The first operator, \, is called the *integer division operator*. The result returned will always be a whole number (1, 2, 3, ...) rather than a fractional or mixed number (2.3). Such whole numbers are called integers. In other words, \ produces an integer that is the whole part of the division:

```
print 7 \ 3
  2
|
```

(By the way, you can put spaces between the numbers and operators, as we've done in this example. Sometimes such spaces make it easier to read a complex equation.)

The Mod operator calculates only the remainder of a division. For example, if you want to display the remainder of 7 / 3, type the following:

```
print 7 mod 3
  1
```

That's all there is to it. The Mod operator gets its name from the mathematical operation *modulo*, which calculates the remainder of a division.

Now, just for the fun of it, we'll show you something a little ahead of time: **Print** can display more than one result at a time, and it can show strings of characters enclosed by double quotation marks as follows:

```
print 7 \ 3 "remainder" 7 mod 3
   2 remainder 1
|
```

We've discussed all the operators in Table 1.1 except the exponential operator. Let's look at it next.

Exponentiation

You may not use the exponentiation operator very often. Nevertheless, because programmers sometimes use it, a brief explanation is in order—at least you'll recognize it when you're reading someone else's program. When you were learning about powers in algebra class, you probably saw something like this:

```
10 2
```

This means 10 to the second power, or 10 * 10. This is written in Basic as 10^2, as you can see in the following example:

```
print 10^2
   100
|
```

Now that you've learned about the arithmetic operators, we'll turn to two related issues: operator precedence and parentheses. These aren't the most scintillating topics, but a little information will go a long way toward saving time when your program crashes and you can't figure out why.

Complex Equations

The next concept will probably take a little time to get used to. It's an important subject, because almost all programs deal with equations of one type or another. You can use several operators in a simple expression to create a complex equation.

If you use more than one operator in a single equation, it's not always obvious how Basic will handle the calculation. For example, if you have an equation that uses both addition and multiplication, such as 3+4*5, you conventionally multiply (4*5=20) before you add (3+20=23):

```
print 3 + 4 * 5
  23
|
```

But what happens when you mix the integer division operator, \ , with multiplication?

Most programming languages use a concept known as *precedence* to determine the order in which operations are performed. Operations with higher precedence, such as multiplication in the previous example, are calculated before operations with lower precedence, such as addition. Table 1.2 shows the arithmetic operators from Table 1.1, grouped by precedence. The most important (highest precedence) operators are at the top of the table.

Table 1.2 Operator Precedence

OPERATOR	MEANING
^	Exponentiation (to the power of)
–	Minus (negative) sign
*, /	Multiplication, division
\	Integer division
Mod	Remainder
+, –	Addition, subtraction

Rules:

1. **Highest precedence first.** Basic first calculates operators that appear higher in this table (such as 4*5 in 3+4*5).

2. **Left to right, same precedence.** If two operators are at the same level (such as * and /), Basic starts with the left-most operator, then moves to the right (such as calculate 2+3 first in 2+3+4).

3. **Parentheses.** You can override these rules using parentheses, such as (3+4)*5 to force Basic to calculate 3+4 and then multiply by 5.

These rules take a little time to get used to, and you can often make a mistake. For example, you might expect the integer division operator \ to be on equal footing with normal division and expect the result of 3\2*2 to be 2. But as you can see from Table 1.2, this isn't the case. In fact, multiplication has the same precedence as regular division but a higher precedence than integer division. So Basic calculates 2*2 before doing the integer division.

We've made this mistake, and if you don't think to look for it, it can take a long time to find the error. If you're in doubt about the order Basic will use in such a calculation, use parentheses to tell Basic how to calculate the result. Instead of writing 3\2*2, you would write (3\2)*2.

If you have a highly complex equation, you might wish to use more than one set of parentheses: 1/((3+4)*(2+5)). That is the same as the following:

$$\frac{1}{(3+4) \times (2+5)}$$

As you can see, using many parentheses can become complicated, and you need to make sure you put them in the right place.

Matching Parentheses

Some equations have many parentheses. How can you make sure you have the correct number of left and right parentheses?

The pros use a method called counting parentheses. You go through the equation counting parentheses in a special way. Each time you see a left parenthesis—(—you count up. Each time you see a right parenthesis,), you count down. If you start with 1 for the first left parenthesis, you should end up with a count of zero. If you don't, you're missing a parenthesis. If it's 1, you need another right parenthesis. If it's –1, you need another left parenthesis.

Let's look at an example that is incorrect. If you count parentheses on the following equation, you won't end with a count of zero:

1/((3+4)*(2+5)

The count will be 1, 2, 1, 2, 1. The final 1 means you're missing a right parenthesis.

One final note before we close this chapter. You might have noticed in Table 1.2 that there are two – signs: one for subtraction and one for a negative sign. The negative sign is a little different, because the other operators work with two expressions, such as 3+4. The negative sign, on the other hand, modifies just one expression: –(2+3) returns the result –5. You can also write something like 3+–2, which means 3+(–2) and equals 1.

RELATED TOOLS

Visual Basic is a rich language, and we won't cover every aspect of it in this book. To help you explore Visual Basic on your own, you'll find a section called "Related Tools" at the end of each chapter. In this section, you'll find a list of commands and features related to the ones you learned about in the chapter. You might find some of these commands of interest, and you can explore them on your own.

We should warn you, however, that sometimes—especially early in the book—these related tools will use knowledge you don't yet have. So if you don't understand this section now, you will later, after you've read more of the book. Here are the related tools for this chapter:

- Tab stops. In this chapter, you briefly used the comma to display two numbers in different columns. You can instead use the **Tab** function to control which column Visual Basic moves to between items displayed on a line. For example, `print 1 tab(15) 2 tab(30) 3` displays a 2 in column 15 and a 3 in column 30, That produces a display very much like what you get with `print 1,2,3`.

- Format command. You use this command if you want more control over number formatting than you get with **Print**. For example, if you're displaying money information, you might want to display the number 2.3 as $2.30 (with a dollar sign and two decimal places). **Format$** will do that for you, and much more. Right now **Format$** is an advanced command. But by Chapter 8, where you'll use **Format$** to display time information, you'll know enough to use it yourself.

■ Exp:e to the x power. This is a rather advanced function related to exponentiation. People working in the sciences often need to calculate powers of the constant e (which is related to natural logarithms). You can calculate e^2 by writing **Exp(2)**. There are many similar functions you might find useful, such as **Log** and **Sqr** (square root).

SUMMARY

We've covered a lot of introductory material in this chapter, and we've learned three Basic commands. Here's a summary of what you've learned so far:

■ Starting Visual Basic. You learned how to start and exit Visual Basic.

■ Immediate window. The Immediate window is a window you'll use often in the next few chapters to learn about new Basic commands.

■ The **Beep** and **End** commands. These two commands are simple. **Beep** emits a sound from your computer; **End** tells Visual Basic to exit run mode and return to Design mode.

■ Arithmetic and the **Print** command. You used **Print** command to learn about Basic's arithmetic operators and took a quick look at how to send text strings to your screen.

■ Precedence. You learned about the precedence of operators, which determines in what order Basic will calculate expressions in a complex equation.

In Chapter 2, you'll learn about forms (which are a type of window), projects, and controls.

CHAPTER 2

Creating a Simple Program

- Creating a new form
- Adding the buttons to the form
- Running the program
- Adding code to each button
- Saving the project

You created a few single-line programs in Chapter 1. Congratulations! Next, you'll create an entire program that includes a window and some buttons. Don't worry if you don't understand the code yet. Getting started is the hardest part. Having finished Chapter 1, you have already begun.

The simple program we will construct in this chapter will demonstrate all the steps required to create a working Visual Basic application. This application will also provide a foundation to which you can add more buttons and test functions. As you build this application, you will use several simple functions (such as one that changes the window color) and see how the different pieces of a complete application fit together.

You may have heard the terms *application* and *program* used interchangeably. *Program* typically refers to the commands that execute to complete a particular task. *Application* refers to the complete solution experienced by someone running the program. This solution includes the code, the windows, the controls, and all the other components. The distinction is subtle and in this book the two terms have the same meaning.

Working with the Form Window

In Chapter 1, when you initially started Visual Basic you clicked the **Open** button to create a standard **EXE**. An **EXE** is a program that can be run on any computer and is referred to as a *stand-alone application*. Programs such as Microsoft Word and Lotus 1-2-3 are examples of standard **EXE**s. A complete **EXE** stands in contrast to the miniature programs you typed into the Immediate window in Chapter 1. To run these single-line programs, you must have Visual Basic installed on each machine that needs to execute them. An **EXE** can be run without the Visual Basic Programming Environment and therefore can be used by anyone.

Visual Basic Programming Environment

The Immediate window that you have been working in so far is one part of what is known as the Visual Basic Programming Environment, which contains the menus, windows, palettes, and toolboxes used to create a Visual Basic application. The term *programming environment* usually refers to the Design mode, in which the program can be changed and augmented.

The programming environment is shed when you create an **EXE** application. You develop the application within the programming environment. When it is finished, you tell the environment to create an **EXE** that can be distributed. The **EXE** cannot be examined or modified. For example, you could not reprogram Microsoft Word and add your own features. Similarly, no one will be able to modify your final **EXE**.

When you click the **Open** button in the first window, a new project is created. A *project* is like a container that holds all the elements of an application—the Form windows, the programs, the commands, the components, and all the other parts. We won't actively modify the project in this chapter except to save it and the window that we will create.

In Figure 2.1, the Project window is on the right side of the screen. The project that is automatically created is called **Project1**. It has a folder labeled **Forms** that shows all the Form windows that are stored in the project. The Forms folder contains only one form, which is named **Form1**. This is the form we will use in this chapter to create our application.

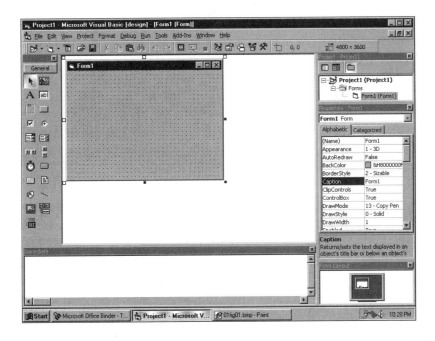

Figure 2.1 Form1 surrounded by a number of palette windows, including the Project window.

Form1 is the blank Form window created when a new project is started. Each standard **EXE** project must have at least one form window. As shown in Figure 2.1, the form design window is shown almost in the middle of the screen and is surrounded by the various palette windows. The form is the central construct within Visual Basic. A form is a window that you place user interface elements (known as *controls*) and add your programming code.

On each form, you can add *controls*, which include buttons, list boxes, combo boxes, and other user interface items. In Figure 2.1, to the left of **Form1** is a window with a number of icons (the box above the icons is labeled **General**). This is the control toolbox. It contains all the controls you can use on a form within a particular project. In the figure, 21 controls are displayed and the title is **General**. These general controls are automatically added to a project when it is created.

Each control has two primary parts: event code and properties. *Event code* executes when a particular event occurs (such as a user click). *Properties* are values that give the control its appearance and basic identity (such as the Font property, which governs the font of a button title). In building this application, you will add controls to a form and then modify the controls' properties and add event code.

All this new vocabulary may be challenging, but to create an application, you start at the top and work down. A project is created to hold all your forms. Each form can contain one or more controls. Each control has events to which it reacts and properties that govern its appearance and behavior. When you create a new **EXE**, a blank project (Project1) and blank form (Form1) are automatically created for you. You simply add the controls and the program code to create your application, as we will do now.

ADDING FOUR COMMAND BUTTONS

Now that we have covered the basic concepts of an application's structure, you will put them into action. We will begin constructing the application by adding four command buttons to the form. A *command button* is simply a button that can be clicked on to activate a function. Each of our four buttons will execute a separate action.

To add the command buttons to the form, we must select the proper control from the toolbox. If you have ever used a drawing program such as Paint (included in the Accessories program group with Windows 95), you will find that drawing controls on a form is very similar. First, you must select the correct tool from the toolbox. Click on the command button tool shown in Figure 2.2. The command button is now selected, so if you move the mouse over the form, the shape of the cursor (normally an arrow) will turn into a crosshair.

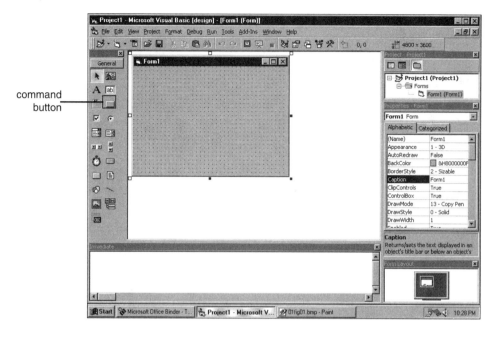

command
button

Figure 2.2 *The toolbox contains numerous controls. Select the command button tool to create buttons on the form.*

Now move the cursor onto the form and put it near the top left corner. To create a button, click and hold down the mouse button and drag down and to the right. As you drag the mouse, a shimmering outline should appear on the form. This outline defines the size of the control that you are placing on the form.

When the outline shown is about 3 inches wide and half an inch tall, release the mouse button. Your first button should appear on the form. It should be labeled **Command1**. After you draw each control, the control just created on the form is selected, and the cursor automatically returns to the arrow shape. If you want to draw another control, you must reselect the necessary control from the toolbox.

We want to construct four controls, so we need to select the control again. Click on the command button control in the toolbox and draw another button just below the first one. Repeat these steps until you have created all four buttons on your form. Your form should now look like the one shown in Figure 2.3.

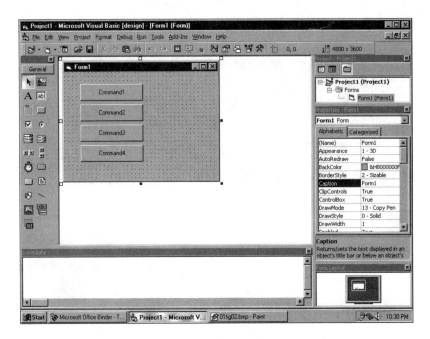

Figure 2.3 *Form1 should now contain four command buttons.*

Now we have the command buttons on the form, but their names (**Command1–Command4**) are not very descriptive. Remember when we said that each control has events and properties associated with it. The label shown on a command button is one of its properties. The property that contains the command button's title is called the Caption property.

If you didn't click on anything after you created the last command button, it should still be selected (you'll see eight squares, called *handles*, surrounding the selected control). On the right side of the screen is a window labeled **Properties - Command4**. Figure 2.4 shows this Properties window. All the properties used by this control are shown in this window. If you were to select a different control, different properties would be shown (although many controls have the same property types, such as the Name property). In this list, the property type is shown on the left and the value stored in it is shown on the right. For example, in Figure 2.4 you can see that the Caption property currently has a value of **Command4**.

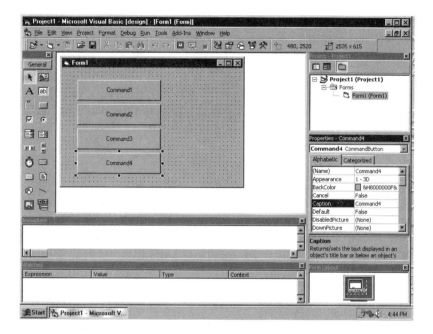

Figure 2.4 *The Properties window shows all the properties of the selected control.*

We'll change this property to a caption that more clearly describes what this button will do. Move the cursor to the Properties window and click in the property cell to the right of **Caption** that says **Command4**. Now press the **Backspace** key until you have completely erased **Command4**. As you delete each character, the title of the command button on the form changes at the same time. Now type **Draw Square** into this property and press the **Enter** key. The title of the command button should now match what you just typed.

We want to change one more property on this control. Every control has a Name property. Like a person's name, the Name property is used to refer to that control. For example, from within a program, the Caption property of a command button could be modified to match something the user has input. To change the caption, the control would be referenced from program code using its Name property.

We will modify the Name property to clearly denote the purpose of each control. This will prevent confusion later when we look at code that references it. Right now, the Name property of the current control is set to the same value as the Caption property: **Command4**. The user never sees the Name property, so when you change it, there will not be a visible change to the control as there was with the Caption property.

Click in the cell to the right of the Name property and delete the current text. Enter the text **cmd_DrawSquare**. Unlike the Caption property, the Name property cannot contain any spaces. The name we have given this control begins with the letters *cmd*, signifying that it is a command button. This is not a requirement; a name can be set to almost anything. However, if we name it in this way, code that references this control will be much clearer to read because the control type is identified in its name.

Now we need to change these properties for each of the other three controls. Click on the control (**Command3**) that is second from the bottom. Change its Caption property to **Swap Color** and its Name property to **cmd_SwapColor**. For **Command2**, change its caption to **FontSize** and its name to **cmd_FontSize**. Finally, for **Command1**, change its caption to **Message Box** and its Name property to **cmd_MsgBox**. Now your form should look like the one shown in Figure 2.5.

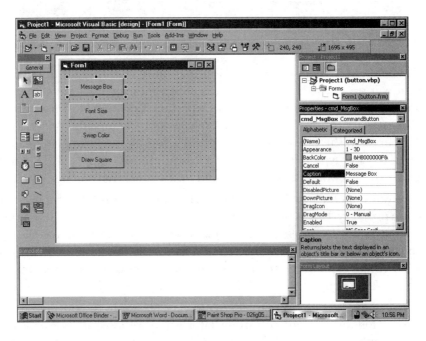

Figure 2.5 *All four controls after their Name and Caption properties have been changed.*

Fantastic! Now that you've created the four command buttons you will need for the project, we'll run the application. But before we do that, we want to save the project and all its forms. It is always a good idea to save your project as often as necessary. Later in this book we will show you how to save any changes to a project or form automatically every time you execute an application.

Pull down the File menu and select the option **Save Project…**. A standard Save dialog box will appear. This is the first time we've saved this project, so two Save dialog boxes will appear in sequence: the first saves the form and the second saves the project itself.

Because multiple files are associated with each project, let's create a new folder for it. Click on the **New Folder** icon and name the new folder **MyProject** as shown in Figure 2.6. Now double-click on it so that the form file will be saved in it. Name the form **button.frm** and click **OK**. After this file is saved, you will be presented with the dialog box to save the project. Name the project **button.vbp** and click **OK**. The **vbp** extension on the file stands for Visual Basic Project.

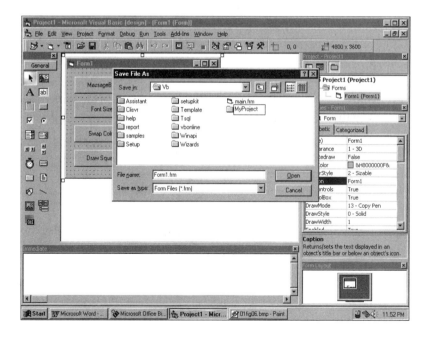

*Figure 2.6 Create a new folder called **MyProject** to hold all the project files.*

Now your project is saved. If anything were to happen (power outage, machine crash, dog knocking out the power cord) all your work will be safe. Save Often! We can't stress this enough. Nothing is more annoying than losing hours of work because of an accident.

You've created a new project, added four controls to the form, and saved the project. Let's run your application. Press the **F5** key or select the **Start** option under the Run menu. You can also click the **Start** button on the toolbar. Your form should now appear, gleaming and new, on the screen. Clicking on the buttons will depress the button on the screen, but nothing else will happen. That is the next step in our programming adventure—adding the event code.

ADDING EVENT CODE TO THE BUTTONS

Now we will step into the realm of real programming. It is here that you will learn how a true application works and interacts with the user. Whenever the user does something within a program (for example, clicks on a command button or selects a menu), an *event* is activated. An event can actually be more than something the user does. When the system loads a window, for example, the Load event is activated.

Each control responds to a number of events. One of the primary events command buttons respond to is a Click event, and text boxes activate the KeyPress event most often. For our application, we will write some code that executes every time a command button is clicked. Therefore, all the code we will write will appear in the Click event of the form.

When we left your application, it was still executing. Stop it by selecting the **End** option under the Run menu or by clicking the **Close** box on Form1. The Visual Basic Programming Environment should now return to the Design mode.

To get to the code window, simply double-click on the **cmd_MsgBox** control. The center window should fill with the code window as shown in Figure 2.7. The code begins with `Private Sub`, which we will explain later. For now, suffice it to say that this line makes this subroutine private to this form (the routine cannot be accessed from other forms). Following the keywords is the name of your control, `cmd_MsgBox`. The control name is followed by an underscore (_) character and then the name of the event to which this code applies. In this case, the event is the `Click()` event, which executes when the user clicks on the command button.

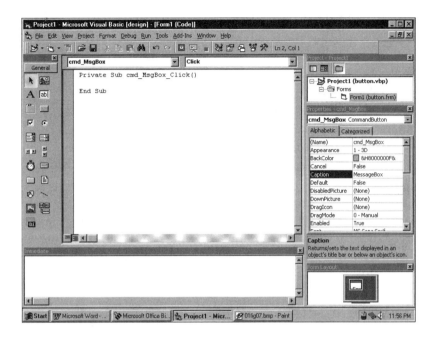

Figure 2.7 *The code window for the Click event of the command button named* **cmd_MsgBox***.*

The next line of code is blank. There is currently no code to execute when the user clicks the command button. We could put a simple keyword such as BEEP in this blank line. The BEEP keyword, introduced in Chapter 1, would simply make the speaker beep every time the user clicks on the button. We'll add a little more complex code shortly.

Following this blank line are the keywords End Sub, which denote the end of the Click event code. These three lines are all that make up the Click() event for this button. Next, we will put code into the Click event that will execute when the **cmd_MsgBox** button is clicked.

The text cursor should be flashing on the blank line in the event code. Enter the following code:

```
' Create variable to hold user response
Dim result As Integer
' Display MessageBox
result = MsgBox("Please press the OK button to continue",
vbOKOnly, "Sample Message")
```

As you progress through each chapter, you will better understand the commands in this code. For the moment, just enter the code as it is listed. Notice that lines that begin with an apostrophe (') seem to be written in English. The apostrophe keyword makes the text on the line following it invisible to Visual Basic. Known as a *remarks* or *comments*, these lines allow you to place comments about the code within the subroutine.

Commenting your code in this way is good programming practice. When you return to the code later or give it to another programmer, it remains clearly understandable. All the code in this book will contain comment lines.

After you have entered the code for the Click event, execute this form (press the **F5** key). Now when you click on the **Message Box** button, a message box similar to the one in Figure 2.8 should appear. The sample message will be shown, and you will be required to click on the **OK** button before the dialog box is dismissed. Wow—that wasn't so hard. You now have a working button on your form. Now let's add the code to the other three buttons.

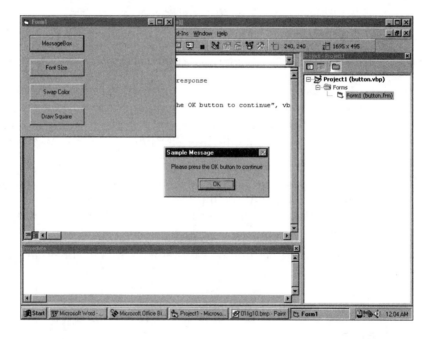

Figure 2.8 *The message box shown after the **cmd_MsgBox** control is clicked.*

Stop the execution by selecting **End** from the Run menu or closing the form window. Visual Basic will return you to design mode in the same place that you left. Your code window with the `Click()` event should still be showing. At the top of the window, you will see two combo boxes—one containing **cmd_MsgBox** and the other containing **Click**. The box on the left shows the control that is currently selected for code editing. The one on the right contains all the events that are related to this control.

We will be editing only the Click events of the command buttons, so in this chapter we will not use the combo box on the right. Out of curiosity, you might click on this combo box just to see some of the events available to the command button—just make sure you return the selection in the box to the Click event after you're finished.

Now, click on the combo box on the left and select the **cmd_FontSize** control. The code window should now show the empty event for the `cmd_FontSize_Click()` routine. Enter the following code:

```
Private Sub cmd_FontSize_Click()
    ' Check current font size
    If cmd_Font.Font.Size = 18 Then
        cmd_Font.Font.Size = 9
    Else
        cmd_Font.Font.Size = 18
    End If
End Sub
```

(handwritten annotations: Error. cmd_FontSize.Font = 18 .Font.Size = 18)

This code checks the current font size of the caption of the button. If the font size is equal to 18, the size is set to 9. If it is not equal to 18, it is set to 18. This code causes the size of the title of the command button to flip-flop between being 9 points and 18 points. You can execute the program again, or you can move on to the other controls.

Select the **cmd_SwapColor** control in the combo box on the left. The following code swaps the Foreground color and Background color of the current form:

```
Private Sub cmd_SwapColor_Click()
    ' Create variable to save current colors
    Dim tempForeColor, tempBackColor
```

```
    ' Save current colors to variables
    tempForeColor = Me.ForeColor
    tempBackColor = Me.BackColor
    ' Swap colors
    Me.ForeColor = tempBackColor
    Me.BackColor = tempForeColor
End Sub
```

You might notice the Me keyword in four of the lines of code. This keyword simply selects the current window in which the code is executing. This keyword is another way of referencing the form. We will describe this technique later in the book.

Finally, select the **cmd_DrawSquare** control. Enter the following code:

```
Private Sub cmd_DrawSquare_Click()
    ' Set ScaleMode to pixels, default is twip
    ScaleMode = 3

    ' Draw a red square that is 100 pixels by 100 pixels
    Line (150, 0)-(250, 100), RGB(255, 0, 0), BF
End Sub
```

This code first sets the ScaleMode to pixels. A single pixel is equal to a single dot on the screen. The standard, or default, unit in Visual Basic is known as *twips*. A twip is one-twentieth of a pixel. This standard is used so that drawings can easily be sent to high-resolution devices (such as laser printers) without any recoding. High resolution is not important in this example, and pixels are easier to work with, so they are used. Following the ScaleMode keyword is the command to draw a red square about 1.4 inches square (72 pixels is approximately equal to 1 inch).

You've entered all the necessary code. Great! You now have a complete application. Before you run it again, we suggest that you save your project to preserve all the work you've done so far. Select **Save Project** under the File menu. Run the application and try clicking on each button. The buttons should execute their assigned tasks. You have just created a complete application that can be expanded to do almost anything. In the coming chapters, we will clearly explain how to write code that executes the functions you need.

For now, you have a working foundation that you can refer to often. For example, if you want to try adding code yourself, add a line with the BEEP keyword to one of the buttons. Now when you click that button, a beep should sound. This process of experimentation will dramatically increase your Visual Basic programming abilities.

RELATED TOOLS

Forms provide the core functionality of the Visual Basic environment. After all, before Visual Basic, there was simply BASIC. When window and form construction was added, the environment was renamed Visual Basic. The appearance of a form is substantially at the whim of the designer or programmer.

- Appearance property. Every form and control has a property named Appearance. This property designates whether the given control will have the Windows 95 3-D look (light gray and white at the top and left edges, dark gray and black at the bottom and right) or the flat look characterized by older Windows 3.1 applications. You can change this property to suit your taste.

- Double-clicking on a property. Many properties have only two or more settings (for example, a True/False property). You can double-click on these properties in the Properties winow to toggle between the settings. If the property has more than two values (the Align property, for example, has three: left, right, and center), each double-click advances to the next option.

- Form layout. The window in the bottom right corner of the screen that is labeled **Form Layout** designates where the form will appear on the screen. This allows you to conveniently work on the design of the form in the top-left corner of the screen even if, on execution of the application, the window will appear in the bottom-right corner.

- VB commands. Each command (such as **Run** or **Stop**) can have as many as four ways to activate it. The command can be entered into the Immediate window. There is usually a menu option for each command. Often, a toolbar icon or keyboard shortcut (such as the **F5** key) can execute the command. Use the method that feels most comfortable.

- Automatic addition of controls. If you prefer not to actually draw the controls on your form, Visual Basic will add a control in a standard size. Simply double-click on the desired control on the toolbox palette. The control will automatically be placed on the form and sized to an appropriate width and height.

SUMMARY

We've covered a lot of introductory material in this chapter, and we've learned how to create a complete Visual Basic application. Here is what you've learned so far:

- The structure of a Visual Basic application. All the resources of an application are stored within a project. Each project has one or more forms. On a form, controls are placed for the user to manipulate.

- Saving a project and form. Projects and forms are stored as separate files on the hard drive. During the development process, it is important to save often to ensure that no work is lost.

- Placing controls on a form. Putting a control on a form is much like using a drawing program. A control is selected from the toolbox, and then sized on the form.

- Adding event code. Event code is executed when a particular event occurs. Placing code in the event subroutines is the way most programs are constructed.

In Chapter 3, you'll learn about variables, which let you give names to numbers and other pieces of information.

CHAPTER 3

Learning About Variables, Values, and Procedures

- What variables are
- Values and types
- Introduction to strings and string operators
- Procedures of both types: subroutines and Functions
- Retrieving values returned from a function

In this chapter, we'll talk about two things that lie at the heart of all but the simplest of programs: variables and values. *Variables*, as you'll see shortly, represent places in memory that store numbers and strings of characters. These numbers and strings are *values*.

You may wonder why you must learn about variables and values. Why can't you just graduate to building windows (forms) and dialog boxes? It's because nearly every program you write, no matter how small, will use variables and values. Programs aren't very useful if they don't do anything, and programs you build in Visual Basic won't be able to do anything unless you use variables and values.

In this chapter, you'll also learn more about strings of characters and the operators that you can use to work with strings.

WHAT ARE VARIABLES?

Variables store numbers and strings, something you'll do often in programs to keep track of intermediate results. The easiest way to demonstrate this idea is with an example.

Make sure you have Visual Basic running and the Immediate window visible and active. Then type the following line in the Immediate window and press **Enter**:

```
n=2
|
```

What does this mean, and what did it do?

The equal sign is a new command called the *assignment* operator. It's not an equation. Rather, the assignment operator saves a value in part of your computer's memory. We'll show you where it saves this value in a moment, but first, let's make sure this number is actually in memory.

You can use **Print** to display the value stored in a variable simply by supplying the variable's name. Try it.

```
print n
  2
|
```

As you can see, the value of 2 is still in n.

NOTE We chose to use the letter *n* here because it's short for the word *number*. For simple variables, programmers sometimes use a single letter, such as *n*, for a name rather than spell it out. In most of this book, we'll use more descriptive names. For now, using a single letter makes the examples a little easier.

Notice that the n=2 line is still in the Immediate window. You might wonder what would happen if you edited this line to something like n=3. Would your edit change the value of n? The answer is yes and no. If you change this line and press Enter while the insertion point is still in the line, Visual Basic will change the value of n. But if you move the cursor to another line without pressing **Enter**, Visual Basic won't change the value of n. Here's why.

The text you see inside the Immediate window is merely a string of characters as far as Visual Basic is concerned. It treats this text as a command only when you press **Enter**, at which point Visual Basic runs the command. The moral of the story is this: previous commands inside the Immediate window are merely text until you press **Enter**. Pressing **Enter** runs only one command: the command on the line that contains the insertion point when you press Enter.

The = Command

REFERENCE The = command is an assignment operator. It assigns a value to a variable:

name = *expression*

Assign the value of *expression* to the variable called name.

The next thing you'll do is really interesting. Let's say you want to add 3 to the value already in n; in other words, you want to add 3 to 2 and put this result back into n. How do you do this? By writing n=n+3, as follows:

```
n = n + 3
print n
   5
|
```

It worked. (We added some spaces around the = sign to make this statement more readable. Basic doesn't care whether you use spaces.) This statement (n = n + 3) works because the code to the right of the equal sign (n+3) is executed before the value is stored into the variable n.

Equal is Not Equal—It's Assignment

The equal sign in programming languages is different from the equal sign in algebra. In algebra, num = num + 3 is an equation with one unknown: num. (This particular equation doesn't have a solution.) Basic, on the other hand, treats the equal sign as a command.

Here's what happens. When Basic sees an equal sign, it looks on the right side of the equal sign and calculates the value of the expression it finds there (num + 3, which results in 5 because num is currently 2). Then Basic assigns this value to the variable num, which appears on the left side of the equal sign.

Because this arrangement can be a little confusing, some programming languages use a left-pointing arrow for assignment:num 2-3. The Pascal language uses := rather than =, as in num:=2+3.

Where Are Variables Stored?

The simple answer is that variables are stored in memory. Each program in Windows has its own areas of memory that it uses and works with. Visual Basic, for example, has a number of pieces of memory that it uses for itself and the programs you write. Some of this memory is available for storing variables.

What happened when you typed n = 2? Visual Basic first looked through its memory for a variable named n. One didn't exist, so Visual Basic created a new variable with the name n. Because Visual Basic "forgets" all variables whenever you switch modes (from Run mode to Design mode or vice versa), this variable exists only when you're running in a particular mode. So if you are running a program, type **End** to exit Run mode, and then check the Immediate window, you'll discover that n no longer has the value 2. Try it for yourself. Enter the following:

n=2

Then press **F5** and **Ctrl+Break** and enter the following:

```
print n
```

|

Why did **Print** display a blank line rather than tell you that n doesn't exist anymore?

It turns out that Visual Basic defines a new variable for you automatically whenever it sees a name it hasn't seen before. So when you entered `Print n`, Visual Basic automatically defined a variable called n. And because you didn't assign a value to n this time, it had no value. All new variables are empty until you assign a value to them. We'll talk more about empty variables shortly.

 All new variables are empty until you assign a value to them.

N O T E

Naming Variables

The only variable name we've used so far is n, but you can use longer, more descriptive variable names. The sidebar "Naming Variables" gives the rules you must follow when naming variables. Here are some examples of names that follow these rules:

`lastName`	Mixed case, starting with a lowercase letter
`first_Name`	Underscore in the name
`NumNames`	Mixed case, starting with an uppercase letter
`Name3`	Includes a number that isn't the first character
`München`	Uses an international character: ü
`last_Name_3`	Combines several of the elements above

The following are some examples of names that are not allowed:

`2Name`	Variables cannot have names that start with a number
`beep`	Variables cannot have the same name as a Basic keyword. Basic ignores the case of a word, so `beep`, `Beep`, and `BEEP` are all considered to be the same keyword.

As you can see, you have quite a bit of freedom in choosing variable names. When we start writing programs, we'll have more to say about variable names and how to choose them. For now, let's work with short, simple names. The names really aren't important yet, and we're more interested in the concepts of variables and values.

Naming Variables

Variable names can be almost anything you want, as long as you follow these rules:

- Length. Names can be as many as 255 characters long.
- Characters. You can use any uppercase or lowercase letters, numbers, and the underscore (_) character. The first character must be a letter. Letters can include international letters such as ü but not symbols such as @.
- No Keywords. You can't use names such as `Print` or `Beep`, or even `beep`, because they are keywords in the Basic language; nor can you use any other Basic keywords as variable names. Visual Basic has many keywords, so it's best to check names that you want to use against the words listed in the *Language Reference Manual* included with Visual Basic.

VALUES AND TYPES

Most of the examples so far have dealt with numbers, although you worked briefly with a string in Chapter 1. There you wrote the following command:

```
print 7 / 3 "remainder" 7 mod 3
```

This command generated the following output:

```
 2 remainder 1
|
```

The text "remainder" is called a *string* because it's a string of characters. You must enclose strings within a pair of double-quotation marks to tell Basic that the characters constitute a string rather than a variable name.

REFERENCE

Strings

Strings are groups of characters that you work within Basic. Whenever you write a string in a Basic command, you must surround all the characters with double-quotation marks (one on each end) as follows:

```
"any string of characters"
```

You can use any character inside a string. However, if you want to use a double-quotation character (") itself as part of a string, you must write it twice for each time you want it to appear in the string. For example:

```
print "A double-quote "" character"
A double-quote " character
|
```

What happens if you try to assign such a string to a variable called s?

```
s = "remainder"
|
```

It seems to have worked, and you can verify that using the **Print** command as follows:

```
print s
remainder
|
```

You can assign a string to a variable just as easily as you assign a number to a variable. Now try to assign a number to the variable s. Can you change the type of value stored in this variable? Give the following a try:

```
print s
remainder
s = 10
print s
   10
|
```

Every value has a specific type—for example, a string or a number. Visual Basic's variables are storage containers that can store any type of value.

You might wonder whether a single variable can contain both a string and a number. The answer is no. Variables in Basic can contain only one value at a time. (Some languages, such as LISP, allow you to assign multiple values to a single variable. Basic does not.)

There is one operator you can use to combine multiple strings. The + operator concatenates two strings; that means it creates a new string by combining the two strings. The following example shows exactly how the process works (notice the use of the different variables):

```
s1 = "Text in"
s2 = " two parts."
s = s1 + s2
print s
Text in two parts.
|
```

This example creates two variables—s1 and s2—and assigns part of a sentence to each variable. The third string, s, is a combination of s1 and s2 using the + operator. String concatenation is easy and useful. (Note that we put a space before "two" when assigning the value of s2 to prevent "in" and "two" from being combined as "intwo.")

string concatenation with +

When placed between two strings, the + sign creates a third string that contains both the other strings:

REFERENCE

```
sCombined = s1 + s2
```

This command creates a string sCombined that contains s1 followed by s2.

Variables and Types

You've seen that each value has a specific type, such as a number or a string, and you'll see more types of values in later chapters. You've also seen that the variables you create can contain either a number or a string. You may think that because variables can contain any value, they have no type, but that isn't true.

The variables you've been using so far have a type. They are called *variant* variables and can contain any number or string. You can also create other types of variables that are more restrictive. You need only to tell Basic what kind of value the variable can contain. If you create a string variable, it can contain only a string type of value. Does this sound unduly restrictive? There are several reasons you would want to use such variables.

First, there are times when you'll need to use a specific type of variable, such as when you're writing programs that read and write data to the disk. More important, using specific variable types is good programming practice. For example, if you want to create a variable IDNum to hold an identification number, you should define this variable as a number type. By setting the type, you cannot accidentally enter a string into this variable. Making the variable a particular type also makes the code execute much more quickly.

You can tell Basic that a variable has a specific type by adding a special character at the end of the variable name. Adding a dollar sign ($) to the end of a variable name signals Basic that the variable is a string. So if you type **s$ = "remainder"** rather than **s = "remainder"**, you're telling Basic that it's working with a string variable called s$, rather than a variant variable called s. Or you can add a percent sign (%) to the end of a variable name to signal Basic that the variable is an integer. Using a variable named T, define it as an integer and assign it the value of 10, as follows:

```
T% = 10
Print T%
   10
|
```

Now we want you to try assigning the number 10 to this same integer, except place the value in quotation marks, indicating that it is a string:

```
T% = "10"
Print T%
   10
|
```

It worked. Did you think it wouldn't? How could Basic assign a string value to an integer variable? Visual Basic features an automatic conversion for variables. Basic evaluated the contents of the string and determined that it could be converted into an integer.

What happens when you try to assign a string that cannot be converted? Try it using the following code, and you'll see the alert box shown in Figure 3.1:

```
T% = "string"
```

In this case, the error message, "Type mismatch," means that you tried to assign a string to an integer variable. The string did not contain a numeric value that could be converted, so Basic decided that the assignment didn't make sense.

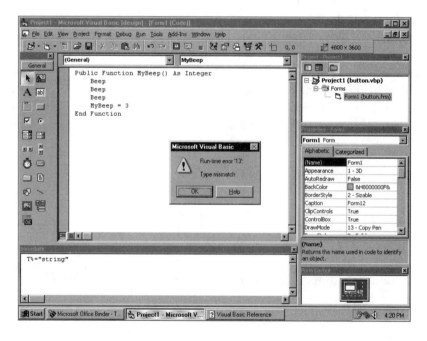

Figure 3.1 *You'll see this warning message box when you try to assign one type of value to a variable of a different type and Basic cannot automatically convert the value.*

The alert box also identifies this error as run-time error number 13. Whenever a run-time error occurs, Visual Basic assigns the error number to the `Err` variable, and advanced programmers use those values in their program code to write error-handling routines.

More about Types and Numbers

You've now seen two types of values: numbers and strings. In fact, there are five different types of numbers. How's that? Calculators get by with just one type of number, so why do computers need five?

The simple answer to this question has to do with speed of execution because of the microprocessor inside your computer. For the most part, computers have limited native abilities to perform calculations. The Pentium microprocessor, for example, can easily and quickly multiply integers (numbers without any decimals, such as 1 or 200). But to multiply two floating-point numbers, such as 1.3 and 6.87, takes much more time. When this multiplication happens repeatedly, the program slows noticeably.

Floating-Point Numbers

You'll often read and hear about *floating-point numbers* in connection with computers. What are they, and why are they called floating-point numbers?

Any number with something after the decimal point is called a floating-point number. Thus, both 1.1 and 3.14159 are floating-point numbers.

The reason they are called floating-point numbers is subtler. All floating-point numbers are represented inside of your computer as whole numbers. Another piece of information tells your computer where the decimal point should be in a number. Because the decimal point can move left or right, depending on the actual number (for example, 123.4, 12.34, and 1.234), it can float around in the number.

It takes time for the Pentium microprocessor to handle this extra processing of the floating point.

When you're writing programs, the difference in speed can be crucial. Almost all programs written by professional programmers make heavy use of the native arithmetic to run more quickly.

For now, be aware that Visual Basic uses several different types of numbers. Table 3.1 lists the types of values that are built into Basic. In this book you'll be working mostly with three types: variant, integer, and string.

Table 3.1 Types of Variables and Values in Basic

Type	Suffix	Range of Values
Integer	%	−32,768 to 32,767
Long	&	−2,147,483,648 to 2,147,483,647
Single	!	Largest number: ±3.402823 ¥ 10^{38}; smallest number: ±1.401298 ¥ 10^{-45}
Double	#	Largest number: ±1.797693134862315 ¥ 10308; smallest number: ±4.94066 ¥ 10^{-324}
Currency	@	−922,337,203,685,477.5808 to 922,337,203,685,477.5807
String	$	From 0 to about 65,535 characters.
Variant	(none)	Null, Error, any number up to the range of a double, or any character text, object, or array.
Byte	(none)	From 0 to 255
Boolean	(none)	True or False.
Date	(none)	January 1, 100 to December 31, 9999.
Object	(none)	Any object reference.

Note: In the old days, the Basic programming language needed to use type-declaration characters, or suffixes, in order to identify the data types. As the language evolved, the suffixes were no longer needed, so the newer data types were never assigned any.

Notice that the ranges for numbers use strange values, such as,−32,768 to 32,767 for integers? Why do numbers in Basic have these particular limits?

They are a result of the way your computer works. If you're interested, you'll find more information about this in the sidebar "Bytes and Numbers." The main thing we're concerned about in this book is the set of limits on the size of numbers. You need to make sure that you don't work with numbers that are too large. We'll explore these size issues a little bit.

Bytes and Numbers

Your computer's memory is divided into many small storage locations called *bytes*. (Most computers running Windows, for example, have at least 8 megabytes of memory). Each byte can hold a single character of information. A string requires one byte for each character plus a few extra bytes to keep track of how many characters are in the string. For example, the string "word" is six bytes long: four bytes for the characters, and two bytes to keep track of the length of the string in characters.

You might guess that numbers would require one byte for each digit, but there's a much more efficient way to store numbers. As it turns out, a single byte can represent any number between 0 and 255. Two bytes together can represent any positive number between 0 and 65,535. In practice, half the numbers are defined as negative, producing a range of -32,768 and 32,767—exactly the range allowed by an Integer type. In other words, an integer is exactly two bytes long.

Microsoft also provides a Byte data type in Visual Basic. Like all bytes, it can represent any number between 0 and 255. This data type is most useful for passing values to external program components such as DLLs and OLE objects (a subject beyond the scope of this book).

Exploring the Limits on Numbers

We're almost finished with our discussion of numbers, and soon we'll move to more entertaining topics. Let's spend a little time exploring different types of numbers and their limits. This section will give you a better sense of the range of numbers that you can work with and will help you understand what happens when you pass the limits.

Let's do some more work in the Immediate window. You already know how to define a variable as an integer. Let's use another letter to represent the variable. Type the following:

```
z% = 5
|
```

You can verify that this worked correctly by typing the following:

print z%

```
5
|
```

That's all there is to defining z% as an integer.

Be careful of using a command such as `Print z% = 5`. Don't expect this command to assign z% = 5. It won't. Instead, this command tests z% to see whether it's equal to 5. It prints `False` when z% is not 5, and True when z% is equal to 5. You'll learn about this kind of command in Chapter 5 when we talk about Boolean expressions.

Now let's do some arithmetic so that you can see how differently integers behave from the floating-point numbers in variant variables. The value of z% is currently 5. If you divide 5 by 3, you would normally expect the answer to be 1.666667. But here, because z% is an Integer (whole number) type of variable, the answer is 2 (again, a whole number). Try the following:

```
z% = z% / 3
print z%
  2
|
```

Why did this code result in 2 rather than 1? It's because Basic rounds the real answer, 1.666..., to the nearest whole number, which is 2.

How Visual Basic Rounds Numbers

When you want to turn a fractional number into a whole number, the most accurate method is to round the number to the closest whole number. If the fractional part greater than 0.5, you round up to the next highest number. If the fractional part is less than 0.5, you round down. But what happens when the fractional part is exactly 0.5?

You may think that you should always round 0.5 up to the next highest number, but this isn't mathematically correct. Instead, you round up half the time and round down the other half of the time. The rule is that you round up when the whole part of the number is odd and round down when it's even. For example, 1.50 is rounded up to 2 (because 1 is odd) and 2.50 is rounded down to 2 (because 2 is even).

Let's see what happens if you always round up 0.5 rather than round up only when the whole part is odd. Let's say you're adding a group of numbers, all of which end with 0.5: 1.5 + 2.5 + 3.5 + 4.5 = 12.0. If you round all these numbers up before adding them, you get 2 + 3 + 4 + 5 = 14, which isn't correct. On the other hand, if you use the rule Basic uses, you get: 2 + 2 + 4 + 4 = 12. The bottom line is that rounding up half the time gives more accurate answers than rounding up all the time.

Now let's see what happens when you multiply two large numbers. First, set z% to 30,000; then multiply this by 30,000 (note that Basic doesn't allow you to type commas between the thousands) as follows:

```
z% = 30000
z% = z% * 30000
|
```

You'll see the warning message box shown in Figure 3.2. "Overflow" means that the result is too large to fit into an Integer type. In other words, the number (900,000,000 in our example) overflows the size limits of an Integer type (32,767).

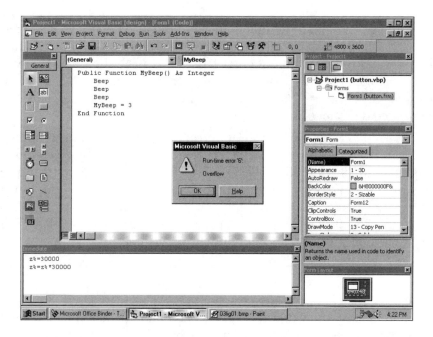

Figure 3.2 *Whenever a result is too large for a type of variable, you'll see this warning message box.*

Another message you'll sometimes see is "Division by zero," which means you tried to divide a number by 0 as follows:

```
z% = 1/0
|
```

You might want to experiment a little with the limits of Integers before you move on.

Scientific Notation

Next, let's look at what happens when you work with really large numbers using the variable r!, which is of type Single because it has an exclamation point at the end of the name. Numbers of type Single are floating-point numbers, and that means you can work with very small numbers, such as 0.000001, as well as large numbers, such as 10000.2. Notice that the decimal point "moved" between numbers.

First, set `r!` to 1,000,000 as follows:

```
r!=1000000
print r!
  1000000
|
```

Multiply this by 1,200,000, which should result in 1 trillion 200 billion (11 zeros in all). The following is what you'll see:

```
r! = r! * 1200000
print r!
  1.2E+12
|
```

The answer, 1.2E+12, is what's known as scientific notation. If you remember back to grade school, you learned that you could write large numbers as 1.2×10^{12}. But this is impossible to write on a computer that can't use superscripts, so you must write it as 1.2E+12. The E+12 means that the number (1.2 here) is multiplied by 10 to the 12th power.

PROCEDURES: SUBROUTINES AND FUNCTIONS

Now that you've learned about variables, it's time we covered the basic structure of programming in Visual Basic. *Procedures* (also called *code, functions, methods, routines, subroutines,* and *routines*) consist of blocks of commands. In Chapter 1, you learned the **BEEP** command. It was typed on a single line:

```
BEEP
|
```

If you wanted multiple beeps, you would have several lines, each containing a command.

```
BEEP

BEEP

BEEP

|
```

What do you do if you want a command button to make these three beeps? You create a procedure and give it a name. When you type that name in a program, all the commands of the procedure execute. If we created a procedure of **BEEP** commands and named it MyBeep, it would look like this:

```
Public Sub MyBeep()
      Beep

      Beep

      Beep
End Sub
```

If you placed this procedure within a form, you could call it and the speaker would beep three times. The first word in the first line of the code is **Public**. This command allows procedures on other form windows to execute this procedure (as opposed to the **Private** keyword, which hides this routine from everything except code on this form). The second command on the line, **Sub**, defines this block of code as a subroutine (another name for a procedure).

The **Sub** command is always followed by the name of the procedure, in this case MyBeep. There is nothing between the parentheses that follow the name of the procedure because no variables are passed to this procedure. If this were a more general-purpose routine, we might want to allow the procedure that calls MyBeep to tell it how many beeps should occur. In such a case, the beginning line of the procedure might look like this:

```
Public Sub MyBeep(numbeeps As Integer)
```

This procedure header accepts a variable (named numbeeps) that is an integer. The MyBeep procedure can then use this variable to beep the number of times stored in the numbeeps variable.

The final line of the procedure code, End Sub, completes the definition of the procedure. Many of the programming constructs that you will learn in this book have this kind of beginning and end command (Sub...End Sub), which functions much as quotation marks do in written English. They mark where the procedure begins and ends.

REFERENCE

How a Procedure Is Called

A procedure can be called (executed) in several ways in Visual Basic, something that can be extremely confusing when you are first learning to program. Most of the methods work exactly the same way, and it generally boils down to personal preference.

To call the MyBeep procedure, you can use this code:

```
MyBeep
```

or this:

```
Call MyBeep
```

or this:

```
Call MyBeep()
```

The three statements act in exactly the same way, even though they appear differently. If you're passing a value of 2 to the procedure, you can use this:

```
MyBeep 2
```

or this:

```
Call MyBeep(2)
```

These two statements also function identically. Note that if you were to add parentheses around the value without the Call statement, Visual Basic would generate an error; you cannot have the command MyBeep(2). As you examine more Visual Basic code developed by numerous authors, you will probably see variations on these calling procedures.

A variation of the procedure, called a *function* allows values to be returned. Functions are necessary for many routines but appear most often when calculations are performed. For example, you might create a function that calculates the number of days in the current month.

We have been using the MyBeep procedure to demonstrate code. To change it into a function, we must change the header and footer to read Function instead of **Sub**. We must also set the return value. In the following code, the final line reads `MyBeep = 3`. This statement sets the return value of the function to 3. You must use the = sign with the name of the function to return a value.

```
Public Function MyBeep() as Integer
    Beep
    Beep
    Beep
    MyBeep = 3
End Function
```

Notice that we have added the code `as Integer` to the end of the header line to specify that the function will return an integer value. When you call the function, you must use a variable to store the value returned. For example:

```
X = MyBeep()
```

This code calls the `MyBeep` function and stores the value returned (in this case, the integer 3) in the variable `X`. If no value is set for the function, a default value is assigned. If an integer was expected to be returned, the default will be zero (0); if a string, the default would be an empty string (""), and so on.

RELATED TOOLS

- Converting between types. Visual Basic has a number of built-in functions that allow you to convert between the different types of numbers and to convert between strings and numbers as follows:

  `CCur`   Valid numeric or string expression to Currency.

  `CDbl`   Valid numeric or string expression to Double.

  `CLng`   Valid numeric or string expression to Long.

  `CSgn`   Valid numeric or string expression to Single.

  `CInt`   Valid numeric or string expression to Integer, rounds to the nearest whole number.

Fix	Numeric expression to Integer, truncates the fractional part.
Int	Numeric expression to Integer, largest whole number less than or equal to Number. (3.2 Æ 3 and -3.2 Æ -4). Truncates to the nearest whole nimber
Str	Numeric expression to String.
Cbool	Valid numeric or string expression to Boolean.
Cbyte	Valid numeric or string expression to Byte.
Cdate	Valid numeric or string expression to Date.
Cstr	Valid numeric or string expression to String.
Cvar	Valid numeric or string expression to Variant.
Val	String expression to Number.

- String functions. Visual Basic has a useful set of tools that you can use to work with strings. These tools, a combination of functions and commands, allow you to do things such as search strings, break strings into pieces, or convert to uppercase or lowercase. The following is a brief overview of these functions:

InStr	Searches to see whether one string is contained inside another.
Left$	Builds a new string that contains the first (left-most) n characters from another string.
Mid$	Builds a new string that contains characters from the middle of another string. You can also use this function to replace part of a string with another string. Using InStr and Mid$, you can do search-and-replace operations.
Right$	Builds a new string that contains the last (right-most) n characters from another string.
LTrim$	Builds a new string, removing any spaces at the start of the string.
RTrim$	Builds a new string removing any spaces at the end of the string.
LCase$	Returns a copy of a string, converting all letters to lowercase.
UCase$	Returns a copy of a string, converting all letters to uppercase.
Len	Returns the length, in characters, of a string.

■ Variant functions. There are several functions you can use with variant variables to determine what's in the variable.

`VarType` Tells you the data type is currently stored inside the variant variable.

`IsEmpty`	Reports whether a variant variable is empty. All new variant variables are empty when they're first created.
`IsNull`	Reports whether a variant variable contains the special `Null` value, which is used to indicate that the variable contains no data. `Null` is like `empty`, except that `empty` applies only when a variable hasn't had any value assigned to it.
`IsNumeric`	Returns True if the value in a variant variable is a number.
`IsDate`	Returns True if the value in a variant variable is a date or time value.
`IsArray`	Returns True if the variable is an array.
`IsError`	Returns True if an error is identified.
`IsMissing`	Optional arguments or parameters can be passed from procedure to procedure. `IsMissing` returns `True` if a specified optional argument or parameter was not passed to the procedure.
`IsObject`	Returns `True` if the expression represents a valid object.

NOTE A valid numeric or string expression is one in which the value falls within the allowable value range of the data type to which the expression is being converted. If the expression exceeds the range, an error occurs.

SUMMARY

This chapter introduced a great deal of new material. Here's a quick review.

■ Variables are named locations in memory where you can store values. Each variable has a type that determines what you can store in it.

- Values are pieces of information and can be numbers or strings. You can use a wide range of values with variables. For Integers, numbers can range from –32,768 to 32,767 (but you can't use the commas when you type the numbers in Basic).

- Types. All of Basic's variables have specific types. There are six different types: one string type and five numeric types. In this book you'll work almost entirely with the Integer, Variant, and String data types, but if you're writing scientific programs, you may need to use the Double type because it provides more precise results. (Note, however, that calculations with Double values are slower than calculations with Integer values.) If you're writing financial programs, you might want to use the Currency type.

- The two basic building blocks of a program are the variables, which are used to store information, and Procedures which are the blocks of commands that create all of the action of a program.

- There are two basic types of procedures: a subroutine that executes commands and a function that executes commands and returns one or more values.

- There is more than one way to call a procedure. You can use the **Call** command or type the name of the procedure by itself. If you're calling a subroutine, use parentheses to enclose passed values only with the **Call** command. If you're calling a function, be sure to include a variable that receives the value the function will return.

CHAPTER 4

Learning About Objects

- What objects are
- Methods and properties
- Classes and instances
- Building a program with objects
- Information hiding

Welcome to the wonderful world of objects! When you use objects in Visual Basic, programming is far more convenient because you can reuse parts of one program in another program without having to start from scratch. Understanding how objects should be used is paramount if you want to learn how to program effectively. As with any skill, if you have a solid foundation to build from, you can progress better, faster, and more enjoyably. You will also be well prepared for programming in the next decade as most programming development moves toward object techniques.

The great benefit of objects is that they're self-contained. Programming with objects is a lot like using an erector set. You can bolt objects together to create the final program that you want. You need program only the nuts and bolts that hold together the various struts. You can use the objects that come with Visual Basic as well as buy objects others have written. By putting together the objects that you need in a project, you can develop powerful and amazing programs in a fraction of the time it would take to build them from scratch.

One thing that makes programming with objects better than using an erector set is that you can forge your own girders. Visual Basic allows you to create your own objects, plug them into a program, and reuse them again and again. In Chapter 8, we will build a clock object; in Chapter 13, we will reuse this same clock object and add it to another program.

Before we construct objects, we must learn how they work and how they are created. This chapter introduces a great deal of new terminology. Not to worry! This is the last foundation chapter before we begin building programs. The examples provided in each chapter should also make things easier to follow. In many of the past examples you have already accessed objects. Now you will be able to understand how the code works.

WHAT IS AN OBJECT?

In Chapter 3, you learned about variables and procedures. Variables are used to hold information and data (such as strings, numbers, and so on). Procedures are blocks of commands that execute, perhaps reading or manipulating variables.

Objects are a way of unifying variables and procedures into a single unit. In other words, an *object* is a combination of variables and the procedures that manipulate those variables. For example, a window is an object. The variables that affect the window (such as the window size and type) are stored within the window (or form) object. Likewise, the procedure code to manipulate the window (such as code to make it visible, to redraw its contents, etc.) is stored within the object.

Examples of visible objects include forms, list boxes, combo boxes, check boxes, and menus. Even an entire application (such as Word, Access, or Excel) can be treated as an object. Invisible objects, such as calculation engines or email routers, are not visible on the screen.

In Visual Basic, most objects you have worked with so far have been visible. When you draw a control on a form, you are essentially placing an object within another object. The control is an object, and the form is an object in which you are embedding the control object. In Figure 4.1, we have placed a check box control on the form. Traditionally, objects are stored within a hierarchy in the same way that files are stored within folders. The control we have added to the form has added an object within another object in much the same way as a file is placed within a folder.

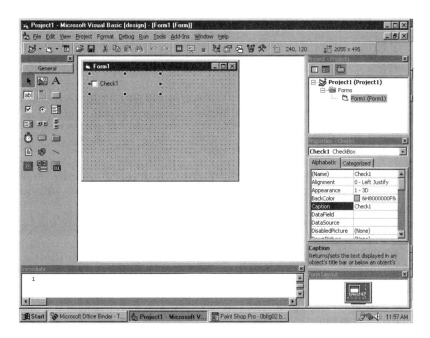

Figure 4.1 *This form object now contains a check box control object.*

In Chapter 2, we placed four buttons on a form and then changed the Name property so that they had names such as `'cmd_FontSize'`. That name allows us to reference that particular command button object. If you're familiar with the Windows directory structure, you know that folders use the backslash (\)

symbol to separate levels. For example, to get to a readme file in the System directory on the C drive, you would use this path:

```
C:\windows\system\readme.txt
```

Object hierarchies work in the same way except that the dot (.), or period, symbol is used instead. For example, in Chapter 2, we used this code to change the font size:

```
cmd_Font.FontSize.Size = 9
```

We did not include the form in the hierarchy, because it is implied (this code is executing from within the form object). However, we could have added it:

```
Form1.cmd_FontSize.Font.Size = 9
```

As you can see, the command moves down three levels into the hierarchy. The first object is the form itself (Form1). The second object (cmd_FontSize) is the button object we placed on the form. The third object (Font) is an object contained within the standard command button control. Finally, the Size variable is set to equal 9 in the statement above.

Using the dot command, you can reference any object within a hierarchy. Now that you have a general idea of how an object is referenced, it is important to understand what makes up an object.

METHODS AND PROPERTIES

Certain terms are specific to object-oriented development. When relating to an object, variables and procedures are called *properties* and *methods*, respectively. A variable that is particular to a certain object is a property. A method is a procedure that is located within an object. Figure 4.2 shows a simplified diagram that compares a traditional program with an object-oriented program.

In traditional programs, procedures and variables are not connected and cannot be organized easily. If you want to reuse a routine, you must find and duplicate all the procedures and variables that relate to that routine. A particular procedure might rely on another procedure to set a variable.

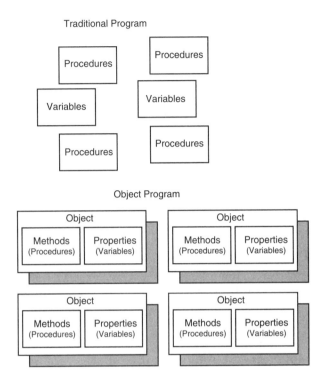

Figure 4.2 *Traditional vs. object-oriented programs.*

An object encapsulates both properties and the routines that use those properties. Object-oriented programs are much better organized, because relevant information and processes are stored within the object itself. Reuse is facilitated, because the object can simply be transferred to another program with all the items it needs.

ActiveX Controls

You may have heard a great deal recently about the Internet and ActiveX controls. Because all the properties and methods for functioning are contained within an object, it can be used almost anywhere. ActiveX controls package an object so that it can be transported over the Internet and used within a Web browser (such as Netscape Navigator or Internet Explorer). We will use Visual Basic to create an ActiveX control later in the book. With traditional programs, using the Internet in this way would have been extremely difficult. You can begin to appreciate the flexibility you gain by using objects.

Properties can be either public or private. In the earlier code, we set the `Size` property of the Font object equal to 9. The `Size` property is known as a Public property. It can be accessed and modified by routines outside the object. The reason for having public and private properties will be explained in detail later in the "Information Hiding" section.

Properties are accessed using the dot (.) command as shown in the example that modified the `Size` property. Methods are invoked using the same approach. All forms have a method called `Show`. The Type style method makes the form visible and brings it to the front of the screen. Suppose a form has a `Name` property of `Form2`. You could use the command:

```
Form2.Show
```

This command would execute the `Show` method of the form object, and that would make the form visible. Methods that return values are called in the same way that a function procedure is executed. For example, form objects have a method called `Point` that returns the RGB color value of a specified point. If we created a variable called `MyRGB`, we could call this method to return the value of the color at point 100, 100. A statement to retrieve this value from a point on Form1 would look like this:

```
MyRGB = Form1.Point(100,100)
```

This code is an excellent example of the use of an object. The `Point` method is constructed to retrieve information (the point color) from data (the background or picture of the form) stored in the object. If the format of a window ever changed, the `Point` method would have to be rewritten. However, none of the routines that call this method need worry about the format of the window. The `Point` method makes the internal properties of the object invisible.

UNDERSTANDING CLASS AND INSTANCES

You should now have a basic understanding of the definition of an object. By combining data with the procedures that affect that data, you create a self-contained object; when supplemented with additional code and objects, it can be used to build a program. Each object has two aspects for creation and use: its class and instancing. An object class is essentially a blueprint of how an object instance will be created. Figure 4.3 shows a diagram of a multiple objects created from a class blueprint.

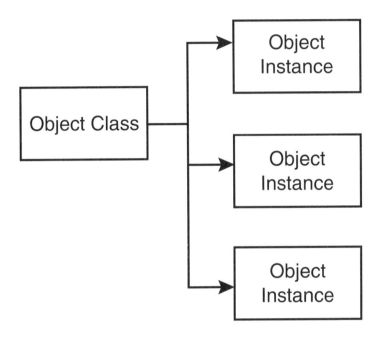

Figure 4.3 A class is used to create instances of an object.

To bring this abstract subject down to earth, we will use the analogy of building a house. To build a house, you need a blueprint detailing its specifications, the layout, and other key information. From this blueprint, you can build a house. In fact, with the same blueprint you can build numerous houses that are functionally identical. However, you cannot live in the blueprint.

An object class is a blueprint to create an object. It defines the procedures and data that will be used in an object, but you cannot execute or use the class except to create an instance of the object. Instancing creates, in the memory of the computer, an actual object that can be used. The process of creating an instance is also referred to as *instantiation*. Multiple instances of an object can be instantiated from a class.

Creating an Instance

We'll now use Visual Basic to work with objects and show how an instance of an object is created. We will create multiple instances of the form that we originally created in Chapter 2. If you don't have the original project opened in Visual Basic 5, load the project now (it should be called **button.vbp**). We'll add another button that instantiates multiple instances of the entire form and all the objects stored within it. Start by adding a command button to the form and setting the `Caption` property to `New Form` and the `Name` property to `cmd_NewForm`, as shown in Figure 4.4.

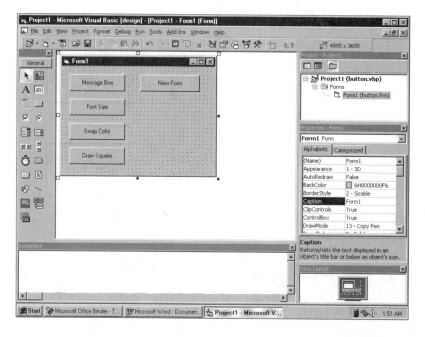

Figure 4.4 Add another button to the form and set its `Caption` and `Name` properties.

After you have created the button and set the correct properties, we add the code that will create a new instance of the form object. For simplicity's sake, we'll create duplicate instances from the original instance that is created when the program is executed. If we were to create a form from its object class, we would have to add all the controls by hand. Later in this book we will create an example class and generate multiple instances from it.

Now let's enter the code to create duplicate instances of the form. Double-click the **cmd_NewForm** button to show the code window. Enter the following code into the Click event of the button.

```
Private Sub cmd_NewForm_Click()
    ' Create variable to hold new instance of a Form
    Dim MyNewForm As Form1


    ' Create new instance of Form1
    Set MyNewForm = New Form1
    ' Make new instance visible
    MyNewForm.Visible = True
    ' Set new form's Caption property to say "Hello"
    MyNewForm.Caption = "Hello"
End Sub
```

The Click event code first creates a variable to hold the object instance of the new form. The next line uses the **Set** command to make the variable to reference the new form. The keyword New that appears before the Form1 reference is the command that instantiates the new instance of the form. If this command were omitted and the line read Set MyNewForm = Form1, a new instance would not be created. The line would merely set the variable MyNewForm to reference the current instance of Form1.

N O T E   The code we have been inserting into the command buttons of this form is actually methods of the command button objects. When an event occurs, Visual Basic executes whatever code is stored in a particular method. In the code we have added so far, all the statements have been added to the Click methods of command buttons.

The lines that follow the creation of the new instance make the new form visible and set the Caption property to Hello. By giving the form window a different caption, we make it easier to see which form is the new instance. You can now execute this program (by pressing **F5**) with the added button. When you click the **New Form** button, your screen should look like the one shown in Figure 4.5. This second form, including all its control objects, is fully operational. If you click the **New Form** command button on this new instance, another new instance will be created.

This example should enable you to understand some of the power of object-oriented programming. Once a blueprint class is created, you may create as many duplicate instances of an object as you need. These objects can also be reused in other programs, so you don't have to reinvent the wheel every time you write a new program.

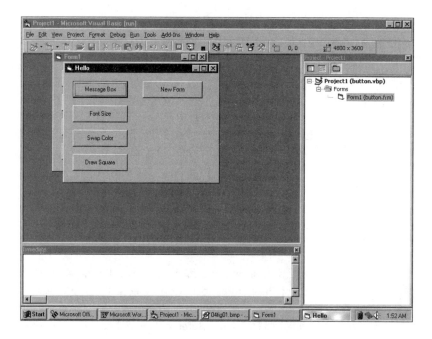

Figure 4.5 *Your program after the creation of a new form.*

Dot Commands

The best way to read an object reference is in the opposite direction of the way you probably normally read. Reading right to left, you begin with the object being accessed, the method being executed, or the property being manipulated. Take a look at this code:

```
Excel.ActiveSheet.Visible = True
```

Notice first that the `Visible` property is being changed to `True`. This change occurs on the active sheet of the Excel application. Reading from right to left allows you to see exactly which object is being affected. Reading from left to right can often be confusing. The similarity of object names may make you leap to the wrong conclusion about which object is being called or executed.

You can now understand how an object is used within a program. You design the class and then create instances of the objects when the program is executed. This example showed how objects are used within an executing environment. If multiple instances of a type of object are created, it is extremely useful to have a convenient way to track and manipulate them in a series.

Collections of Objects

Many programs require the creation of a series of instances of a particular object. Visual Basic provides an effective technique for organizing multiple instances if the objects are of the same type. References to each instance can be stored in a *collection*. Each object referenced in a collection is known as a *member*. Members of a collection can be referenced either by the index number of the order in which they occur in the collection or by the name of the particular object.

We will discuss collections of objects in more depth later in the book. Collections are used extensively within other object collections. The forms themselves are stored within a collection by the Visual Basic environment. As you examine more Visual Basic programs, you may see code such as this:

```
Excel.Sheets(2).Visible = True
```

Or

```
Excel.Sheets("Sheet2").Visible = True
```

This code simply accesses the second instance of an Excel worksheet in the Sheets collection of Sheet objects. Note that it is common practice to use the plural (Sheets) of an object name (Sheet) to denote a collection.

BUILDING A PROGRAM USING OBJECTS

As mentioned earlier, putting together a program using objects is like using an erector set. Objects are added to a project and then code is written to connect the object, supply the proper data, and perform any necessary functions. Building programs in this manner is a boon for the individual programmer and for the team building a large project.

For the individual programmer, object program development can provide the structure needed to make quick and dramatic changes to the entire program. If it's decided on short notice that video and sound effects are required, it's easy to add object controls to the project. Controls can be purchased or even downloaded for free through the Internet.

Additionally, as you gain experience, you might consider creating your own series of object classes. Nearly every programmer keeps a toolbox of common routines handy. Object-oriented programming provides the technology for even a beginning programmer to create an effective toolbox. Do you need to reuse the part of your program that calculates the average number of cars on the freeway and displays it as a graph? Just create it as an object class, and you can use it easily in many programs.

Market for Good Objects

NOTE   There is a constantly growing market for specialty controls. If you develop an object that would be useful to others in your field, you may find a ready market for it. Controls that are constructed in Visual Basic can be used not only over the Internet, but also from within any application that is capable of being an ActiveX container. Programs that feature this ability include Excel, Word, Access, Project, Internet Explorer, Netscape Communicator, Lotus 1-2-3, Lotus Notes, Visio, and others and the list is growing.

No matter what type of control you build (from calculating structural analysis to estimating the cost of furnishing a home), you might find others interested in using it.

For team development, an entire program can be prototyped by creating dummy objects for all the functions. Then these dummy objects are brought together to create the framework for the completed application. Individual programmers are then assigned to create the actual functioning objects.

A functioning prototype can be built using these techniques. For example, for a mathematical launching program for a new rocket, dummy objects could be created to output numbers needed by other parts of the application. Objects might need to be developed that receive velocity numbers and output the necessary fuel to maintain this velocity. The dummy objects could receive numbers and output dummy numbers. In this way the entire process of the program could be tested before code development begins. If fundamental structural changes are needed, perhaps eliminating certain objects, much time can be saved. A completed prototype would also improve the accuracy of planning and resource scheduling.

When you are constructing a program, it is best to imagine it as a series of black boxes: closed portions whose inner workings you cannot see or manipulate. The construct simply has an input and an output. This approach prevents developers from tampering with the core part of a module and also discourages them from relying on specific interior details that may change in the future. Using this metaphor, each object in a program is a black box which you can pass data into and retrieve the resulting information. The black box should be self-contained and hold all the necessary variables and routines stored within the object. If the black box metaphor is violated (by calling a routine outside the object or accessing a global variable), its effectiveness is severely hampered. Sharing, re-using, or debugging such an object becomes much more difficult.

INFORMATION HIDING

With a simple object, all the properties and methods relevant to it are contained within it. Because the properties are still exposed, however, the object is not entirely stable. Suppose an object calculates a car's number of miles per gallon given the average miles per hour (MPH) the car is driven and several other factors. What happens if the input MPH property is set to an outrageous figure, such as 20,000 or -18? The methods within the object could crash, because this property should not occur in those ranges.

One possible solution is to include a range check in each method in the object to make sure that the range is valid. What happens if you forget to include it in one of the methods or if a new method is added? What if you later want to modify the range of accepted values? In an object, the best solution is to hide the actual properties used by the calculation routines within the object. Simply expose methods that get and set these properties. When the properties are retrieved or set by other code, a check is automatically performed and invalid values are rejected.

This technique of not allowing access to the internals of an object is known as *information hiding*. Only the properties (variables) and the methods (procedures) needed for strictly defined input and output can be accessed from outside the object. Anything that is critical to the functioning of the object is hidden from other routines. Visual Basic provides mechanisms for information hiding in a Visual Basic program.

The `RemoveItem` method of a list box control is a perfect example of information hiding. To remove the first item from the list in a list box named List1, you would execute code such as this:

```
List1.RemoveItem 1
```

You never have access to the actual properties that store the items contained in the list. Instead, the `RemoveItem` method accesses the internal representation of the list and removes the item. By supplying this method, the designers of the list box control eliminate the possibility that a programmer might accidentally break the internal structure of the list, causing another method, such as `AddItem`, to crash.

Information hiding also prevents people from having direct access to your internal design if you are producing your object commercially. By creating a black box, you force potential competitors to create their own similar solutions rather than duplicate the structure you spent a great deal of resources to refine.

For Individual Programmers

Although information hiding is extremely useful and potentially makes the execution of your objects more solid, it is not strictly necessary if you are doing individual programming. If you have no plans to share or distribute your code, the extra time it takes to implement information hiding may not be worth the gains that you might receive.

By preventing access to the data used within the object, you can create something known as a *wrapper*. The wrapper converts data to and from the object so that an otherwise incompatible routine can be used. Suppose you have a routine that calculates the amount of paint required to coat a wall. The routine came from Europe, where the wall size is measured in meters, but your customers are located in the United States, which uses the English system of measure. You can create an object wrapper that automatically converts the input (feet and inches) into meters. When the calculation method is called, it uses the internal (metric) values to complete the figuring. The results can then be converted automatically to feet and inches for output. You can create this wrapper without having to modify the original routine; otherwise, modifying the core routine could introduce bugs into the calculations. If you later decide to make the routine work with English units of measure, you can modify the method and the property get and set routines without any reprogramming of code that accesses the object.

Now that we've completed our discussion of basic object concepts, we can start having fun. In Chapter 5, you'll learn some new commands that will let you draw on the screen and create a program called Sketch. You'll put all your learning to work!

RELATED TOOLS

- Object-oriented programming is often referred to by the acronym OOP. If you read more on OOP, you will be amazed by how complicated the technology can be. Luckily, Visual Basic simplifies almost all this complexity without sacrificing the power of OOP.

- Objects take up memory. If you finish referencing them and they are no longer used, they will automatically remove themselves from memory. If you leave a dangling reference, however, they can remain in memory and take up memory and system resources. Just to be safe, it is recommended that you set your object to Nothing after you have finished working with it. In the case of the form instance we created in this chapter, the statement would read as follows:

```
Set MyNewForm = Nothing
```

- Most of Visual Basic itself is stored as an object. It can be modified to include additional functions or shortcuts. Although that topic is beyond the scope of this book, you'll find references on the Internet and information in the Visual Basic help file on how to make these modifications. Look under information about Visual Basic add-ins.

- All the objects that can be accessed by your Visual Basic program are available in the Object Browser (we will cover the Object Browser in depth in a later chapter). You can use it to examine object for active object models. Select the **Object Browser** option under the View menu, press **F2**, or click on the icon on the toolbar. Classes and members of those classes (including properties and methods) are shown in the various panes of the browser.

SUMMARY

This chapter was filled with new material. We'll slow down a little in Chapter 5, where you'll learn how to draw on the screen. Here's a quick review of the material in this chapter.

- An object is a fusion of properties (variables) and methods (procedures) that are self-contained. If you encapsulate the methods and properties in an object, it can be reused in numerous programs, and you can change the internals of the object without affecting other parts of the program that accesses it.

- Each object has two aspects: a class and instancing. A class is a blueprint of the object and contains all the methods and properties used by the object. An instance is the actual object that is created and used in the computer memory. Multiple instances of an object can be created from a single class.

- Collections are used to contain multiple instances of a particular object type.

- Items shown in an object model are known as members of the class. Members can include methods, properties, other objects, or collections of objects.

- Information hiding is used to create more robust and bug-free programs. By not allowing access to properties used within an object, you can change the internal structure of the object without affecting other code or objects that call the object. This technique can also be used when information sent to an object needs to be modified before it can be used by the methods of the object.

Building Programs

- Events
- Building the Sketch program
- The **If..Then** command and Boolean expressions

At this point, you're ready to roll up your sleeves and start writing real programs in Visual Basic. We'll build a complete application while occasionally using the Immediate window to explore new commands. This program, called Sketch, will let you sketch lines inside a window. We'll spend the next two chapters building Sketch, and most of the work will be learning how to set up the windows, menus, and code for the application.

ANATOMY OF AN EVENT HANDLER

In Chapter 2, you created a simple application that consisted of four command buttons. We placed code for each of the command buttons in their respective Click event methods. For the message box command button, the first button on the form, the code looked like this:

```
Private Sub cmd_MsgBox_Click()
    ' Create variable to hold user response
    Dim result As Integer
    ' Display MessageBox
    result = MsgBox("Please press the OK button to continue",
vbOKOnly, "Sample Message")
End Sub
```

This small piece of code is called an *event handler*, because it handles mouse click events on the button. There are a number of different types of events in Windows programs. Clicking is an event. Pressing a key is an event. Even redrawing (or repainting) a form window is an event. Visual Basic allows you to write instructions (subroutines) for handling each of these events. In this example, you're handling the Click event, and that means you're running the cmd_MsgBox_Click method whenever you click on the button.

REFERENCE

Visual Basic programs are built around events, which are various things that can happen in a program. As you'll see in this book, you can write code to handle a number of events, such as clicking, double-clicking, painting (drawing a window), pressing a key, and moving the mouse.

An event handler consists of three parts: the event definition lines of code you write, and the End Sub line.

The first line defines the name of the event handler. In this case, Visual Basic has created an event handler called cmd_MsgBox_Click(). (In a minute we'll look at the rules Visual Basic uses to define event names. But first, let's finish looking at the structure of this event handler.)

The first word, `Private` in this case, indicates that the subroutine can be accessed only by statements that are inside the form or module containing the private subroutine. In other words, commands inside other forms and modules can't access that subroutine. If it were `Public` instead of `Private`, it would be available to all other commands in all other forms or modules.

The name of this event procedure, `cmd_MsgBox_Click()`, has two parts (see Figure 5.1) separated by the second underscore character (_). The first part of the name is the object you're working with. When you're working with controls, this name is always the name of the control, such as `cmd_MsgBox`.

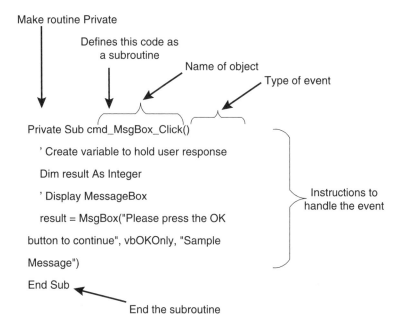

Figure 5.1 *The various parts of an event-handling procedure.*

There are only two cases in which the name of the object does not appear before the event in the procedure name. When the object is either a Form object or a MDIForm, the object names are not used in the event procedures. Instead, the generic event names `Form_event` and `MDIForm_event` are used. Therefore, any code for the Click event method for a form will be titled

`Form_Click()`. Sometimes you may forget about these exceptions and look for an event under the name of the form. We thought we'd mention this before it became confusing.

The second part of the procedure name is the name of the event this subroutine will handle. In this example, you're handling the `Click` event for mouse clicks on the button. If this procedure were instead to be activated when the `KeyPress` event occurred, it would be called `cmd_MsgBox` `_KeyPress()`.

As with any procedure, the subroutine ends with the line `End Sub`. All event methods are stored as subroutines. Events occur and are passed to the event routine. You cannot pass information back to an event, so there are never event procedures that are functions.

A Look at Event-Driven Programs

Most of the time that your program is "running," it's not actually doing anything. This is because your Visual Basic program has returned control to Windows. Unless the user clicks on an object, is typing at the keyboard, or is accessing the disk, the computer is simply waiting for an event that will cause it to perform an action.

All Windows programs are built around what's known as the *event model* of programming. In this model, Windows watches your computer to see what's going on; as soon as something interesting (an event) happens, Windows figures out which program the event belongs to and then sends that event to the correct program (see Figure 5.2).

When you click a command button, Windows notices that the click belongs to a window owned by Visual Basic, so it sends the click event to Visual Basic. Visual Basic, in turn, notices that the click is for your command button, so it sends the event to your code in the `Click()` method, which executes your code. The event code is executed until Visual Basic encounters the `End Sub` statement, which signals the end of the code for this event. Visual Basic then returns control to Windows and awaits the next event.

You should now have a general understanding of how an event-based program functions. All these concepts will become clearer in the next few chapters, where you'll continue to work with events. The concept of an event is one that most people have a little trouble learning at first. But when you get the hang of it, it's a useful and simple way to write programs. So hang in there.

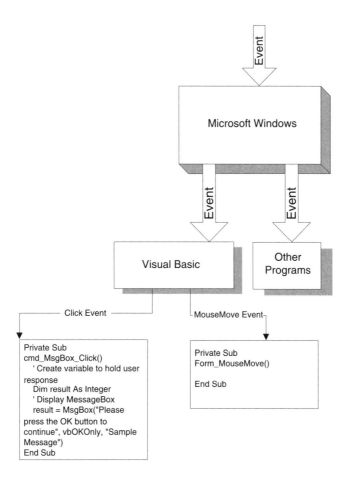

Figure 5.2 *The event model used in Windows programs. In this model, your program receives control of, and runs in response to, only events generated by Windows.*

BUILDING A SKETCH PROGRAM

Your first real program, Sketch, will allow you to sketch on the screen. Figure 5.3 shows what this program will do when you finish it at the end of Chapter 7. In developing this program, you will encounter all the primary concepts used in building a complete program. You will see how to use the power of Visual Basic to create the applications you want.

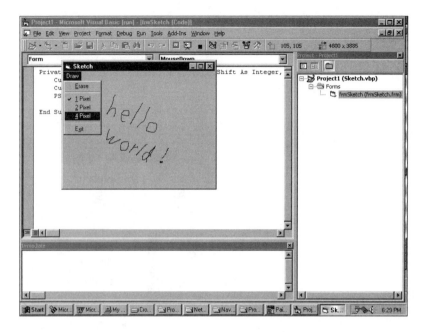

Figure 5.3 *Sketch lets you use the mouse to draw on the screen. It includes a pull-down menu that lets you erase the picture, change the width of the pen, and exit the program.*

We'll be using the `Line` method which is built into every form object. The `Line` method draws a line within a form. You will create sketch by using this method, tracking the mouse, and drawing a line where it has been. After you've polished the part of the program that draws lines, we'll add the pull-down menu. This task is remarkably easy, especially compared with the effort it takes in complex languages such as C or C++.

Create a New Project

The first step is to start a new project. There are two ways to do this. You can either quit and then restart Visual Basic, or you can select the **New Project** option from the File menu. Either way, the main New Project window should be shown. Click the **Open** button, which will create a new Standard EXE project. A new form name, Form1, will appear on the screen.

Choosing the Event

The first event that we'll work with, `Form_MouseMove`, occurs whenever you move the mouse. (Big surprise, right?)

First you'll need to get to the code window. Double-click somewhere within the blank Form1, displaying the code window with the `Form_Load()` event shown. This event occurs when the form is first loaded. However, we don't need to modify this event now. We want the `MouseMove` event.

You get to this event by clicking the down-pointing arrow in the combo box at the top right of the code window. The combo box shows `Load`, the event that is currently displayed in the window. Figure 5.4 shows this combo box pulled down with the `MouseMove` event highlighted. Click on this event to show it in the window.

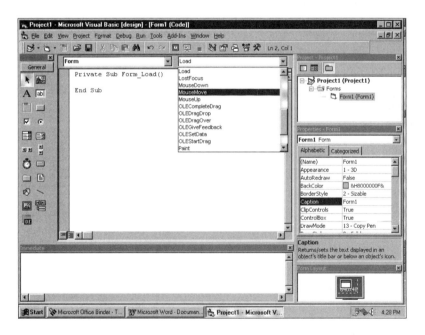

Figure 5.4 *Click the down-pointing arrow for the combo box to show the procedures (event handlers) available. Then click **MouseMove** to select this event procedure.*

If you use the horizontal scroll bar, you can see that the `MouseMove` event procedure receives a number of arguments (the names inside the parentheses):

```
Private Sub Form_MouseMove(Button As Integer, Shift As
Integer, _
X As Single, Y As Single)
```

(Even though this is one code statement, we've written it as two lines so that it will fit on this page.)

N O T E

Lines of code in this book are restricted to about 65 characters, the width of the page. So the lines you write will usually not be longer than 65 characters. But Visual Basic often creates subroutine definitions that are longer than 65 characters.

To make it easier to read code in the code window, Visual Basic has added a line-continuation character so that you can write single code statements that require more than one line. To continue a statement onto the next line, use a space, followed immediately by an underscore character at the end of the first line; then continue the statement on the subsequent line.

The MouseMove subroutine definition includes four arguments. In Chapter 1, you learned that the **Print** command can work with a number of arguments. Like **Print**, the MouseMove event handler can receive arguments:

- Button. Gives us information about which mouse button is pressed. This will be 1 if only the left button is down, 2 if only the right button is down, and 3 if both buttons are down.

- Shift. Which shift keys (such as the **Left Shift**, **Right Shift**, **Alt Shift**, and **Ctrl Shift**) are currently down. We won't be using this information here.

- X, Y. Gives information about where the mouse is inside the window. You'll use these two numbers for the endpoints of your lines.

Writing Event Code

Make sure you have the Form_MouseMove subroutine visible in the code window. Then type the following line of code between the Private Sub and End Sub lines:

```
Line -(X, Y)
```

(You can indent this line by pressing the **Tab** key.) Now press **F5** to run this program. Move your mouse. See how it draws lines to follow the mouse (see Figure 5.5). When you want to exit this program, click on the control menu in the upper-left corner of the window and choose **Close** (or press **Alt+F4**).

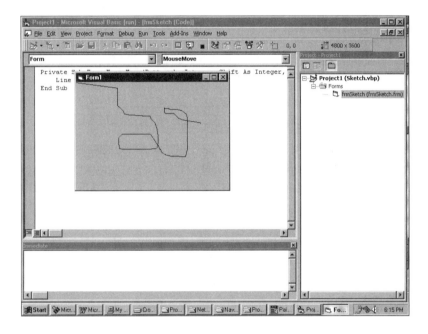

Figure 5.5 *The line follows the movements of the mouse; however, this program started by drawing a line from (0,0) to our mouse's location.*

There are a couple of problems with this program, and we'll show you how to fix them. First, notice that Sketch began by drawing a line from (0, 0) to the mouse location. This happens because the Line $-(X, Y)$ command draws lines from the last location. Because the "last location" is initially (0, 0), the first line starts at (0, 0). Second, you want Sketch to draw lines only when you press the mouse button.

These problems are easy to fix, and we could fix both of them at the same time. But it's better to fix one problem at a time and test your solution. This method—testing a program by changing one thing at a time—is an important programming technique that will save you hours of time in the long run.

If you change too many things at once, you may forget what you're doing and then fail to test a change you made. Effective programming promotes the habit of not waiting to test a routine. You should make a change and then test, make a change and then test, and make a change and then test. The more work you do, the more you will fall into the rhythm of this method.

NOTE We said that the Line routine was a method for the form object (in this case, Form1). You can simply type the command **Line** without including an object reference, because the routine is executing on the form itself. Therefore, the object reference is implicit. The line code would function identically if it included the reference to the form:

```
Form1.Line -(X, Y)
```

Let's start by changing Sketch so it that won't start drawing until you click. Let's think about what you need to do. You need some way of knowing when the mouse is down and drawing only then. If you look again at the arguments received in the MouseMove event subroutine, you'll notice that one of them is called Button, and it tells you which mouse button is pressed. How can you use this information?

Clicking to Draw

A command called **If..Then** will run a command (or set of commands) only if a condition is true. This is the perfect command to use for drawing a line only if the left button is down. Before we look at all the details of **If..Then** and how it works, let's try it in the program. Replace the current Line command in Form_MouseMove() with the following:

```
If Button = 1 Then
  Line -(X, Y)
End If
```

NOTE

The code we have entered begins with an If...Then statement and ends with an End If statement. Code may not always include the End If statement. If the condition is true and only one command needs to be executed, you can include the command on the same line as the Then statement and eliminate the End If command. The code would appear as follows:

```
If Button = 1 Then Line -(X, Y)
```

We don't use this approach in this book (except when we're using the Immediate window, which won't accept multiline If...Then statements), because it can be confusing. If more than one command needs to be executed on the true condition, the End If must be included. For the sake of consistency, all routines, even single commands, will use the End If statement.

Try running this program. Sketch will draw lines only when you hold down the left mouse button. Great! Programming usually works this way. Add a feature at a time until your application performs like magic.

Now we need to cover more theory, so we'll save this project before we continue.

Saving Sketch

We'll save this project to the hard disk, but first let's name the form. Before changing the form's name, you'll need to return to Design mode (if you haven't already stopped execution with the **Stop** toolbar button). If the code window is now visible (instead of the form), use the Window menu to select the **Form1 (Form)** option. Make sure the Sketch form is active (click once on it); then press **F4** to make the Properties window visible and active. Finally, use the scroll bar on the right side of the Properties window to scroll to the top of the list until the line with (Name) becomes visible (see Figure 5.6).

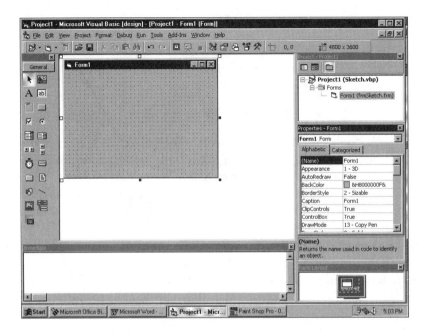

Figure 5.6 *Use the Properties window to change the name of this form. Scroll the list until the* Name *property is visible. Click on it and type in the new name (**Sketch** in our example).*

Click on the **Name** property. Notice that the combo box at the top of the Properties window now reads **Form1**. This is the current name of your form, as you saw in the Immediate window. To change this name, type **frmSketch** and press **Enter** (see Figure 5.7).

The Properties window allows you to change various properties. The (Name) item that you selected is a property of this form, as are the CurrentX and CurrentY properties. As you can see, you can change a number of other properties by using this window.

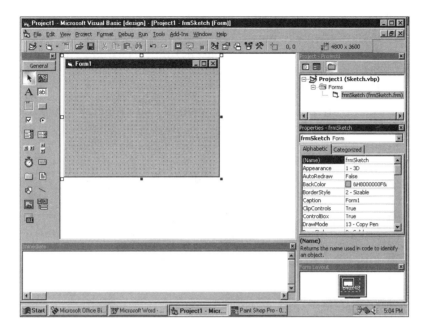

Figure 5.7 *The Property bar after you've typed in a new form name,* **Sketch**, *but before pressing* **Enter**. *You can use the mouse or cursor keys to edit what you've typed.*

N O T E You may have noticed that the CurrentX and CurrentY properties don't appear in this combo box. Why not? These two properties are *run-time* properties, and that means they have meaning only when you're running a program. On the other hand, the properties you see in this combo box are *design-time* properties. Some properties are both run-time and design-time properties, but only the design-time properties are shown in the Properties window.

In addition to changing the form's name, you'll need to change the caption in the window (which currently reads **Form1**) so that it reads **Sketch**. To do this, again use the scroll bar to display the line with **Caption**, and click on it to select the Caption property. Then type **Sketch** and press **Enter**. Your Sketch window should now say **Sketch**, rather than Form1, at the top.

Now you're ready to save your project. Instead of allowing the files to be saved in Visual Basic's directory, we suggest that you create a directory for your projects and a subdirectory called Sketch for all your Sketch files. Select the

Save Project option under the File menu. Make a new directory named PROJ using the **Create New Folder** icon (the folder with the sparkle on the top right corner), as we did in Chapter 2. Double-click on this icon to enter the folder. In this folder, create another new folder titled **Sketch**. Double-click the **Sketch** folder so that your project will be saved in this folder.

Visual Basic will first try to save the form Sketch (see Figure 5.8). Because we've already provided the form name, it has supplied us with the filename **frmSketch.frm** to be saved as a FRM type file. Click **Save** to save the form.

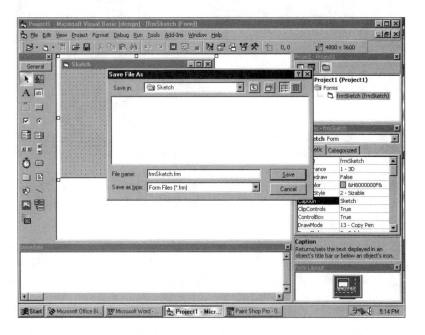

Figure 5.8 *When you ask to save the project, Visual Basic will first prompt you for the name and directory of the Sketch form.*

Next, Visual Basic displays a Save Project As dialog box with a default name of **Project1.vbp** for the project file. Type **Sketch.vbp** and press **Enter** (the directory will already be the one where you stored **Sketch.frm**). That's it. You've now saved Sketch, so you can exit Visual Basic and then load your project into Visual Basic by selecting **Open Project** in the File menu.

Opening Your Sketch Project

When you start Visual Basic again, you'll need to know how to load the Sketch project. Quit Visual Basic and start over (using the **Exit** option under the File menu). When you have Visual Basic running again, click the **Recent** tab in the opening dialog box. The dialog box should look like the one in Figure 5.9.

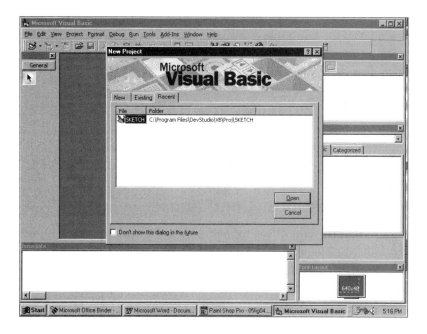

Figure 5.9 *When you select the **Recent** tab, the most recently used projects will be displayed. Click **Open** to reopen the Sketch project.*

The Sketch form should be shown again in the center of the screen.

THE IF..THEN COMMAND

Now that you've saved your project, let's spend a few minutes on the theory behind the **If..Then** command. You've probably already figured out how the `If Button=1 Then Line` command works, but let's try a few simple experiments anyway. Make sure you have the Immediate window visible and active and enter the following to test the **If..Then** command:

```
if 1=1 then print "True"
True
|
```

As you can see, the **If..Then** command checked to see whether 1=1. Because it does (meaning that 1=1 is true), Visual Basic ran the command `Print "True"`.

You can also try using this command with something you know isn't true:

```
if 1=0 then print "True"
|
```

You'll notice that Visual Basic ignored the `Print "True"` command, and that is exactly what you want it to do. In other words, it executes the **Print** command only if the condition is true. Because 1=0 is not true, it didn't print.

Boolean Expressions (Conditions)

You'll notice that the equal sign here is a test rather than an assignment. Such tests are called Boolean expressions. Although it may sound intimidating, all Boolean means is that an expression can be either true or false. In other words, it can have only one of two values.

Another piece of jargon should make a little more sense. When you use a Boolean expression such as 1=0 in an `If..Then` statement, it's called a *condition*. In other words, `If..Then` runs a command only on the condition that an expression is true.

Let's try more tests to see how Visual Basic handles true and false. Because there are only two values, you can use two **Print** commands to display both of them:

```
print 1=1
True
print 1=0
False
|
```

You can see from this reply that Visual Basic uses the words `True` and `False` as values for the Boolean data type. So if everything works as expected, you should be able to use the words as conditions just as easily as expressions. The following are the same **Print** commands as before, but this time we're using the Boolean data value rather than expressions:

```
if true then print "True"
True
if false then print "True"
|
```

A Boolean expression will always return either `True` or `False`.

BOOLEAN EXPRESSIONS

The term *Boolean* is derived from the name of the English mathematician George Boole. In the mid-1800s, Boole developed a type of mathematics called Boolean algebra. This type of algebra deals with values that are either true or false. It is invaluable for use with computers, because computers work fundamentally with 0 and 1 (false and true) signals.

With Visual Basic, the Boolean data type shows us the words `True` and `False`, but internally, Visual Basic is storing the value numerically. The number 0 represents `False`, and 1 represents `True`.

You can see this for yourself by using the **CInt** command (it stands for "convert to Integer") in the Immediate window, as follows:

```
Print CInt(True)
  -1
Print CInt(False)
  0
```

The reason Microsoft chose these two numbers has to do with an operator called `Not`, because the expression `Not True = False`. In other words, the **Not** command reverses the evaluated results returned by a condition (it changes `True` to `False` and `False` to `True`).

The Not operator works with something called a *bit*, which is the smallest unit of storage inside your computer and is either 0 or 1. An Integer number, which is how true and false are represented, is built from 16 of these bits. If we write the numbers for true and false as bits, we get the following:

BOOLEAN	BASIC	BINARY
False	0	0000 0000 0000 0000
True	—1	1111 1111 1111 1111

The Not keyword inverts all the bits in a number, changing 0s to 1s and 1s to 0s, which means that Not 0 = —1. This means that Not True = False, which is exactly what we want Not, True, and False to mean.

Why is Not 0 negative? You learned in Chapter 1 that half of the values in an Integer number are defined as being negative. The microprocessor inside your computer determines whether a number is negative by looking at the first digit in the binary number: all numbers that start with a 1 are negative numbers. So Not 0, which starts with a 1, will be a negative number, which happens to be minus 1.

The Else Part of If..Then

The If..Then command is very powerful. So far we've looked only at the simplest case, in which you run one command if a condition is true. But you can also have **If..Then** run a different command if the condition is false, as you'll see in the next example.

The following example executes one command if a condition is true and another command if it's false:

```
if 1=0 then print "True" else print "False"
False
|
```

All you have to do is to add an Else keyword, followed by another command. The **If..Then** command is a useful command that you'll use often in this book, so you'll learn more of the details in coming chapters.

You'll learn more about the **If..Then..Else** command and how to use all its pieces in following chapters.

```
If condition Then
     command1
[Else
     command2]
End If
```

There are several pieces to this command. The first piece, *condition*, is a test that the **If** command performs. If the result of this test is true, Visual Basic runs command1; otherwise, it will do nothing, or, when you have an **Else**, it will run command2.

```
If condition1 Then
   [statements]
[ElseIf condition2 Then
   [statements] ]
[Else
   [statements] ]
End If
```

Boolean Operators

In addition to the simple = comparison that you've been working with so far, there are a number of other operators, as you can see in Table 5.1. Some of these operators should be fairly clear, but others, such as Xor, are more advanced. We will cover them in later chapters when you need them.

Table 5.1 Boolean Operators

OPERATOR	MEANING
=	Equal to; returns True if the values on both sides are the same
<>	Not equal; the values on the two sides differ
<	Less than; True if the left side is less than the right side
>	Greater than; True if the left side is greater than the right side
<=	Less than or equal

Table 5.1 Boolean Operators (continued)

OPERATOR	MEANING
>=	Greater than or equal
Not	Invert all the bits in the number to its right; Not 0 = –1
Or	Bit-wise Or
Xor	Bit-wise Exclusive Or
Eqv	Equivalent
Imp	Implication

We will, however, take a quick look at the `Or` operator, which is useful when you have more than one condition and need only one condition to be true. For example, if you have the Boolean expressions 1=1 and 1=0 and you write (1=1) or (1=0), the result should be true because the first expression is true. Try it by using the **Print** command, and you'll discover that it is true:

```
print (1=1) or (1=0)
True
|
```

The `And` operator is useful when you have multiple conditions all of which must be true. The following two examples should give you a better idea of how `And` works:

```
print (1=1) and (2=2)
True
print (1=1) and (1=2)
False
|
```

The first example returns `True` since both expressions are true, but the second example returns `False` because the second expression (1=2) is not true.

One final word of advice. When you have a number of operators in one expression (there are two equal signs and one `Or` in the preceding example), it's a good idea to use parentheses to make sure that Basic correctly interprets what you write. If you're not intimately familiar with operator precedence (which you learned about in Chapter 1), you could easily write a statement that looked correct but that Visual Basic calculated in an order different from what you might expect.

Finishing Sketch

Enough theory! Let's get back to the Sketch program and fix the remaining problem. You'll notice that the program draws a line from (0, 0) to your mouse location when you first click. You'll also notice that you can't draw unconnected lines. These problems turn out to have the same cause. All these extra lines appear because the Line −(X, Y) command draws a line continuing from the last point. Visual Basic remembers the last point using the CurrentX and CurrentY properties, and they're set to 0 when you first start your program. What you need to do is to set CurrentX and CurrentY to the location of the mouse when you first click it. You do that by using a new event called Form_MouseDown.

Visual Basic runs the code you write in the MouseDown event subroutine whenever you click the mouse button, but not during the rest of the time you hold down the mouse button. (On the other hand, the Click() event that you worked with before runs only when you click and then release the mouse button.) In other words, if you click and hold and then move the mouse, Visual Basic first runs MouseDown and then runs MouseMove (and finally Click when you release the button). And this is exactly what you want. You'll set CurrentX and CurrentY to the mouse position (X, Y) inside the MouseDown subroutine.

The MouseDown and Click events are quite different. MouseDown is called as soon as you click the mouse button, but Click is not called until you release the mouse button.

N O T E

Make sure you're in Design mode and that the Sketch form is visible. Then double-click on this form to show the code window. Next, pull down the Procedure combo box and select the **MouseDown** event. The following code is all you need to add:

```
CurrentX = X
CurrentY = Y
```

After you've entered these two lines in the Form_MouseDown event, run your program and see how it works. You should now be able to draw lines without the initial line from (0, 0). You'll also notice that Sketch now allows you to draw unconnected lines.

That was easy, but there is one last problem. If you click and release the mouse button without moving the mouse, Sketch doesn't draw anything. It should draw at least a point, so let's add yet another command that will draw a point even if you don't move the mouse.

To draw a point, you'll use the Basic command **PSet**, which stands for point set. **PSet** draws a single point (pixel) on the screen. The command PSet(X, Y) will draw one pixel at (X, Y). Add this command to the Form_MouseDown subroutine, which should now look like the following:

```
Private Sub Form_MouseDown (Button As Integer, Shift As
Integer, _
X As Integer, Y As Single)
  CurrentX = X
  CurrentY = Y
  PSet (X, Y)
End Sub
```

(The first line is too long to print as a single line, so we've wrapped it to two lines, using the continuation character–a space immediately followed by an underscore character–indicating that the second line is a continuation of the first line.)

Pset Command

REFERENCE

[object.]PSet [Step](x!, y!)[,color&]

The **PSet** command draws a single point (pixel) at (x!, y!). You can also use the same Step keyword and color& argument used by the **Line** command.

Isn't this great? You should feel a touch of accomplishment for all the progress you have made. You've done all the work on Sketch for this chapter, so you should save your work. You can use the **Save Project** command in the

File menu to save the project file as well as any other files (**Sketch.frm**) that you've changed. In Chapter 6, you'll add a menu bar to Sketch.

RELATED TOOLS

- **Select Case**. This command is similar to the **If..Then** command. It's most useful when you're testing a single variable against several values. In other words, if you want to run a different statement for any value in a variable, use this command.

SUMMARY

You learned a lot about building real programs in this chapter, and you'll learn even more in the coming chapters.

- Code window. You'll use the code window throughout the rest of this book to write your programs. You display this window by double-clicking on the form window, which is called **Form1** in new projects.
- Events. Visual Basic programs are built around event subroutines (also known as event handlers) that handle such events as clicking the mouse button, moving the mouse, and pressing a key. In this chapter you worked with the `Click`, `Form_MouseMove`, and `Form_MouseDown` event subroutines.
- **Sub**. Any subroutine begins with the word Sub and the subroutine's name. Event subroutines are formed from the object name (such as `Form`) and the event name (such as `MouseMove`). Subroutines end with the line `End Sub`. Any lines of code you write must appear between these two lines.
- **If..Then**. The **If..Then..Else** command allows you to choose which code you want to run based on the result of a condition. Conditions are Boolean expressions that result in a `True` or `False`. In the Basic language, `True` = 1 and `False` = 0, and Boolean expressions return numbers of type Integer.
- Properties window. You use the Properties window to change the form `Name` and `Caption` properties of your Sketch program.

CHAPTER 6

Adding a Menu Bar

- Control names and menus
- Using the Menu Editor window
- Control arrays
- The Index argument

In this chapter you'll add a menu bar to the Sketch program. A menu bar is the list of menus that runs along the top of an application window, typically containing File, Edit, and other menus. As you'll see, creating a menu bar and its associated menus is easy to do. You won't have to learn as much new material in this chapter as in previous chapters.

BUILDING A MENU BAR

Visual Basic provides a visual design tool for building menu bars, so building them is simple. Anyone who has written a program using a language such as C or Pascal will tell you it's much more work using those languages. Visual Basic makes the entire process graphical, so you can create menus quickly and edit them easily.

If you don't already have Sketch loaded in Visual Basic, open it again. Use the **Open Project** selection under the File menu and locate Sketch under the **Recent** tab. To use the menu tool, you'll need to close the Code window (if you still have it open) so that your Sketch form will be visible and active. You might want to click once on it to make sure it's active. Next, pull down the Tools menu and click on **Menu Editor** (or use the **Ctrl+E** keyboard shortcut). This action will bring up a window like the one shown in Figure 6.1.

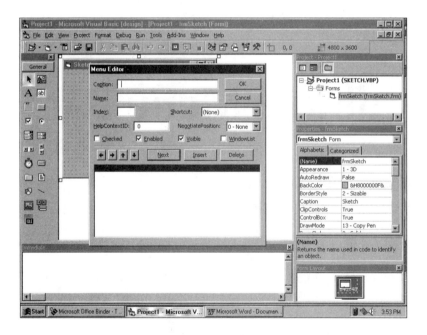

Figure 6.1 *The Menu Editor window.*

This window lets you create a menu bar that contains all the menus and menu items you want. Let's quickly review the menu you'll create (see Figure 6.2). You'll start with a simpler version of the Draw menu, using only a single menu item: **Exit**. This will allow you to get a menu up and running quickly, without learning everything you'll need to know for the full menu.

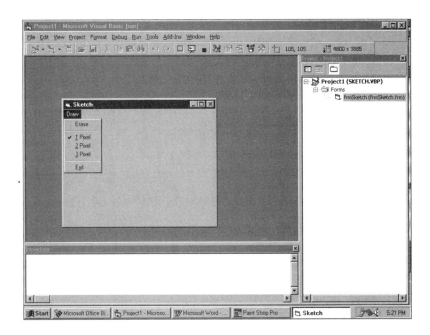

Figure 6.2 *The Draw menu you'll create. Notice that there's only one menu on the menu bar.*

Creating the Menu Title

The first part of creating a menu is easy. Type the name of the menu—in this case, **Draw**—into the **Caption** field at the top of the Menu Editor window. Notice in Figure 6.2 that the *D* in Draw is underlined. This tells Windows that users can use the **Alt+D** key combination to pull down this menu.

Such underlined letters are called *mnemonic access characters*. This is quite a mouthful, but its meaning is simple. Mnemonic characters are characters you can remember more easily than function keys, such as **F4**, as shortcuts for an action. Such letters usually have some obvious connection, such as the first letter, to the full name. For example, the letter *d* has a mnemonic connection to the word *draw*.

Sometimes, however, two or more menus or menu items start with the same letter, such as File and Format in Microsoft Word. In these cases, you'll have to use other rules to choose which letter to underline. See the sidebar "How to Choose Mnemonic Characters" for the rules that Microsoft suggests.

The Menu Editor uses an ampersand character (&) in front of a letter to mark it as a mnemonic access character. To make the *D* in Draw the access character, type the following into the **Caption** text box of the Menu Editor window:

```
&Draw
```

Next, press the **Tab** key. This moves the insertion point to the next text box, **Name**, which is the name of the control.

How to Choose Mnemonic Characters

Microsoft has a number of suggestions about how to choose a mnemonic access character. These rules apply to menu names and to the names of the menu items in any one menu. Here are the rules, in order of preference:

- First letter. Use the first letter when you can. If you have more than one menu or item that starts with the same letter (such as File and Format), you'll have to choose a different mnemonic character for all but one name. You may also decide that another letter is more meaningful than the first letter, such as *x* for Exit. When you have a two-word title, you can use the first letter in the second (or third) word. For example, many programs have a **Save** and a **Save As...** menu item. Notice that the *A* in **Save As** is underlined.

- Distinctive consonant. If you can't use the first letter, use a consonant that stands out. For example, the *t* in Format stands out more than the *r* or *m*, because it's at the end of the word. On the other hand, the *b* in Ribbon is more distinctive than the *n*. There are no hard-and-fast rules here.

- Vowel. If all else fails, choose a vowel in the title. For example, Word for Windows has the following menus: File, Format, Tools, and Table. You can see how they chose the characters by following all three rules.

In all cases, you mark the mnemonic access character with an ampersand (&) in code. For example, `T&able` marks the *a* in Table.

Controls and Control Names

A control is a special type of object. You learned about objects in Chapter 4, which explained that all controls used in Visual Basic (such as check boxes and list boxes) as well as forms are objects. The menu bar and its items, for example, will appear as objects inside your Sketch program (as soon as you finish building it). You will give each menu and each menu item an object name so that you can access it from your code.

Let's name the Draw menu. In the **Name** field for the &Draw title, type the following:

```
menDraw
```

Here, we're using a naming convention we'll use throughout this book for the names of controls. We've put men in front of Draw to indicate (to you, not Visual Basic) that this control is the name of a menu.

When you've finished typing this control name, press **Enter**. This is the same as clicking the **Next** button, which takes you to the next menu or item name. Pressing **Enter** places the Draw menu in the current menu definition (the box at the bottom of the Menu Editor, which should now read **Draw**). The **Caption** and **Name** fields are automatically cleared for a new item, and the cursor should be in the **Caption** text box.

N O T E   You may wonder why we had you underline the *x* in E<u>x</u>it rather than the *E*. It turns out that Microsoft has a number of standard menu names and items, and E<u>x</u>it is one of them. Most Windows programs have a <u>F</u>ile menu whose last menu item is E<u>x</u>it.

Creating the Exit Item

The next thing you'll create is the menu item **E<u>x</u>it**. First, type **E&xit** into the **Caption** text box and then press the **Tab** key. Next, type **miExit** in the **Name** field (**mi** is a naming convention for a menu item), but don't press **Enter**. First, you need to tell Visual Basic that you want this to be a menu item rather than a menu. To do that, you'll need to click on the right-pointing arrow (see Figure 6.3).

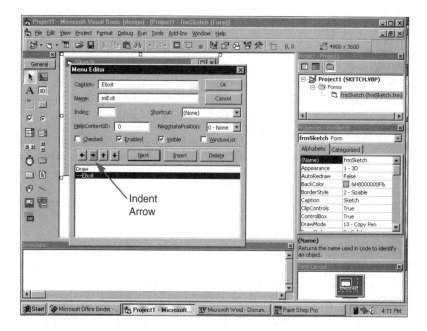

Figure 6.3 *Click on the right-pointing arrow to indent the* **Exit** *menu item so that Visual Basic will know it's a menu item rather than a menu title. Click on the* **OK** *button to finish editing the menu bar.*

Finally, click **OK** to close the Menu Editor window. You'll notice that the Sketch window has a menu bar with a single menu, Draw. We'll use the Menu Editor to expand the menu in a moment. For now, let's add the code to make the **Exit** command work.

The Menu Editor window has a close box (the **X** in the upper-right corner) to close the window. Unfortunately, this close box does not work the same as the **OK** button but rather activates the **Cancel** button. This means that if you accidentally click on the close box , all your current work on the menus is lost. Therefore, treat the **OK** button as a file save. Click **OK** often and simply reopen the editing window (using **Ctrl+E**). This technique will prevent the loss of your work.

N O T E

Adding Code to a Menu Item

You're now ready to write code to handle the new menu bar. The only menu item is **Exit**, which should exit the program. This is the same as double-clicking on the control box in the upper-left corner of the window or clicking the close box in the upper-right corner.

Each menu item has an event handler that is called by Visual Basic whenever you click on the item. The control name you gave to the **Exit** menu item is miExit, so the event handler should be called miExit_Click(). How do you get to this event handler? The design environment lets you select menu items. However, instead of executing the code attached to the menu item, Visual Basic shows the code attached to that event. If you click on the **Draw** menu and then on the **Exit** item, Visual Basic displays the code for miExit_Click() in its code window, which should look something like the following:

```
Private Sub miExit_Click ()


End Sub
```

Do you know what code we want to put into this subroutine? When you select the Exit menu item, you want the program to exit, and that means you want to use the **End** command. The **End** command completes execution of a program, closes its windows, and exits. Type the **End** command into this subroutine and run your program.

```
Private Sub miExit_Click ()
   End
End Sub
```

Did selecting the **Exit** menu item work the way you expected? It should have returned you to the Visual Basic development environment. Later, when we make a standard **EXE** from the Sketch project and run it from Windows, the **Exit** command will quit the program and return to Windows, as with any other application.

Adding the Erase Menu Item

Now let's add another item to the menu. You'll add the **Erase** item, which erases whatever you've drawn into the Sketch form. The **Cls** command (it stands for "clear screen") erases all the drawing on a form. You'll use **Cls** here. But first, you must add the **Erase** menu item.

Click on the Sketch form to make sure it's the active window (or select it through the Windows menu in Visual Basic). Then select **Menu Editor** from the Tools menu. At the bottom of this window you'll see a list of the menus and items you've created so far. It should look something like the following:

```
&Draw
....E&xit
```

Click on the second line, E&xit. Then click on the **Insert** button just above this list. This action will insert a new line (and therefore a new menu item) into your menu. It should look something like the following:

```
&Draw
....
....E&xit
```

As you have probably noticed, the dots (...) that precede the menu items do not appear when the menu is running. They simply indicate the menu level. Although we won't create any such menus in this book, the Menu Editor can be used to create multiple-level menus like the main Start menu in Windows. The right arrow that you used to indent the **Draw** option to make it a menu item can be used to make deeper levels. When you inserted the new menu item, it was placed on the same level as the **Exit** item by the dot indentation shown.

Click in the **Caption** text box and start typing. (You must click in the **Caption** box, because the insertion point won't be there until you click.) Type **&Erase** for the caption and then press the **Tab** key and type **miErase** in the **Name** field. Finally, click **OK**. You should now have a menu bar with two items: **Erase** and **Exit**.

Finally, pull down the Draw menu and click **Erase**. Then type the **Cls** command into the miErase_Click() event handler as follows:

```
Private Sub miErase_Click ()
  Cls
Sub End
```

That's all there is to it. Now you have a simple menu bar that works. Try drawing in your Sketch window and then use the **Erase** command. Nice, isn't it?

Now you should save your project (using the **Save Project** item in the File menu) before you move on. Selecting **Save Project** saves not only any changes to the project but also any changes to the forms and modules contained within it (files with **.FRM** and **.BAS** extensions). In the next section, you'll add menu items that allow you to change the width of the lines drawn in Sketch.

COMPLETING THE MENU BAR

In this section, you'll add five new menu items: three line-width menu items (**1 Pixel**, **2 Pixels**, and **3 Pixels**) and two separating lines. The first step (can you guess?) is to bring up the Menu Editor window. In the previous section, you saw how to insert menu items in front of an existing menu item. You'll use this same technique to insert all five new items, so we won't step you through entering each one. But you'll learn a couple of new techniques.

Inserting Lines in Menus

First, let's look at how you insert the two separating lines. Typing a hyphen (-) into the **Caption** text box tells Windows to draw a line across the menu. You must provide a control name for these two separating lines even though you can't click on them. Consistency in naming is a good habit to get into, so we suggest that you use the names `miLine1` and `miLine2`.

Insert the first line between the existing **Erase** end **Exit** menu items. Remember to set the **Caption** to - and **Name** to **miLine1**. If you insert the menu item in the wrong place (such as before the **Erase** menu item), don't worry. You can use the up and down arrows shown in the Menu Editor window to reorder items on a menu.

Adding Control Arrays

Next, add the three line-width menu items. The first one should have a caption of `&1 Pixel` and a control name of `miPixel`. But before you add the next menu item, you'll want to add another piece of information. If you look at the Menu Editor window, you'll notice a text box labeled **Index**. Press the **Tab** key to move the insertion point into the **Index** box, and then type **1**.

What's this for? You can create a number of menu items—or other controls for that matter—that are closely related, and the **Index** field labels each control in the group. We'll create two other menu items with subsequent index numbers (2 and 3). This will become clearer after an example, so let's continue creating the menu bar.

At this point your Menu Editor window should look something like Figure 6.4. You can now enter the other two menu items and the final line using the information in Table 6.1 (which shows an index of 2 for the **2 Pixels** item, and an index of 3 for the **3 Pixels** item).

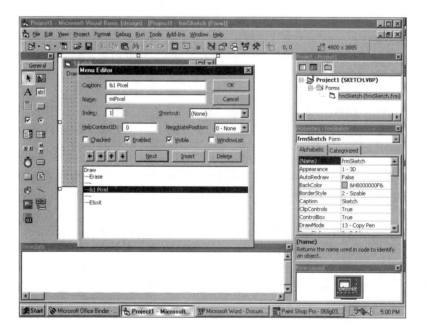

Figure 6.4 *Your Menu Editor window should look like this after you've entered the first line-width menu item, &1 Pixel. Notice the 1 (the numeral one) in the **Index** field.*

Table 6.1 Menu Names and Control Names

CAPTION	NAME	INDEX
&Draw	menDraw	
....&Erase	miErase	
....–	miLine1	
....&1 Pixel	miPixel	1
....&2 Pixel	miPixel	2
....&3 Pixel	miPixel	3
....–	miLine2	
....&Print	miPrint	
....–	miLine3	
....E&xit	miExit	

Finally, close the Menu Editor window by clicking **OK**. You should now have a menu bar like the one shown in Figure 6.2. After doing all this work to build your menu, you might want to save your project. It's a good idea to save changes to your project often, in case Windows experiences an error or you have the kind of power failure or other problem that most people encounter now and then. Either of these problems could result in a loss of all your work from the last time you saved your project.

Changing the Line Width

Now that you have all the menu items for the line-width pixel selections, you'll add the code that allows you to change the width of the drawing pen. After you see how it's done, you might want to add several more line widths to your program by adding more menu items.

Pull down the Draw menu and select the **1 Pixel** menu item. The code window should appear showing the following event handler:

```
Private Sub miPixel_Click (Index As Integer)

End Sub
```

There are differences between this click event handler and the previous click procedures you have encountered (with the command buttons starting in Chapter 2). First, if you look at the upper-left combo box, you'll notice it says miPixel(), which is the object name you selected for the pixel menu items. You'll also notice that this event handler has a new piece of information: Index As Integer. What does this mean, and what is it used for?

Index is an argument to our click event handler. Because all three controls have the same control name, you need a way to determine which menu item you clicked on. This is exactly what Index is for. It reports the value of the **Index** field from the Menu Editor window. Index will be 1, 2, or 3, the three values you entered for the **1 Pixel**, **2 Pixel**, and **3 Pixel** menu items. And you can now see why you used 1, 2, and 3 in the Index field; they are the line widths you'll need to support.

ANATOMY OF AN ARGUMENT

Any argument you see in Visual Basic appears in three parts as follows:

```
ArgumentName As Type
```

ArgumentName is the name of the argument (Index in miPixel_Click). In Chapter 5, you worked with the Button, Shift, X, and Y arguments in the Form_MouseDown event handler.

The next part, As, is a Visual Basic keyword. It tells you that the next word will be the type of value this argument holds. The variable's type can be Integer, Long, Single, Double, Currency, String or Variant.

To change the width of a line you draw, you use the DrawWidth property of a form. Visual Basic initially sets DrawWidth to 1 when you run a program. Unlike start points and endpoints, the line widths are measured in pixels rather than twips. One of the things you'll discover about Visual Basic is that it's not consistent, and that makes learning it a little more challenging.

REFERENCE

DrawWidth Property

The DrawWidth property of a form determines the width of the lines drawn on the form. DrawWidth is measured in pixels and not twips. By default, DrawWidth equals 1 when you first start a program.

When in Design mode, you can change the default DrawWidth value for any form. To do so, click on the form you want to change, select the DrawWidth property in the Properties window, and type in a new number.

By now you've probably figured out which code you need to put into the Click event handler, and you may even have tried it. The following is the code in its entirety:

```
Private Sub miPixel_Click (Index As Integer)
  DrawWidth = Index
End Sub
```

That's all there is to changing the width of the drawing pen. Try running this program and changing the line width by using the menu items. Now draw a line on the screen. You'll see that the line width matches the setting you selected.

The Click event for each menu item sets the line width to match the Index number you entered in the Menu Editor. If you look again at the menu in Figure 6.2, you'll notice that the current width has a check mark next to it. We'll add code to keep this check mark up-to-date so that it shows which pixel width is selected. It takes only two lines of code: one line to remove the current check mark, and one to check the new line width.

Checking Menu Items

Each menu item has a property called Checked, which controls whether Visual Basic draws a check mark next to the menu item. By default, the menu items you create will not be checked, but you can easily check the correct menu item with this code:

```
Private Sub miPixel_Click (Index As Integer)
  miPixel(DrawWidth).Checked = False ' Uncheck current width
  DrawWidth = Index                  ' Change width of the pen
```

```
    miPixel(Index).Checked = True      ' Check the new width
End Sub
```

Try this code, and then we'll go back and see how it works (remember to save the project before you run the program). You should be able to select a pixel width. Next time you pull down the menu, there should be a check mark to the left of the width that you last selected. You'll notice that none of the menu items is checked initially; we'll fix this shortly. But now, the selected width will be checked, and you can also change which width is checked.

REFERENCE

Menu Property: Checked

Every menu item has a property called Checked that determines whether a check mark will be drawn next to it. The menu shown in Figure 6.2 has a check mark drawn next to the **1 Pixel** menu item. Use this code:

```
    menName.Checked = False|True
```

Setting Checked to False removes the check mark, and setting it to True adds a check mark.

Now let's look at this code to see how it works. There are a couple of new concepts here. Let's look at the first line:

```
miPixel(DrawWidth).Checked = False   ' Uncheck current width
```

You know that DrawWidth tells you the current width of the pen. The current width can be 1, 2, or 3, the possible DrawWidth values you defined for Sketch. You also know that you want to change the Checked state on the menu item for the current width. In other words, if DrawWidth is 2, you want to remove the check mark from the menu item **2 Pixels**. That's what this command does. Let's go through each part.

The miPixel control, as we mentioned, is a control array. This means that you have more than one control and that you can refer to each control in the array by a number. The number is the Index value that you typed into the Menu Editor window. By writing miPixel(DrawWidth), you're telling Visual Basic that you want to work with the menu item that has an Index value equal to DrawWidth.

Control Arrays

The three menu items—**1 Pixel**, **2 Pixel**, and **3 Pixel**—are a control array because you gave them all the same control name. You can refer to any control in a control array using the following syntax:

```
Name(Index)
```

`Name` is the name of the control, and `Index` is number that must match one of the `Index` values for a control in the array. For a control array of menu items, the `Index` numbers can be any of the numbers you typed into the **Index** field of the Menu Editor window.

As you'll recall from Chapter 3, properties are like variables except that they're directly connected to particular objects. All objects, such as forms, menu items, and the Printer object, have properties. The `Checked` property you're using here is available only for menu items. You set a property by writing the menu item's name, followed by a period and the name of the property.

Accessing Properties in Objects

You can read or change any property in an object, such as a menu item, using the following syntax:

```
ObjectName.Property
```

`ObjectName` is the name of the object, and `Property` is the name of the property that you want to set or read. Notice that you put a period between `ObjectName` and `Property`.

You can read a property by writing, for example, `miPixel(1).Checked`, and you can set it using the assignment operator:

`miPixel(1).Checked=False`.

This command contains a *comment*: a description you can add to code. Comments make your programs easier to read in the future, when you no longer remember what you were thinking when you wrote the original code. Anything on a line that appears after a single quotation mark (') is treated by Visual Basic as a comment and is therefore ignored when the program is executing.

You can consider the comments to be English-language descriptions of the Basic code you're writing. We can't say enough about using comments (and, indeed, we'll say more in later chapters). Without comments, programs are difficult to read. You'll probably be able to figure out what individual state-ments do, but you may not be able to understand the overall plan. Good com-ments should help you understand why the programmer (you) did something.

Now we must have a way to get the **1 Pixel** menu item checked when the program first runs. This is easy. Bring up the Menu Editor window (**Ctrl+E**) and click on the **1 Pixel** menu item in the list at the bottom of the window. Then click on the check box called **Checked**. This action will cause the **1 Pixel** menu item to be checked initially. Click **OK** to accept the change you just made.

Save your project now, because this is a version you'll want to keep. Before we move to the next chapter, we'll show you a great user interface feature: pop-up menus.

POP-UP MENUS

Pop-up menus, also known as *context menus,* are becoming more common in programs every day. Usually activated by clicking the right mouse button on a particular area of a window, a pop-up menu presents options directly relevant to the area that was clicked. A pop-up menu is the same as the other menus you've created except that it doesn't drop down from the menu bar. Instead, it is displayed on top of a form. Figure 6.5 shows what the Sketch program Draw menu would look like as a pop-up.

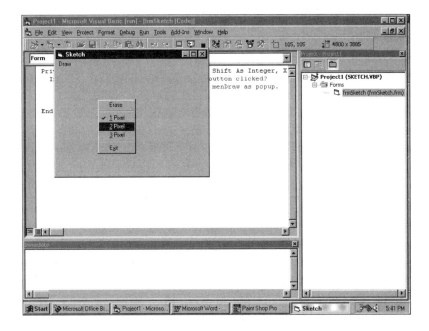

Figure 6.5 *Your Sketch program with the Draw menu added and displayed as a pop-up menu.*

The `PopupMenu` method makes it easy to display menus this way. First, you decide which event will trigger the pop-up. A right mouse event, either `MouseUp` or `MouseDown`, seems to be a common choice. Try adding the following code to your Sketch program's `Form_MouseUp` procedure:

```
Private Sub Form_MouseUp (Button As Integer, Shift As
Integer, _
X As Single, Y As Single)
  If Button = 2 Then          'Right mouse button clicked?
    PopupMenu menDraw         'Yes. Display menDraw as popup.
  End If
End Sub
```

Now press **F5** to run Sketch and then click on your right mouse button in the form area. Your screen should look similar to the one in Figure 6.5. You can click on the menu items. Continue drawing; use the regular Draw menu and verify that check marks are still being maintained while you are using the Draw menu both ways (the pop-up and from the menu bar). Now stop the program (select **End** from the Run menu) and then double-click on the form to bring back the code window.

N O T E For the purposes of this exercise we had you use the right mouse up event to display the pop-up menu, but we suggest that you use the right mouse down event for any real programs you create. The reason is purely one of user perception: the pop-up menu seems to appear on screen faster, so your program will seem faster. We used the MouseUp event so that it wouldn't interfere with the code we have already included in the MouseDown event and make the example more complicated.

Did you notice while you were experimenting that every time you clicked the right mouse button you were also leaving marks—that is, drawing—on the form? That's because of the code in the Form_MouseDown subroutine. Unlike the code in the Form_MouseMove subroutine, the Form_MouseDown event does not check to see which mouse button you're using. If you really like the pop-up menu and want to keep it, you can alter the code in the Form_MouseDown event to make it dependent on which mouse button is clicked. Use the MouseMove event as a model and add an If statement to check for Button = 1, indicating left mouse usage. If you don't want to keep the Draw pop-up menu, delete the code you put in the Form_MouseUp subroutine, and we'll move on.

You can also create a menu for pop-up use that does not appear on the menu bar. If you look at the Menu Editor window (see Figure 6.1), you'll notice a check box marked **Visible**. If you select your menu name and uncheck this box, your menu will not appear on the menu bar. It will, however, still be available for use with the PopupMenu method. The PopupMenu method also uses optional flag parameters with X and Y variables to control the location and behavior of the pop-up menu. For details, see the *Language Reference Manual*.

In Chapter 7, you'll continue working on Sketch, learning to print your sketches. In the process you'll learn even more about the Basic language and how complete programs are developed. You should feel fairly accomplished at this point, having created a functional (if simple) drawing program.

SUMMARY

You're now finished writing your first real Windows program. You've learned a great deal in the process:

- Menu Editor window. You use the Menu Editor window to add a menu bar to your programs. The trick is to make sure you're in Design mode (and not Run mode) and that your window is active (you might have to click on it) before you select the **Menu Editor** item from the Tools menu.

- Mnemonic access characters. You create mnemonic access characters (which allow menus and buttons to be accessed using the **Alt** key) by placing an **&** in front of the letter to be underlined.

- DrawWidth. The DrawWidth property allows you to change the width of the drawing pen. This width is measured in pixels.

- Control arrays. Related controls (menu items) can be grouped into a control array. All menu items in a control array share the same control name, but each item must have a unique Index number. This number allows you to reference individual controls in a control array.

- Checked. The Checked property for menu items allows you to check or uncheck items in a pull-down menu.

CHAPTER 7

Using Array Variables to Save Lines

- Defining array variables
- Working with arrays
- The **For..Next** command
- Creating new subroutines

The goal of this chapter is twofold. First, you'll modify Sketch so that it will remember all the lines you've drawn. This capability will allow you to add printing capabilities to Sketch, and it will make it possible for Sketch to redraw a picture when part of its window is erased (when, for example, another window is dragged over it). Second, you'll learn more about variables and writing Visual Basic programs. Variables are probably one of the most important aspects of any computer language, and they take a little getting used to. In this chapter, you'll learn how to work with some new forms of variables.

DESIGNING A NEW SKETCH

To redraw or print a drawing, you'll need for Sketch to remember all the lines you drew. For that you'll use an array.

In Chapter 6, you learned about control arrays. You created three related menu items that shared the same name. You can also have a list of variables that share the same name and are referenced using a number in parentheses (just as you referenced controls in a control array). These *variable arrays* are simple to work with, as you'll see shortly.

Here's an outline of what we'll do to record a sketch as it is being drawn. First, you'll create two arrays, called saveX and saveY, in which you'll save all the points in the lines you've drawn. You'll also need a way to keep information about where one line ends and the next line begins and about the thickness of each line (remember that you can change the line thickness, so not all lines may have the same thickness).

We'd like to say a few words about our approach to writing programs. Whenever we begin a new program, we think for a while about what we'd like the program to look like and what we'd like it to do. After we've figured that out, we don't sit down and write the entire program; that's a difficult thing to do. Instead, we start with a simple piece and get it working. Then we add another piece. Adding one piece at a time is much easier than writing the entire program at once, because each piece is small and easy to work with. This process is known as *stepwise refinement*, and it's how most programmers write real programs.

With Sketch, we started with simple pieces. You've added a form, then drawing capabilities, and then the menus. Now we will continue adding small pieces. First, you'll write some code to keep a list of points as you draw them. Then you'll try to redraw these points when Sketch's window is erased. But here you'll just connect all the points you've stored without concern for where one line ends and the next begins or for the thickness of each line. Later, we'll refine these additions to add these features.

With that in mind, let's examine array variables so that you can start to modify Sketch.

A WORD ABOUT VARIABLE NAMES

You'll notice that we chose to use variable names, `saveX` and `saveY`, that start with a lowercase letter. But all the variables you've seen so far, such as `CurrentX`, have started with an uppercase letter. Why did we choose to start these variable names with a lowercase letter?

When you start to read other people's programs, you may find it difficult to tell the difference between properties and variable names. How can you tell whether a name is a property or a variable name? If all names start with uppercase letters, you can't. You'll have to look up each name in the *Language Reference Manual*. If you start all variable names with a lowercase letter and all property names with an uppercase letter, however, you'll be able to tell at a glance whether a name refers to a variable or a property.

Visual Basic uses blue lettering to display keywords and green lettering to show comments, so this convention may not seem important. But you may sometimes need to read code from a printout or use a monochrome monitor. It's always a good idea to develop habits that can make your life easier in the long run.

You'll also notice that we use an uppercase letter at the start of each new word, which makes it easier to read variable names. For example, `longVariableName` is much easier to read than `longvariablename`. (Of course, in languages such as German you can have long names without mixed case, such as *Damfschiffskapitänwitwe*, which means the widow of a steamship captain. No kidding.)

ARRAY VARIABLES

The variables `saveX` and `saveY` will play an important role in your new version of Sketch. These variables are arrays in which you can store a number of `X` and `Y` points.

To create an array variable, you must define it and also tell Basic how many "slots" the variables will occupy. For example, the following code defines `saveX` as an array with index values from 0 to 1000. This means it has 1001 slots of type Single (all slots must have the same type):

```
Private saveX(1000) As Single
```

These slots, by the way, are called *elements* of an array. In the preceding example, there are 1001 elements in the `saveX` array.

If you have ever used or seen program code from an earlier version of Visual Basic, you may have expected us to use the `Dim` keyword to define a variable. Although `Dim` still works in Visual Basic, the preferred declaration statement uses either `Private` or `Public`. We'll talk more about defining variables in a moment.

REFERENCE

Variable Arrays

A variable array is a group of variables that share the same name and type. You define a variable array by placing a number in parentheses after the variable name. This number is the maximum index value you'll be able to use with this array. Because the first element of an array has the index value of 0, the number of elements in an array will be 1 greater than the number you provide in the `Private` statement.

You refer to elements in an array by putting the index value in parentheses after the name. For example, `saveX(10)` refers to the 11th element in the `saveX` array, because the first element is `saveX(0)`.

By the way, you can change the index of the first element in an array so that it will be a number other than 0. There are two ways to do this. You can use the `To` keyword (look up `Private` in the *Language Reference Manual*) or use the `Option Base` statement.

There are a number of things that are new about this statement (see Figure 7.1). First, we used the `Private` keyword, which tells Visual Basic that you're defining a variable. All the variables you've used so far have been defined implicitly; in other words, when you first used a variable, Visual Basic automatically defined it (K=1 defined the variable K).

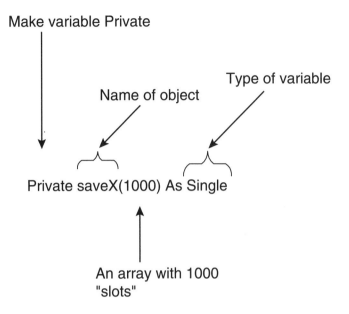

Figure 7.1 *The different parts of a* Private *statement in Visual Basic. If you leave out the type* (As Single), *Visual Basic will create a variable of type Variant.*

However, you must define array variables explicitly so that Visual Basic will know how large to make the array (how many elements you want). The Private keyword, therefore, explicitly defines a variable. (You can use Private to explicitly define any variable and not just arrays.)

You'll also notice the keywords As Single after the variable. The As keyword is used to tell Visual Basic the variable type. Now there are two ways of setting the variable type; you can use either the type character (for example, % or $) or As Single. In other words, both of these statements have the same effect:

```
Private someString As String
Private someString$
```

Which form you use is a matter of taste. If you look at other people's programs (a good way to learn, by the way), you'll notice that some people tend to use As String, and others tend to use $. You'll also find people who use both methods for defining variables. So it's up to you. In this book, we'll mostly use

As String, because we find it easier to remember words such as String rather than characters such as $.

THE AS KEYWORD VERSUS TYPE CHARACTERS

Whether you use the As keyword or a type character to define a variable's type is up to you. The following table lists the corresponding words and characters for all the types defined by Visual Basic.

Defining the Variable Types in Visual Basic

TYPE KEYWORD	TYPE CHARACTER
As Integer	%
As Long	&
As Single	! or none
As Double	#
As Currency	@
As String	$
As Byte	
As Boolean	
As Date	
As Object	
As Variant	

When you're using the type character, remember that it becomes part of the name. So if you create a variable called someStr$, you must always write someStr$ with the trailing dollar sign. You will have to use the As keyword when working with the newer data types, because they do not have a type character.

Defining Form Variables

In Sketch, you want to define two variables—saveX and saveY—so that you can read and write them from several procedures inside your form. In particular, you'll want to add points to saveX and saveY from inside

Form_MouseMove and Form_MouseDown. And you'll want to use these same points inside Form_Paint to redraw the picture.

If you define variables inside a subroutine, you use the Dim or Private keyword, and the variables are available only from inside that subroutine. (You can't use Public inside a subroutine.) There is, however, a special place where you can define such variables so that they'll be available to all subroutines in a form. If you have closed the program, restart Visual Basic and open Sketch. Make sure that the Code window is visible (double-click on the Sketch form). Click on the down-pointing arrow in the left combo box at the top of the window (see Figure 7.2). Finally, click on (**General**) at the top of this list.

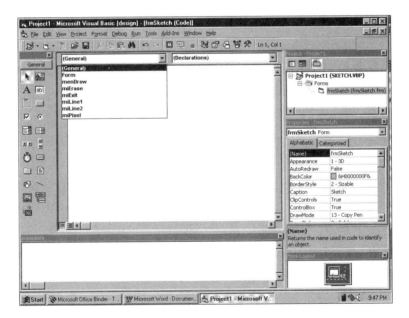

Figure 7.2 *The Object combo box allows you to switch between different objects in the form. You'll notice our Form object as well as* miErase *and so on.*

This combo box lists all the objects (the form and controls) we created inside this form. It provides an easy way for you to move between the code for the various objects inside a form. You'll probably find yourself using this combo box often to change from one object to another as you're writing programs.

The special entry at the top of this list, called (**General**), is used for things other than objects. This is where you use Private to define variables you want to be available to all the code you write inside a form. (If you define a variable inside a subroutine, it's available only inside that subroutine—see "A Word on Scope and Location of Variables.")

When you click on (**General**), it may seem as though nothing happens. So what happens? So far, the only change is a subtle one. Your cursor was moved to the top of the code window. Also, the right combo box now reads (**declarations**), which means you're looking at the declarations part of the form. All variable declarations that are available to all the procedures on the form are located here.

Enter the following three lines at the top of the Code window:

```
Private numPoints As Integer    ' Number of points saved
Private saveX(1000) As Single   ' Saved X coordinates
Private saveY(1000) As Single   ' Saved Y coordinates
```

Notice that comments (signified by the apostrophe) are used to describe the use of each variable. We'll use comments often, because even if you have a good name for a variable, you can always make it clearer with a comment.

A WORD ON SCOPE AND LOCATION OF VARIABLES

Limiting the access to variables is important to prevent conflicts and debugging problems. For example, you might use a variable named myVar in an important routine. If you created another routine that also modified a variable by the same name, both routines might access the same variable. You might not realize that two separate routines are modifying the same variable, and your program might begin doing strange and inexplicable things.

For this reason, you should limit variable access to the procedures that need such access. Defining the accessibility of a variable is known as defining its *scope*. Limiting the scope of a variable to its necessary range is an important skill. You should use Private or Public to define form-level and module-level variables, and Dim should be reserved for defining local variables inside a subroutine. Here are the particulars:

- Subroutine. When you define a variable inside a subroutine, it's available only inside that subroutine. Visual Basic creates the variable again the next time it runs that subroutine. Use the `Dim` keyword.

- Form. When you use `Private` to define a variable in the (**General**) section of a form under (**declarations**), the variable is available to any subroutine inside the form. Use `Public` if you want the variable to be available to other forms and modules.

- Module. You can define variables in any module (but not in forms), and you'll do that later in this book. Use `Public` to define these variables, and they will be available anywhere in your program and not just in a form. This option will become important when your program has more than one form.

What happens when you define a variable inside a subroutine that has the same name as a form-level variable? In such cases, Visual Basic ignores the form-level variable. In other words, you won't be able to read or write the form-level variable in any subroutine in which you've defined a subroutine variable with the same name.

SAVING POINTS IN SKETCH

Next, you'll modify `MouseMove` and `MouseDown` so they save points in these variables. To do this, you need to switch the current object back to the Form object. Pull down the left combo box and select **Form**. Now make sure that the right combo box is set to `MouseDown` so that you see the `Form_MouseDown` event handler in the code window.

The `MouseDown` subroutine saves the starting point for a line, so let's add some code to save this point in `saveX` and `saveY`. The following new version of `Form_MouseDown` saves these points in the arrays and draws the starting point:

```
Private Sub Form_MouseDown (Button As Integer, Shift As
Integer, X As ...
  CurrentX = X                    ' Start point for next Line
  CurrentY = Y
  PSet (X, Y)                     ' Draw first point in line
```

```
    numPoints = numPoints + 1      ' The next free point
    saveX(numPoints) = X           ' Remember this point
    saveY(numPoints) = Y
End Sub
```

The three lines at the end of this subroutine are new, and you'll notice we added comments to the other lines.

N O T E   As mentioned in Chapter 6, if you chose to include the pop-up menu feature in your Sketch project, you'll need to add an **If...Then** statement to the code in the `MouseDown` subroutine. The first statement inside the subroutine (just before `CurrentX = X`) should be the following:

```
        If Button = 1 Then
```

Also, add this last statement just before `End Sub`:

```
        End If
```

Next you'll modify `MouseMove` so that it will save the endpoints of all the lines you draw. You can scroll to the `MouseMove` subroutine or move there automatically by selecting it from the right combo box. Or you can use a keyboard shortcut: Press **Ctrl+PgUp** and **Ctrl+PgDn** to move back and forth between subroutines in the form.

The new version of `Form_MouseMove`, which is much like the new form of `Form_MouseDown`, is as follows:

```
Sub Form_MouseMove (Button As Integer, Shift As Integer,
X As ...
  If Button = 1 Then              ' Is the left button down?
    Line -(X, Y)                  ' Yes, draw a line

    numPoints = numPoints + 1     ' Next free point in array
    saveX(numPoints) = X          ' Remember this point
    saveY(numPoints) = Y
  End If
End Sub
```

N O T E

You can easily move between the subroutines in your form by pressing **Ctrl+PgUp** and **Ctrl+PgDn** in the Code window. If you have long subroutines, these keys will scroll one subroutine at a time until you reach the top or bottom of the form or module. Using the **PgUp** or **PgDn** key alone will scroll one page or screen at a time.

We've also introduced another level of indenting. Programs are usually much easier to read (and therefore write) if you use indenting to make it visually obvious how a program is built. Whenever you have some code that will be run if a condition is true, it's a good idea to indent it to show that this block of code is at a different conceptual level than other parts of the code. You'll see many similar examples in this book.

Now you can run the program to make sure there are no errors in what you've typed. The program won't do anything different from the previous version, because you're not using any of the points being saved. But at least you can make sure there isn't anything Visual Basic objects to, such as a typographical error.

N O T E

If you get an error because of a typographical error, Visual Basic will most likely display an error dialog box that says "Syntax Error." This dialog box has two buttons: **OK** and **Help**. The **Help** button will tell you what a syntax error is but won't tell you about your specific error. If you click **OK**, Visual Basic will suspend execution and place you on the line where the error took place.

Many errors can be corrected right there. If you correct the error, you can continue execution by selecting the **Continue** option on the Run menu or pressing **F5**. If the error requires many lines to be changed, you should probably stop execution (**End** under the Run menu) and execute the program again after the problems are resolved.

Redrawing Forms

Most Windows programs have a way to redraw parts of a window that have been covered and then uncovered. Whenever a part of a window is uncovered and needs to be redrawn, Windows sends a paint message to that window telling it to redraw itself. Visual Basic works the same way.

Whenever your window (or a part of it) needs to be redrawn, your form will receive a `Paint` event that will execute the `Paint` method on your form.

Pull down the right combo box and select **Paint**. This will display the
`Form_Paint` event handler, which is responsible for redrawing the contents of
your windows.

Let's try a simple experiment. Put a **Beep** command in the `Form_Paint`
subroutine to hear a beep whenever Visual Basic sends a `Paint` event to your
program:

```
Private Sub Form_Paint ()
  Beep
End Sub
```

Now run this program. You'll hear a beep when Sketch first starts running.
This means you're asked to paint the window as soon as Sketch starts. After all,
when Sketch starts, the window is blank (except for any controls you put into
it, such as the menu bar).

Next, click on the **Minimize** button (the button that collapses the window
in the upper-right corner) to iconize Sketch. This action makes the form invisible, so Visual Basic doesn't run `Form_Paint`. Finally, click on the minimized
Sketch on the Taskbar at the bottom of your screen. Sketch will return to a
form, and you'll hear a beep, telling you that Visual Basic sent a paint message.

You might want to try other experiments on your own. Try covering up
part of Sketch's window with another window, and then uncovering part of
Sketch's window. Sketch should beep whenever part of its window becomes
uncovered.

NOTE   The left (procedure) combo box has a useful feature you might be interested
in. If you look at Figure 7.3, you'll notice that some of the lines in the combo
box are bold. The bold event handlers are the ones in which you've added
code, so you can tell at a glance which event handlers have code attached to
them—in this case, MouseDown, MouseMove, MouseUp, and Paint.

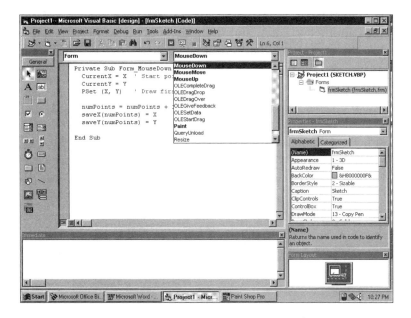

Figure 7.3 *The Proc combo box uses bold characters to show which event handlers have attached code.*

Redrawing Sketch's Lines

From the preceding example, you can see that you'll need to write code in Form_Paint to redraw the lines saved in the saveX and saveY arrays. For this, you'll need a new command, **For..Next**, which allows you to run a set of commands a number of times.

But before we get to the theory, let's look at the new Form_Paint subroutine, which uses **For..Next**:

```
Private Sub Form_Paint ()
  PSet (saveX(1), saveY(1))      ' Draw first point in line
  For i = 2 To numPoints         ' Repeat numPoints 1 times
    Line -(saveX(i), saveY(i))   ' Draw the ith point
  Next i                         ' Got to the next point
End Sub
```

Now try running this program. Draw something, cover a portion of the Sketch window with another window, and then uncover the window. See how nicely that works? This program will now redraw any lines you've drawn. There are a few things it doesn't do correctly, but we'll fix those problems next. At least now you have some code that redraws something.

Let's take a close look at what this new subroutine does. The first line should be clear, because you've used PSet before. If you look at the MouseDown event handler, you'll notice that PSet draws the first point in a line. But you'll notice one difference from the MouseDown subroutine. In MouseDown, you set CurrentX and CurrentY to the mouse location and then you called PSet.

As it turns out, the CurrentX = X and CurrentY = Y lines in MouseDown aren't necessary, because PSet automatically sets CurrentX and CurrentY after it draws a point. Now that you know this, let's go back and change MouseDown so that it's a little cleaner (in other words, as simple as it can be).

```
Private Sub Form_MouseDown (Button As Integer, Shift As
Integer, X As ...

  PSet (X, Y)                     ' Draw first point in line

  numPoints = numPoints + 1       ' The next free point
  saveX(numPoints) = X            ' Remember this point
  saveY(numPoints) = Y
```

NOTE   We'll mention again that if you are using a pop-up menu, your MouseDown subroutine should include the If..Then statement to identify the left mouse button. Now it's up to you to remember this throughout the rest of the Sketch project, because our code examples will not show the If..Then statement for this subroutine.

Now that you've made Form_MouseDown a little simpler, let's get back to Form_Paint. As you just learned, PSet draws the first point in lines saved in the saveX and saveY arrays. But think about that for a second. When you first run Sketch, Visual Basic calls Form_Paint even though Sketch hasn't saved any points yet. So the first line, PSet(saveX(1), saveY(1)), tries to draw a point that hasn't been saved. What happens?

New variables of type Single are initially set to zero, including all the elements in an array. So the first time Visual Basic runs `Form_Paint`, both `saveX(1)` and `saveY(1)` are set to zero. If you look closely at the Sketch form when you run Sketch, you'll see a small dot in the upper-left corner of the window because of `PSet(0, 0)`. That's one problem with this program. You can fix it easily by adding an **If..Then** command to see whether there are any points before trying to draw the first point:

```
Private Sub Form_Paint ()
  If numPoints > 0 Then        ' Are there any points?
    PSet (saveX(1), saveY(1))  ' Yes, draw the first point
  End If

  For i = 2 To numPoints       ' Repeat numPoints  1 times
    Line -(saveX(i), saveY(i)) ' Draw the ith point
  Next i                       ' Go to the next point
End Sub
```

Now let's look at the rest of this subroutine.

The For..Next Command

The rest of this subroutine relies on the new command **For..Next**. This type of command, called a *loop*, allows you to run a set of commands more than one time. There are several different types of loop commands, but we'll cover only **For..Next** here.

The **For..Next** command allows you to specify the number of times you want to run the commands inside the loop. It also uses a variable you supply as a loop counter, which starts with a value and counts up, adding 1 each time through the loop. When you write the following, you're telling Basic to set `i` to 2 before running any commands:

```
For i = 2 To numPoints
  ...
Next i
```

The variable i will then be increased by 1 each time Basic sees the Next i statement. The To part tells Basic when to stop repeating the loop. As soon as i is greater than numPoints, Basic stops running this command.

WHY WE USE THE VARIABLE i

You're probably wondering why we chose to use a variable called i, rather than something more descriptive such as count. Most programmers use the variable i whenever they need a counter. If they need more than one counter, they use j, k, 1, and so on.

The reason is historical, having to do with a programming language called FORTRAN, one of the first popular computer languages used by scientists and other programmers. FORTRAN, unlike Basic, uses the first letter of a variable name to determine the type of the variable. Any variable name that starts with i through n is defined to be an integer. Because most counters (such as i in the For..Next loop) are integers, programmers use the letters i through n as loop counters.

Even though many programmers these days have never learned or used FORTRAN, this tradition persists. It's not likely you'll see this practice disappear, because it's been passed from one generation of programmers to the next.

Let's use the Immediate window for a few experiments to see exactly how **For..Next** works. Enter the following lines into the Immediate window:

```
for i = 1 to 3: print i: next i
1
2
3
print i
4
|
```

You can place several commands on a single line by separating them with a colon, as in the first line of the preceding example.

NOTE

You can see that Basic ran `Print i` three times, with `i` starting at 1 and ending at 3. You can also see that `i` has the value of 4 after the `For..Next` loop finishes.

Try another experiment. See what happens when the `To` value is less than the initial value. Will Basic run the **Print** command once in this case, or not at all? To find out, enter the following command:

```
for i = 1 to 0: print i: next i
|
```

As you can see, `For..Next` won't run any of the commands inside its loop if the initial value is greater than the final value.

REFERENCE

For..Next

The **For..Next** command runs a set of commands inside a loop a specific number of times.

```
For varName = initialValue To finalValue [Step incre-
ment]
     statements
Next [varName]
```

This command repeats the statement between the `For` and `Next` lines. The variable `varName` starts at `initialValue` and increases by 1 (or by `increment`) each time through the loop. Basic stops running the loop when `varName` is greater than `finalValue`.

Here is how Basic runs a **For..Next** command:

1. Set `varName` to `initialValue`.
2. If `varName` > `finalValue`, you're finished.
3. Run statements.
4. `varName` = `varName` + 1 (adds `increment` rather than 1 if you use `Step` command)
5. Go to step 2.

If `Step` is negative, step 2 becomes `If varName < finalValue`.... In other words, the values go down to `finalValue` rather than up to `finalValue`.

Enough theory. You can see from this short description that `Form_Paint` will call `Line` for each line saved, starting with the second point. You'll also notice that `For..Next` won't draw any lines if `numPoints < 2`. `For..Next` will draw lines only if there are lines to be drawn.

Remembering Separate Lines

The program will now redraw all the lines originally drawn using the mouse. But you're not keeping the data about where one line ends and the next begins. So if you draw several separate lines (by releasing the mouse button between lines), your program will draw a single line rather than separate lines (see Figures 7.4 and 7.5). To fix this problem, you'll need to add two more arrays to keep track of the starting and ending points of lines. We'll call these arrays `lineStart` and `lineEnd`, and we'll save enough room for 500 lines (which is a truly arbitrary number).

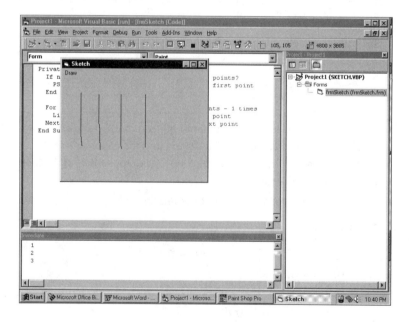

Figure 7.4 *A drawing of four unconnected lines.*

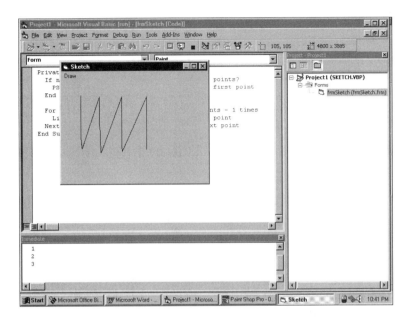

Figure 7.5 *The four unconnected lines from Figure 7.4 after a redraw with the* Form_Paint *subroutine. The current version of Sketch connects the lines because it doesn't keep track of where one line ends and the next line begins.*

Add the following three lines to the (**General**) section of your form:

```
Private numLines As Integer        ' Number of separate lines
Private lineStart(500) As Integer  ' Start of each line
Private lineEnd(500) As Integer    ' End of each line
```

Now you'll need to modify Form_MouseDown, Form_MouseMove, and Form_Paint to save and use these starting and ending points.

First, modify Form_MouseDown so that it will save the starting point (as well as an initial ending point). The "points" you'll save in the lineStart and lineEnd arrays are indexes into the saveX and saveY arrays. The following code changes Form_MouseDown to save the starting index of each new line (add the three new lines at the end):

```
Private Sub Form_MouseDown (Button As Integer, Shift As
Integer, X As ...
  PSet (X, Y)                        ' Draw first point in line

  numPoints = numPoints + 1          ' The next free point
  saveX(numPoints) = X               ' Remember this point
  saveY(numPoints) = Y

  numLines = numLines + 1            ' Next free line
  lineStart(numLines) = numPoints    ' Index of the first point
  lineEnd(numLines) = numPoints      ' Initially a single point
End Sub
```

Next, you'll modify Form_MouseMove to update the index for the endpoint in a line. Each time Visual Basic calls MouseMove, you add another line segment to the line you're drawing. The following code is the new version of Form_MouseMove with one new line at the end.

```
Private Sub Form_MouseMove (Button As Integer, Shift As
Integer, X As ...
  If Button = 1 Then                 ' Is the left button down?
    Line -(X, Y)                     ' Yes, draw a line

    numPoints = numPoints + 1        ' Next free point in array
    saveX(numPoints) = X             ' Remember this point
    saveY(numPoints) = Y

    lineEnd(numLines) = numPoints    ' New ending index for line
  End If
End Sub
```

Finally, you'll modify Form_Paint to use this information. As you can see from the following new version of Form_Paint, it needs more changes than the other two subroutines. This version is almost a new subroutine, so you might as well replace everything in Form_Paint with the following code:

```
Private Sub Form_Paint ()
  For Lin = 1 to numLines        ' Draw each line
    aStart = lineStart(Lin)      ' Start index of this line
    anEnd = lineEnd(Lin)         ' End index of this line
    PSet (saveX(aStart), saveY(aStart))

    For i = aStart To anEnd      ' Draw parts of this line
      Line -(saveX(i), saveY(i))
    Next i
  Next Lin
End Sub
```

This new version of Form_Paint has two For..Next loops. The outer loop (For Lin = 1 to numLines) runs the variable Lin from 1 to the number of separate lines you've drawn. The inner loop (For i = aStart to anEnd) draws all the parts of a single line.

We've added a couple of variables in this subroutine to make it easier to write and read. By setting aStart to the starting index of a line and anEnd to the ending index of the same line, we can use these values in both the PSet command and the **For..Next** command. This means that you don't have to write something like the following:

```
PSet (saveX(lineStart(Lin)), saveY(lineStart(Lin)))
```

This line is hard to read because there are too many parentheses. We prefer to add a few lines of code to break long lines into several steps. We find the following much easier to read (and write):

```
aStart = lineStart(Lin)
anEnd = lineEnd(Lin)
PSet (saveX(aStart), saveY(aStart))
```

You've made quite a bit of progress so far. You have only a few things left to do in this chapter, and then you'll be finished with Sketch. First, you'll need to modify Sketch so that it will remember the thickness of each line. This isn't very hard to do, so you might want to try making this change yourself before you read the next section. You'll add another array that tracks the pixel thickness with each new line that was created.

Then you can have some fun. You'll add a **Print** menu item and the code to print your drawings. Finally, you'll turn Sketch into an **EXE** file that you can run directly like any other program.

Remembering Line Widths

It's easy to get Sketch to remember the thickness of each line. All you have to do is to add another array, called `lineThickness`, and then save the value of `DrawWidth` on each mouse click. Here are the changes you'll need to make.

Add the following line to the (**General**) area of your form to declare the `lineThickness` array:

```
Private lineThickness(500) As Integer   ' DrawWidth for
                                        ' each line
```

Next, add the following line to the end of the `Form_MouseDown` subroutine (on the line before the `End Sub` statement):

```
    lineThickness(numLines) = DrawWidth
```

Finally (yes, you're almost finished adding this feature), add the following line to `Form_Paint` immediately before the **PSet** command:

```
    DrawWidth = lineThickness(Lin)
```

That's all there is to remembering the line thickness for each line. Try this program and see how it works. (Remember to save your project by pressing **Alt+FV**, before you run this program.)

Before we move on, there is one other small problem with your program. Do you know what it is? Have you tried all of the menu items to make sure they work the way you expected?

It turns out that if you select the **Erase** menu item, Sketch fails to discard the points you've drawn. You can see this by drawing some lines, erasing them, and then minimizing and restoring your window. Instead of being erased, the lines will be redrawn.

You'll need to modify miErase_Click so that it clears all the lines you've drawn. Set the numLines and numPoints variables to zero, as follows:

```
Private Sub miErase_Click ()
  Cls                    ' Clear the form
  numPoints = 0          ' Set to no points
  numLines = 0           ' Set to no lines
End Sub
```

In the next section you'll modify Sketch so that it can print your sketches, and then you'll turn Sketch into a stand-alone **EXE** program.

Printing a Drawing

Now that you've modified Sketch so that it will redraw a picture, let's add another menu item, **Print**, that will draw sketches on the printer. You'll put Printer. in front of each drawing command. Bring up the Menu Editor and add another line and a **Print** menu item (see Figure 7.6).

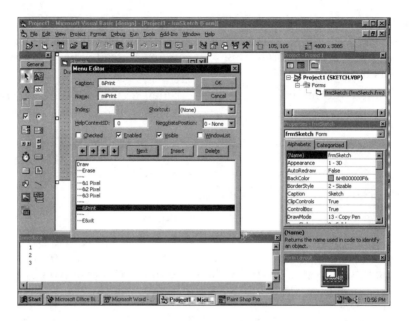

Figure 7.6 *The menu item **Print** and the line that you'll add to your Sketch program. The control names should be* miLine3 *for the line and* miPrint *for the **Print** menu item*

When you've added miPrint to the menu bar, add the following code to
miPrint_Click:

```
Private Sub miPrint_Click ()
  For Lin = 1 To numLines      ' Draw each line
    aStart = lineStart(Lin)    ' Start index of this line
    anEnd = lineEnd(Lin)       ' End index of this line
    Printer.DrawWidth = lineThickness(Lin)
    Printer.PSet (saveX(aStart), saveY(aStart))

    For i = aStart To anEnd     ' Draw parts of this line
      Printer.Line -(saveX(i), saveY(i))
    Next i

  Next Lin
```

```
    Printer.EndDoc
End Sub
```

This subroutine is identical to `Form_Paint` except for the `Printer.` in front of each command that draws or changes properties (such as `DrawWidth`). We also added a `Printer.EndDoc` command at the end of this subroutine. This command tells the printer to print the page you've drawn.

Sketch should now be able to print anything you draw. Give it a try. Did you notice anything interesting? If you try different line widths, you'll notice that the lines are much narrower on your printer. Why?

In Chapter 6, you learned how to change a line's width. You learned that line widths are measured in pixels, and the starting and ending points are measured in twips. This means that anything you draw on the printer, using points measured in twips, will keep the same size no matter what printer you use. But line widths, because they're measured in pixels, will be much smaller on high-resolution printers such as laser printers.

So what do you do if you want a line to keep its width in twips? For now, the easiest solution is to modify the `DrawWidth` line in `miPrint_Click` as follows:

```
    Printer.DrawWidth = lineThickness(Lin) * 3
```

Multiplying by 3 is correct if you're using a laser printer, but it may not be correct for other printers. Figure 7.7 illustrates these ideas.

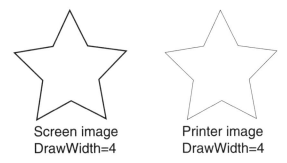

Screen image
DrawWidth=4

Printer image
DrawWidth=4

Figure 7.7 `DrawWidth` *set to 4 on the screen and on a laser printer. The lines won't be as thick on the printer, because* `DrawWidth` *is measured in pixels, and pixels are smaller on a printer.*

CREATING AN **EXE** PROGRAM

Now that you have a finished program that's fun to play with, you'll turn this program into an **EXE** file so that you can run it without starting Visual Basic. To create an **EXE** file, pull down the File menu and select **Make Sketch.EXE**. You'll see a dialog box like the one shown in Figure 7.8.

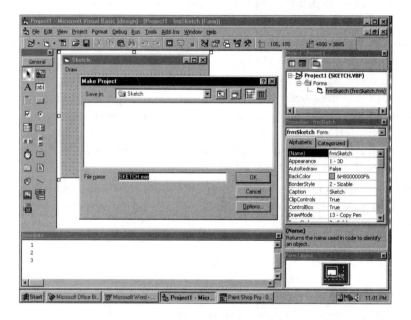

Figure 7.8 *You'll see this dialog box when you select **Make EXE File** from the File menu. Simply click **OK** to create **SKETCH.EXE**.*

To look at the options, click the **Options** button. The Options window will let you set up the version number, the title of the application, the copyright notice, and so on. Once you've finished with the options and dismissed the window, press **Enter** (or click **OK**) in the main file dialog box to create an **EXE** program called **SKETCH.EXE**. Now you can run Sketch from the Explorer, just as you can run any other Windows program.

If you want to give your new **EXE** program to other people, you should create an install disk. In chapter 15, we will show you in detail how to make an installer.

N O T E

THE FINAL SKETCH PROGRAM

You've made a number of changes to Sketch, so this section contains a full listing of the program, as it stands now. Table 7.1 shows all the captions, control names, and index values for the pull-down menu.

Table 7.1 Menu Names and Control Names
The following lines should be in the (**General**) section of your form:

```
Private numPoints As Integer     ' Number of points saved
Private saveX(1000) As Single    ' Saved X coordinates
Private saveY(1000) As Single    ' Saved Y coordinates

Private numLines As Integer       ' Number of separate lines
Private lineStart(500) As Integer  ' Start of each line
Private lineEnd(500) As Integer    ' End of each line

Private lineThickness(500) As Integer  ' DrawWidth for
                                       ' each line
```

The following lists all the event handlers in alphabetical order:

```
Private Sub Form_MouseDown(Button As Integer, Shift As
Integer, X As …
  PSet (X, Y)                   ' Draw first point in line

  numPoints = numPoints + 1     ' The next free point
  saveX(numPoints) = X          ' Remember this point
  saveY(numPoints) = Y

  numLines = numLines + 1         ' Next free line
  lineStart(numLines) = numPoints ' Index of the first point
  lineEnd(numLines) = numPoints   ' Initially a single point
```

```
      lineThickness(numLines) = DrawWidth
End Sub

Private Sub Form_MouseMove(Button As Integer, Shift As
Integer, X As …
    If Button = 1 Then            ' Is the left button down?
      Line -(X, Y)                ' Yes, draw a line

      numPoints = numPoints + 1   ' Next free point in array
      saveX(numPoints) = X        ' Remember this point
      saveY(numPoints) = Y

      lineEnd(numLines) = numPoints  ' New ending index for line
    End If
End Sub

Private Sub Form_MouseUp(Button As Integer, Shift As Integer,
X As …
    If Button = 2 Then            'Right mouse button clicked?
      PopupMenu menDraw           'Yes. Display menDraw as popup.
    End If
End Sub

Private Sub Form_Paint()
  For Lin = 1 To numLines         ' Draw each line
    aStart = lineStart(Lin)       ' Start index of this line
    anEnd = lineEnd(Lin)          ' End index of this line
    DrawWidth = lineThickness(Lin)
    PSet (saveX(aStart), saveY(aStart))

    For i = aStart To anEnd        ' Draw parts of this line
      Line -(saveX(i), saveY(i))
    Next i
```

```
   Next Lin
End Sub

Private Sub miErase_Click()
    Cls
  numPoints = 0            ' Set to no points
  numLines = 0             ' Set to no lines
End Sub

Private Sub miPixel_Click(Index As Integer)
  miPixel(DrawWidth).Checked = False   ' Uncheck current width
  DrawWidth = Index                    ' Change width of the
pen
  miPixel(Index).Checked = True        ' Check the new width
End Sub

Private Sub miPrint_Click()
  For Lin = 1 To numLines       ' Draw each line
    aStart = lineStart(Lin)     ' Start index of this line
    anEnd = lineEnd(Lin)        ' End index of this line
    Printer.DrawWidth = lineThickness(Lin)
    Printer.PSet (saveX(aStart), saveY(aStart))

    For i = aStart To anEnd     ' Draw parts of this line
      Printer.Line -(saveX(i), saveY(i))
    Next i

  Next Lin
  Printer.EndDoc
End Sub
```

Related Tools

- Array lower index. The arrays in this chapter have a starting index of 0 and count up from there. You can change the first index number for an array in two ways. First, you can use the `Option Base` statement to change the lower bound from 0 to any other number; this will apply to all arrays. Second, you can use the `To` keyword when you define an array. For example, `Dim A(- 10 to 10)` defines an array with index values that range from −10 to 10.

- Array bounds. The `UBound` and `LBound` functions allow you to find out the lowest and highest index value for any array. So if you define an array with `Dim A( - 10, 10)`, then `LBound(a, 1)` returns −10. For more details, see the *Language Reference Manual*.

- Erasing arrays. If you ever need to erase all the variables in an array (set them to 0, or, for String variables, to an empty string), you can use the **Erase** command. For example, to erase an array called `A`, you would type `Erase A`.

- Dynamic arrays. Sometimes you may want to change the size of an array when your program is running. For such cases, Visual Basic has a type of array called a *dynamic* array. Dynamic arrays can change in size as your program runs.

  You define a dynamic array by omitting the size in the `Dim` statement. For example, `Dim A()` defines an array `A` as a dynamic array. To use this array, you set a size for the array using the `ReDim` command. This command erases any elements that might have been in the array and creates a new array of the size you ask for. You can use `ReDim Preserve` to resize an array without erasing the values stored in it.

- Loops. In addition to **For..Next**, Visual Basic supports several other loops. Each type of loop has its own advantages. The following is a summary of the types of loops in Visual Basic:

- **For..Next**. Repeats a set of statements a specific number of times. The following is the syntax:

```
For counter=start To end [Step increment]
   [statements]
Next [counter]
```

■ **Do..Loop**. Allows you to repeat a loop as long as (or until) a condition is true (as you'd use in **If..Then**). There are five forms. Which form you use depends on which is most convenient for solving a specific problem.

■ **While..Wend**. Works exactly like the **Do While..Loop** statement. We suggest that you use **Do..Loop** instead, because it is a more recent addition to Basic language and is more flexible.

In general, it's best to use **For..Next** if you want to repeat some commands a specific number of times and to use the **Do..Loop** command whenever you need to test a condition to tell when you're finished running the loop. The following is a summary of the five versions of **Do..Loop** you might want to use and a discussion of how they're different:

Repeat statements as long as condition is true (could be zero times):

```
Do While condition

   statements

Loop
```

Repeat statements until condition is true (could be zero times):

```
Do Until condition

   statements

Loop
```

Repeat statements as long as condition is true (at least one time):

```
Do

   statements

Loop While condition
```

Repeat statements until condition is true (at least one time):

```
Do
```

```
        statements
    Loop Until condition

    Repeat statements forever:
    Do
        statements
    Loop
```

SUMMARY

This is the final chapter we'll devote to the Sketch program. You have a fully working program that allows you to sketch, redraws the window when necessary, features a complete menu bar, can print the sketch to the printer, allows you to change line widths, and includes a context pop-up menu. In Chapter 8, you'll build a new program, in which we will create our own control. Instead of a check box or list box control, this control will be a clock. You will be able to place the control on the form as if it had come with Visual Basic.

In this chapter you learned more about building Visual Basic programs. In particular, you've learned the following:

- Stepwise refinement. With this technique, you build a program one step at a time, and each step is fairly small. After each step, you test the program. Building a program one small step at a time is much easier than trying to build it all at once.

- Array variables. Array variables share the same name and type. Each array consists of a fixed number of elements, and you access any element using an index in parentheses. For example, saveX(9) returns the tenth element of the saveX array. You use the Dim keyword to define array variables.

- Form variables. Any variable defined in the (**General**) area of a form, which you get to by using the left combo box, is available to all subroutines inside a form. You defined several variables and arrays so that they would be available to all your subroutines.

- Form_Paint. Every time your program needs to redraw parts of its window because part of it has been erased by another window, Visual Basic calls your form's `Form_Paint` event handler. You used this subroutine to redraw the lines in Sketch.

- **For..Next**. The **For..Next** command is used to repeat a group of commands and draw the saved lines. **For..Next** allows you to specify how many times a group of statements (called a code block) should be run. This command uses a counter variable, which counts up from a starting value to an ending value. You use this counter as the index into the `saveX` and `saveY` arrays.

- Creating **EXE** programs. You turned your Sketch program into an **EXE** program that you can run just as you run any other Windows program (without using Visual Basic).

CHAPTER 8

Building a Clock Control

- Creating a user control
- Placing multiple controls on a form
- Using timers
- Reading the clock
- Formatting times
- Custom-drawing scales
- Constants
- Drawing in color
- Erasing lines

Building programs is what Visual Basic is all about, and that's what you'll be doing in Part II of this book. By creating your own control, you'll be able to reuse it in later programs. In this chapter, you'll build a clock control that displays the current time inside an icon. Then you'll create an application that shows two of these clocks on a form. This program is a little larger than the Sketch program, and you'll learn some new concepts. You'll also gain more experience with ideas you learned in previous chapters.

In Chapter 9 you'll start on a new program called Address Book. That project will take a number of chapters to build. Through this program, you'll learn more about the Basic language, about creating and using databases, and about building programs with Visual Basic.

DESIGNING ICON CLOCK

Before you start to build a program, it's a good idea to take a few minutes to think about what you want to build. Building a program without a game plan is difficult, because it's hard to know where to start.

The first step is to think about what you want your program to look like and what you want it to do. For the Icon Clock program, we'll plan to make it look like Figure 8.1. You also have a pretty good idea about how it should work, because it works much like a real clock.

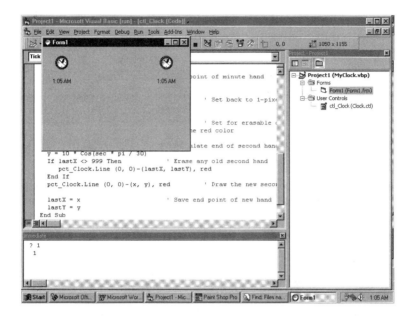

Figure 8.1 *We plan to make a form with two Clock controls.*

Let's review a few things to make sure that we're all headed in the same direction. First, notice that our program draws the clock hands inside the icon. As you'll see in this chapter, it's easy to draw inside an icon when you're using Visual Basic.

The icon you'll use is a blank clock face—everything you see in Figure 8.1 except the clock hands—so you'll need to draw the clock hands. The hour and minute hands are drawn as black, two-pixel-wide lines. To make the second hand stand out as in a kitchen clock, you'll draw the second hand in red.

Writing a program that does all this can be somewhat daunting unless you start with something simple and then work your way to a more complicated (and complete) program. As we mentioned in Chapter 7, this process in known as stepwise refinement.

We'll start with the basics. You'll experiment with minimized programs to learn a little about how they work and how to change the caption in the taskbar. Then you'll learn how to get the current time from your computer and place it into the caption under the cursor. Only then will we tackle the problem of drawing the clock hands inside the window and changing them every second. Now that you know the game plan, you can get to work. You'll begin by creating a simple control and placing in on a form. Then we'll add features to the control until we have a complete, reusable component.

Fire up Visual Basic with a new project (the default when you start Visual Basic); you will have an empty window (form) called Form1. To begin creating our program, we need to create a basic user control to be placed onto a form. You cannot run a user control separately; it must be placed on a form for testing.

Select the **Add User Control** option in the Project menu. A window like the one shown in Figure 8.2 will appear. The **User Control** icon will be the only one in this window, so it should already be selected. Click the **Open** button, and a new window will appear. This window will look like a form except that it won't have any edges.

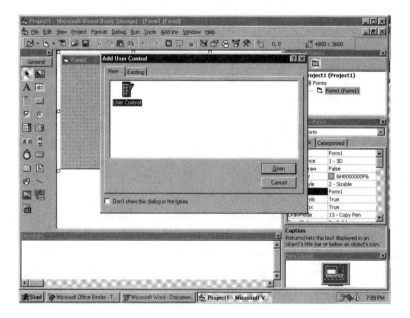

Figure 8.2 *Click the **Open** button to create a new user control.*

In the project window on the right side of your screen (currently labeled **Project 1 (Project 1)**), you'll see that under the Forms folder you have a Form1 and under the User Controls folder you have a UserControl1.

The area displayed in the window is the size that the control will be on the form. We don't need the control to be as large as Visual Basic automatically creates it, so we'll shrink it a bit. The gray area that makes up the background of the form should be surrounded by eight blue squares. Each of these squares (called *handles*) can be used to resize the control area. You are probably accustomed to using the edges of a window to resize it. The handles make it more convenient, especially because they are also used to resize controls on the form itself. You'll notice that only three of the squares are filled in: those along the bottom, the right, and the lower-right sides. The handles that are solid can be changed, whereas the hollow ones cannot be changed. In this case, the control that you create will be placed somewhere on a form, so it doesn't make sense to be able to change the top and left sides.

Click on the lower-right handle, hold down the mouse button, and drag the handle until the form is about the size shown in Figure 8.3. The form must be large enough to hold an icon and a text label that displays the time. Try to get it approximately the size shown in the figure, but don't worry if it is too large or too small. You can always change it later.

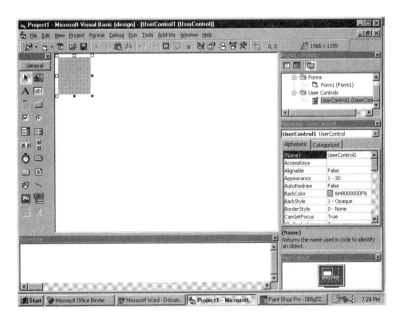

Figure 8.3 *Drag the lower-right handle up and to the left to shrink your control to the size shown.*

Let's set the Name property of the control. Click in the Properties window on the right of your screen and change the **(Name)** property to **ctl_Clock**. Notice that the name is also automatically changed in the Project window.

Now it's time to label the control and test it. In the control toolbox, select the **Label** control tool (the letter **A**) and draw a label in the bottom of the control area. In the Properties window, change the **(Name)** Property to **lbl_Time**, change the **Alignment** property to **2 - Center**, and change the **Caption** property to **12:00 am**. Your control should now look like the one shown in Figure 8.4.

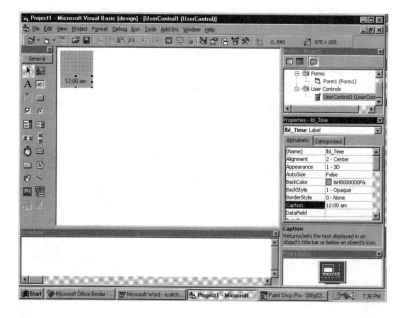

Figure 8.4 *Create a label in the bottom of the control and change the three properties shown.*

Now we're ready to test our first control by placing it on a form. First, let's save this project. Select the **Save Project** option on the File menu. Select the **Proj** folder that we created in Chapter 6. Now create a new folder in the Proj folder called Clock. Double-click the new **Clock** folder so that all the files will be saved there. The first object to save is the control. By default, the control is named **ctl_Clock.ctl**. Eliminate the first **ctl** and the underscore (_) character so that the filename is **Clock.ctl**. Then click **Save**.

Visual Basic will ask for the name of the form and default to **Form1.frm**. This name is fine for the purposes of this program, so click **Save**. Now it asks for the project name. Enter **MyClock.vbp** and click **Save**.

We're now almost ready to place the control on the form. Before the control can be used, however, we must close the window that we're using for design. This arrangement simplifies things so that any changes made to your control won't affect the creation of new controls on your form. To close the control window, click on the form icon just to the left of the File menu. It will present you with a menu of options; select **Close**. At the bottom of the toolbox you will see a new icon like the one shown in Figure 8.5. This icon represents your new control! It has defaulted to a generic icon that we will replace later. If you move your arrow cursor over the control, the tooltip will appear with the name of the control, as shown in Figure 8.5.

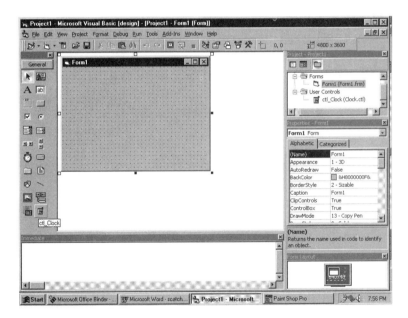

Figure 8.5 *The user control called **ctl_Clock** has been added to the toolbox.*

Let's use a trick to make it easy to draw the control on the form. If you double-click on any icon in the toolbox, that control will automatically be placed on the form and sized to a default width and height. Try it now by double-clicking on your control. It will appear on the form.

To better understand how a control can be reused, drag the control to the upper-left corner of the form. Now double-click your control icon in the toolbox again and drag the new control to the upper-right corner. The form will now look like the one in Figure 8.6. Both of these controls are directly tied to your original control. Any changes made to the control will instantly appear in both of them.

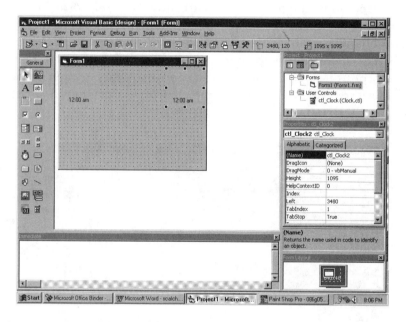

Figure 8.6 *Two copies of the **ctl_Clock** control on the form.*

The power of creating controls should be apparent. If you upgrade the control, all the projects that use it gain the new features. Let's make a change to our clock control and watch the effects on the original form. In the Project window on the right side of the screen, double-click on the line that says **ctl_Clock (Clock.ctl)**. The control window will reappear.

You have reopened the control for modification. While the control window is open, you cannot add the control to a form. To see how the existing controls react to the design window of the control being opened, select the **Project1 - Form1** option under the Window menu. Both controls now appear as boxes full of diagonal lines. The control on the toolbox has been dimmed so that new controls cannot be added until the design window is closed.

Select the **Project1 - ctl_Clock** option on the Window menu to return to our control design window. Click on the label that we added to the form. Now change the **Caption** property to **1:00 am**. Close the control design window using the menu to the left of the File menu.

Notice anything different? With the control window closed, you will see the Form1 window again and both controls now read **1:00 am**. In Chapter 4, we learned that a class is the blueprint for an object and that instances of the object are built from the class. When you created this user control, you were making a class of your user control. By drawing the control on the form, you create instances of that class.

Instances are not actually instantiated (created in the computer's memory) until the program is run. If you press **F5** now, your program will execute. The form will appear, showing both controls. When the program is running, each instance of the control object has been instantiated in the computer's memory.

Fantastic! Now that you understand the basics of creating a control, let's add the functionality we need. As we update the control, the instances placed on the form will automatically reflect all the changes we'll make.

WORKING WITH ICONS

Before you make any more modifications to the control, change some of the aspects of the main form. Press **F5** to run the program again. Click on the **Minimize** button of the Form1 window to turn it into a button on the taskbar (see Figure 8.7).

Figure 8.7 *If you click on the **Minimize** button of Form1, it will turn into an icon near the lower-left corner of your screen. It should look like the icon labeled **Form1** in this figure.*

The form displays the generic **Form1** name, and the icon used for Form1 is a generic icon that Visual Basic supplies to any new form you create. You can change this icon to one of your choosing, but for now we'll work with this icon.

Setting the Caption

The first thing you'll do is to experiment with changing the caption in the taskbar. Press **Ctrl+Break** to access the Immediate window.

The title of a window is controlled by the `Caption` property. You've used the Properties window to change the caption. Another way to change a window's caption is to use a command inside your program to assign a new string to the `Caption` property. In the Immediate window, type the following:

```
caption = "testing..."
|
```

The caption of the minimized form should be instantly changed, and you'll see something like Figure 8.8. Changing a window's caption couldn't be easier. By the way, a window's caption appears inside the title bar when a window is open and to the right of the icon when a window is minimized, as in Figure 8.8.

Figure 8.8 _Changing the caption of a minimized form._

Isn't it nice that Visual Basic makes this so simple? You've now learned everything you need to know about changing the caption inside a Visual Basic program.

READING THE CLOCK

You're making good progress. You know how to create a control and set the caption of a form with code. The next step is to get the current time and add that to the control.

Visual Basic has a special string function called `Time$` that will give you the current time. The easiest way to see how it works is to try an example. Let's use the **Print** command to display the value of `Time$`:

```
print time$
```

```
13:48:43
|
```

Now try it again after a short pause:

```
print time$
13:49:22
|
```

Notice that Visual Basic reports the time using a 24-hour format. We don't know about you, but we find it easier to read times with AM and PM, probably because we grew up with that format. (The standard time display in almost all countries except the United States and Latin America is 24-hour time.)

For now, we'll use this 24-hour time to build our program. Later in this chapter we'll show you how to display the time by using the AM and PM format.

USING TIMERS

Now you can go back to Design mode (type **End** in the Immediate window or select **End** from the Run menu) to start modifying the clock control. Double-click on **ctl_Clock** in the Project window so that we can begin enhancing the control. We'll add a timer control. Timer controls have an event handler, `Timer`, that you'll use to display the current time in the caption every second.

Creating a Timer

To create a timer, double-click on the icon in the toolbox that looks like a stopwatch (it's shown in Figure 8.9). You'll see a small clock inside a box. Don't worry if the timer icon overlaps the label control. The timer is an *invisible* control, which means that it does not appear on the form when the program is running. It can be placed anywhere on the form or control without effect.

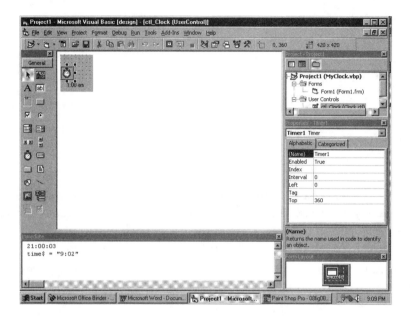

Figure 8.9 *Your control should look something like this after you create a*
timer object by double-clicking on the stopwatch icon.

Before we move on, let's take a look at what you've done. First, you've just created a new object, and it is different from all the other objects you've been
working with so far.

Using the Toolbox to Create Objects

With the exception of the pointer (in the upper-left corner), all the icons
you see in the toolbox (Figure 8.9) are objects that you can create inside a
form. You create any object by following these steps:

1. Click on the icon for the object you want to create (the timer, in our
   example).
2. Click and drag to outline the area you want the object to cover. The
   timer object will remain the same size, but you can resize other
   objects.
3. Release the mouse button, and you'll see your new object.

Alternatively, you can double-click on the icon and the control will be created on the form in the default size.

Finally, take a look at the Properties window (see Figure 8.10). You'll see that the default **(Name)** property for this new object is **Timer1**. Visual Basic automatically assigns a name to new objects, but, as you can see, it may not be a very informative one. The control name tells you it's a timer, but it gives you no idea what kind of timer it is.

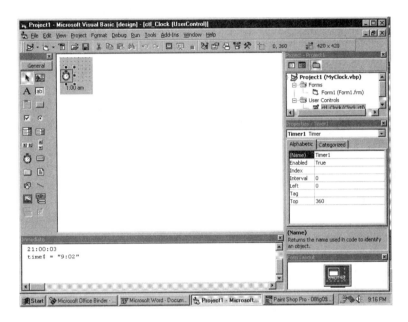

Figure 8.10 *The default control name for the new timer object is* ***Timer1***.

Let's rename this control to more closely reflect the planned function. You'll use this control to update your clock, so let's change the **Name** property to **Tick**.

Setting the Timer

Your next step will be to run a simple test program. It's best to work in small steps, and we can't overemphasize the value this approach. Instead of making all the needed changes in one sitting, let's start with making the timer beep every second.

You'll need to do two things to make your timer beep. First, you need to tell the timer how often to generate a `Timer` event. To do this, make sure that your timer object has handles around it (by clicking on it), and then click on the Properties window and use the scroll bar to select the **Interval** property (click once on it).

The initial interval will be 0, and that means this timer will never generate a `Timer` event. We need a non-zero value, but what value? What units are the intervals measured in?

Intervals are measured in milliseconds (0.001 second), so if you want to generate a `Timer` event every second, you need to set this property to 1000 milliseconds. To do this, type **1000** and press **Enter**. You should now see the number 1000 in the Properties window (see Figure 8.11).

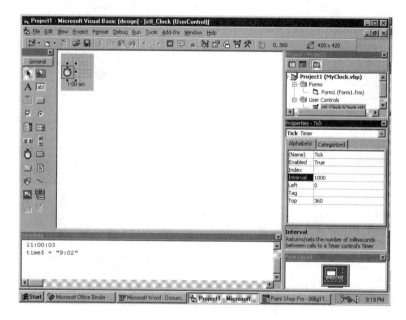

Figure 8.11 *The Properties window after changing the timer's interval to 1000.*

Finally, double-click on the timer object inside your form. This will bring up the Code window, showing the `Tick_Timer` subroutine. Add the **Beep** command to this subroutine:

```
Private Sub Tick_Timer ()
   Beep
End Sub
```

Now run this program. Your program should beep faithfully (or almost so; see the sidebar "The Timer Interval") every second. Although you have two instances of the control on the form, you will probably hear only one beep. Both instances of the control will be activated at exactly the same time; although both beeps are occurring, you hear only one.

THE TIMER INTERVAL

The Interval property, measured in milliseconds (0.001 second), tells a timer object how often to generate a Timer event. But for a couple of reasons, you don't actually have precise control over how often your program receives Timer events.

- Windows uses a timer inside your PC to determine how much time has elapsed from the last Timer event. But this internal timer ticks only 18.2 times every second, which is about 55 milliseconds. So you can never set the interval more accurately than 55 milliseconds.

- Windows won't always generate a Timer event as soon as the interval has elapsed, because Windows doesn't actually allow more than one program to run at a time. Instead, it lets one program process an event, and then it lets the next program process an event, and so on. If another program takes a long time to process an event, your program won't receive a Timer event until after the first program finishes processing its event.

If this sounds confusing, remember that your program will usually get a Timer event at about the right time, but don't rely on the timer for perfect precision.

Try experimenting with different interval values. Also, see what happens when you work with other programs while your Visual Basic program beeps away. If you run another program, you may discover that your program doesn't beep for a short while.

SHOWING THE TIME

Now that you have the `Timer` event handler working, let's make it a little more interesting. In the following code, you'll update your window's caption every second to display the current time. But before we show you the code, can you write it yourself?

Think about it for a minute. You want to read the current time each second and then set the `Caption` property of the **lbl_Time** control on the form by using this time. You've already learned how to create all the pieces you need to build this program. All you have to do is to put them together in the correct order, so give it a try.

Are you done yet? Now we'll show you our solution to this problem. As you may have guessed, the new version of **Tick_Timer** requires only the following single line:

```
Private Sub Tick_Timer ()

  lbl_Time.Caption = Time$

End Sub
```

Try this program. Both controls on your form should be updating! You'll see the caption flicker every second (unless you have a very fast computer). Flickering tends to draw your attention to the source of the flicker, and that's great fun when you've just finished writing a program. But after a while, this kind of flickering bothers most people, especially when they're trying to work on something else. It can be distracting.

If you update the caption every minute instead of every second, you probably won't notice the flicker anymore. This is exactly what the final version of Icon Clock does, as you can see in Figure 8.1.

The problem, though, is that `Time$` always returns a time showing seconds. So you need some way to get a time that doesn't include the seconds.

Using Time Functions

Visual Basic has time and date functions in addition to `Time$`, including one called `Now`. The `Now` function returns the current time and date information as a special date number (which is represented inside Visual Basic as a number of type Double). Visual Basic provides some functions that take a date number apart. We'll use these other functions shortly, but first an example.

If you print the value of Now, you'll notice it's displayed as a full date and time, which is more information than you need for Icon Clock, as follows:

```
print now
10/27/94 9:23:11 AM
|
```

The return value of the Now function, by the way, has the type Date, which you'll need to keep in mind for later, when you define a variable to remember the value of Now at a single instant.

REFERENCE

Now Function

The Now function returns a special date number of type Date. This single number contains all the information on the current time and date. The following returns the current time and date information in a date number of type Date:

```
someVar = Now
```

There are a number of functions you can use with the information returned by Now. The following functions are the ones that you'll use in this chapter. The following returns the seconds, which is a number between 0 and 59:

```
s% = Second(Now)
```

The following returns the minutes, which is a number between 0 and 59:

```
m% = Minute(Now)
```

The following returns the hours, which is a number between 0 and 23:

```
h% = Hour(Now)
```

The following returns the current time, using the United States. 12-hour format (such as 9:55 AM):

```
s$ = Format$(Now, "h:mm AM/PM")
```

Visual Basic has four functions you'll use with the value returned by Now: one each to return the hour, minute, and second information, and a fourth one to format the time nicely.

Let's start with the function that will format the time reported by Now. This new function, called Format$, returns a string. It's a useful and powerful function for formatting numbers of all kinds. Here you'll use only the part of this function that formats a date serial number using the AM and PM time display (rather than the 24-hour display), which doesn't show seconds. Try the following command in the Immediate window:

```
print Format$(now, "h:mm AM/PM")
9:55 AM
|
```

The Format$ function takes two arguments. The first argument is the date returned by the Now function. The second argument is a pattern that tells Format$ how you want the time formatted. If, for example, you want to display the time in 24-hour format rather than 12-hour format, you could use this string instead: "h:mm". Give this a try.

Let's rewrite the timer code in the control so that it will use the Format$ function, as follows:

```
Private Sub Tick_Timer ()
 lbl_Time.Caption = Format$(Now, "h:mm AM/PM")
End Sub
```

When you run this program, it now displays the time in exactly the same format shown in Figure 8.1. (Note: if you're in a country other than the United States, you may see the time displayed in your country's standard format instead.)

REFERENCE

Print Function

We have used the **Print** command extensively in the Immediate window. There is a shortcut to save you some typing. Instead of the **Print** command, you can substitute a question mark. For example, the preceding formatting code could use the **?** command:

```
? Format$(now, "h:mm AM/PM")
```

In this book, we will continue using the complete **Print** command, but feel free to substitute **?** for quicker testing.

Now let's look at how you can keep the caption from flickering. There are two approaches. First, you could change the interval to 60,000, which is 1 minute. But because you'll need to draw a new second hand every second, this isn't the solution that you'll use.

The second approach takes a little more work. You'll create a form-level variable, called `lastMinute`, that keeps track of the minute currently displayed. As soon as the current minute is different from `lastMinute`, you'll change the caption. If this sounds a little confusing, it'll become clearer after a little more work.

Getting Information from Dates

Visual Basic has yet another function, called `Minute`, that returns the minute part of a date. So if you type the following, you'll see just the minutes part of the time:

```
print time$
9:58:04
print minute(now)
 58
|
```

(The minutes will be different in this example if you wait too long between running these two commands.)

Here's what to do. First, define the variable `lastMinute` in the (**General**) section of your control, as follows:

```
Private lastMinute As Integer     ' Last minute shown in
                                  ' caption
```

Next, you'll use this information in `Tick_Timer`, as follows:

```
Private Sub Tick_Timer ()
  Dim t                 ' The time information

  t = Now               ' Get the current time
```

```
    min = Minute(t)                ' Get the current minute
    If min <> lastMinute Then      ' Update caption if new minute
        lbl_Time.Caption = Format$(t, "h:mm AM/PM")
        lastMinute = min            ' Remember new current minute
    End If
End Sub
```

(If you changed the `Interval` property, make sure you set it back to 1000.) Try this new program and then think about what it does before you read on.

A few things in this subroutine may not be obvious. For starters, notice that we defined the variable `t` without a type after it. Any variables you define without an explicit `As` type are created as Variant variables, which is exactly what you want in this case. The `Now` function returns a Date value, and Variant variables can contain Date as well as other types of values.

You'll also notice that we used a very short name, `t`, to save the date number. Why didn't we use a longer, more descriptive name, such as `time`? In this case you can't use `time` because Visual Basic already has a function called `Time`. You could use an even longer name, such as `dateNumber`, but because you're going to be using this variable a couple of times, we suggest using a very short name. When you use one variable a number of times in a single subroutine, a short, single-letter variable name can make the code easier to read and write.

Let's look in detail at how this subroutine works. First, it assigns the value of `Now` to the variable `t`. You do this, rather than continue to use `Now` in the rest of the subroutine, to make sure you're working with a single time. Otherwise, the time might change before `Tick_Timer` finishes.

Next, the subroutine gets the minutes from this time and saves this value in the variable `min`. It then compares the value in `min` to the value in `lastMinute`. The symbols `<>` mean "not equal to." So if `min` is not equal to `lastMinute`, Visual Basic runs the next two statements. In other words, it updates the caption only when `min` is different from `lastMinute`.

Finally, `Tick_Timer` updates the caption and saves the new minute value in the `lastMinute` variable. This arrangement ensures that it won't update the caption again until the minute changes.

Displaying the time in the caption is the easy part. Now for the hard part: drawing the hands on the clock face.

DRAWING THE CLOCK FACE

Writing the rest of the clock control is a little more difficult, because you'll use trigonometry to draw the hands on the clock. Fortunately, you can start with something much simpler: inserting the icon used for the minimized program.

Setting the Icon

The icon we use in this program is included on the accompanying disk. We'll show you how to use this icon in your own program.

Make sure you're in Design mode. Then click on the icon in the toolbox that looks like a picture with a cactus and a sun. (If you pause the mouse over this button, a tooltip will appear with the name **PictureBox**.) Click and drag the mouse inside the form to create a PictureBox control, just as you previously created command buttons (see Figure 8.12). Don't worry if you overlap the Timer control. It's invisible on the form anyway.

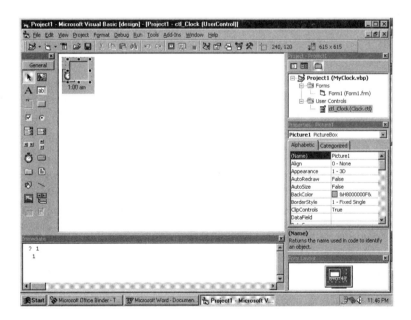

Figure 8.12 Draw a PictureBox control on the **ctl_Clock** background.

In the Properties window, change several properties for the PictureBox control:

(Name)	pct_Clock	
Appearance	0—Flat	
AutoSize	True	
BackColor	&H8000000F	(Button Face)
Border Style	0—None	

Next, select the **Picture** property in the Properties window. At this point you'll see a small button with three dots (…) to the right of the **(Picture)** property value. Click on this button, and you'll see the open file dialog box.

If you haven't installed the files from the accompanying disk, you'll need to do so now. Then use the Directories part of the Load Icon dialog box to switch to the Clock directory. You'll find a file called **Ckock.ico** in this directory. You can also use any of the Clock icons in the \VB\Graphics\Icons\Misc folder. Double-click this file to load it into Visual Basic.

Your PictureBox control should now show a clock face. You also want to make this icon the main application icon. Close the control window with the menu to the left of the File menu.

Now click on your Form1 window to make it the active window. If one of the controls has handles around it, click anywhere else in the form (except on the timer control). This will ensure that your form, rather than the picture box or timer, is the currently selected object.

Instead of the `Picture` property, we want to set the Icon property. Click on the **Icon** property, click the three dots (**...**) command button, and select the **Clock.ico** file. You will notice that the icon in the upper-left corner of your form now looks like a clock instead of the standard Visual Basic form icon (see Figure 8.1). Your next project will be to draw the hands on the clock face.

DRAWING THE CLOCK HANDS

Drawing the clock hands isn't hard, but it will take a much longer subroutine than you've written before. You'll actually use several subroutines to do all the work.

Why does it take so much code? For one thing, you'll be drawing three hands on the clock: the hour hand, the minute hand, and the second hand. This is in addition to updating the caption, which you're already doing.

Let's start by drawing the second hand; it will move each second so it will take only a minute to see whether it works correctly in all positions. To do this, we'll need to review a little math, which is necessary to calculate where to draw the second hand. You'll be able to use the same code for both the hour and the minute hand.

Figure 8.13 shows a blowup of the clock face, along with the hands drawn on the screen and a review of the trigonometry involved in drawing the second hand.

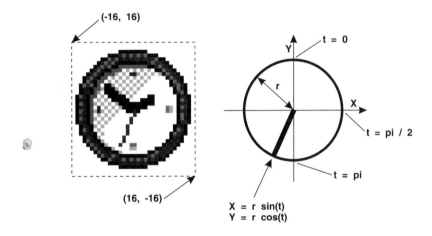

Figure 8.13 *A brief review of the trigonometry that you'll use to draw the hands on the clock. You'll define the coordinate system to go from –16 to 16, because the icon is 32 pixels wide and high.*

If you remember the drawing you've done so far, you'll remember that (0, 0) has always been in the upper-left corner, with increasing Y values moving down rather than up. But here you'll want to use a Cartesian coordinate system, with (0, 0) at the center of the icon, and increasing Y values moving up. How do you do this? You can fake it by writing the equations to work with the standard coordinates. Better yet, you can redefine the coordinate system so that it's more to your liking.

It's easy to change the coordinate system. A command called **Scale** lets you tell Visual Basic what numbers you want to use for the upper-left and lower-right corners of your form. In the case of the icon, you'll use a range of numbers from –16 to 16, as you can see in Figure 8.13.

Scale Command

The **Scale** command allows you to define a custom coordinate system for any form.

The following code sets up a custom coordinate system, with the upper-left corner at (x1, y1) and the lower-right corner at (x2, y2).

```
Scale [(x1, y1) - (x2, y2)]
```

If you don't provide any coordinates, Visual Basic resets the coordinates to the default coordinate system, with each unit equal to a twip, (0, 0) at the upper-left corner, and Y increasing down.

Any icon for a minimized window in Microsoft Windows is 32 pixels (dots) wide and 32 pixels high. So by creating a coordinate system that spans the range from –16 to 16, you're creating a coordinate system in which each unit is exactly 1 pixel wide. It's not important in this case that each unit be 1 pixel wide, but you'll do it anyway; it doesn't matter how large a unit is, as long as (0, 0) is at the center of the icon.

Let's write the code to draw this second hand using the real time. Return to Design mode for the Clock control (by double-clicking on it in the Project window). Make sure you're viewing the code for `Tick_Timer()`. Enter the following changes (notice we're using the equations in Figure 8.13 to calculate the position of the second hand):

```
Private Sub Tick_Timer ()
    Const pi = 3.141592653    ' Define the value of pi
    Dim t                     ' The time information

    t = Now                   ' Get the current time
    sec = Second(t)           ' Get seconds, 0..59
    min = Minute(t)           ' Get the current minute, 0..59

    If min <> lastMinute Then  ' Update caption if new minute
```

```
  lbl_Time.Caption = Format$(t, "h:mm AM/PM")
  lastMinute = min            ' Remember new current minute
End If


pct_Clock.Scale (-16, 16)-(16, -16)    ' Set scale for clock icon
x = 10 * Sin(sec * pi / 30) ' Calculate end of second hand
y = 10 * Cos(sec * pi / 30)
pct_Clock.Line (0, 0)-(x, y)             ' Draw the second hand
End Sub
```

Then run this program.

You'll find one problem. `Tick_Timer` isn't removing the second hand after it draws it. After a minute, your clock face will be filled with 60 second hands.

Before we fix that problem, notice that there is a new keyword in this program. The `Const` keyword defines a special type of variable, called a *constant*, that has a fixed value. In other words, you can never change the value of a constant. You'll use `Const` whenever you have a constant value in a program, such as pi. (It is written as π in mathematics, but as `pi` in programs, because you can't use Greek letters in programs.)

REFERENCE

Const Keyword

The `Const` keyword allows you to define constants in your programs. You can assign a name to a number or a string of characters, as follows:

```
Const name = value
```

Us the preceding statement to define `name` to be a constant equal to `value`.

Showing One Second Hand

Now let's return to the problem with the second hand. The program draws the hand but never erases it, so we're filling the icon with black lines.

Think about this problem for a moment. How would you fix it? The first step is to identify exactly what the problem is; only then can you solve it. In this case, the problem is simple. You're not erasing the previous second hand before you draw the new one, so you need a solution that erases the old second hand.

We've discussed only one way to erase something: using the **Cls** command. You learned that **Cls** automatically redraws the icon in your minimized program, so it erases everything except the icon. In other words, **Cls** will erase only the second hand, because that's all you've drawn on top of the icon. Try adding **Cls** to your program; then run it. (Here's how to make the change. Put a pct_Clock.Cls command into your Tick_Timer event handler on a line immediately before the pct_Line command.) What happens now?

At this point you'll notice that the second hand moves around the clock face. But the clock face flickers now, just as the caption flickered earlier when you changed it every second. What you want is a way to erase the second hand without having to use the **Cls** command. In other words, you want a way to "undraw" a line. We'll show you how to do it after a brief side trip into colors.

Drawing with Color

At the start of this chapter, we promised that your second hand would be red, so let's examine how to change the color of the line. Doing this before discussing a better way to erase a line may seem that we're getting off the track, but we're not. What you learn here will help make the next step clearer, because the technique you'll use has to do with colors.

The **Line** command has an optional argument that you haven't used yet. This argument allows you to draw lines with other colors. There is also a function, called **RGB**, that allows you to calculate a color number. **RGB** stands for red, green, and blue and takes three arguments: a red, a green, and a blue component. For a red line, you'll want to use 0 for green and blue, and 255 (the maximum value allowed for each part) for red.

The following line is the new version of the **Line** command in Tick_Timer that draws a red line (instead of the normal black line):

```
pct_Clock.Line (0, 0)-(x, y), RGB(255, 0, 0)
```

Now your program will draw a red second hand.

RGB Function

The following code returns a color number, which you can use in the **Line** command to draw a line of any color:

```
colorNumber = RGB(redNumber, greenNumber, blueNumber)
```

The red, green, and blue color numbers can be any number between 0 and 255. White is (255, 255, 255) and black is (0, 0, 0). The number returned by **RGB** is of type Long.

The **RGB** function builds color numbers used by the **Line** command. **RGB** stands for red, green, and blue, the primary colors used for television screens. You may have been taught that the primary colors are red, yellow, and blue. Why do we use red, green, and blue here?

The primary colors you learned about in school are for *subtractive* colors; if you use paint and combine all the primary colors, you'll end up with a dark mess. On the other hand, when you're working with light rather than paint, you're working with *additive* colors. In this case, the primary colors switch to red, green, and blue. This should be familiar if you've done any work with theater lighting, where you create a white spot by combing red, green, and blue spotlights.

Using Xor to Erase a Line

Now that you've learned about colors, you might guess that you can erase the line you drew before (without having to redraw the icon) by drawing a white line. You can try that using RGB(255, 255, 255), but it will also erase anything on the clock face that wasn't white before. So you need a different technique to undraw lines without erasing what was there before. It sounds impossible, but there is a way to do it.

Windows has a way to undraw lines as long as you draw them properly. All the drawing you've done so far has been drawn lines on top of other objects. But you can also draw lines by *inverting* dots on the screen. If you invert the dots twice, they turn back into their original color. This means that you can erase a line by drawing it a second time.

You can change the way a line is drawn by using the DrawMode property. By default, DrawMode is set to 13, which tells Visual Basic to draw lines on top of anything on the screen. You'll set DrawMode to 10, which tells Visual Basic to use the inverting mode. When a line is drawn, each point on the line checks what it is drawing over and uses the inverse color.

Using this mode, if you draw a line over a picture, the line is inverted at any point that isn't white. If this same line with the same mode is drawn in the same place, it inverts the original invert and disappears! This may seem confusing, but when you see it work it will become more comprehensible.

Let's look at how it works. But first, a comment: if you look in the *Language Reference Manual* (or the online help) under DrawMode, you'll find a list of 16 different drawing modes. You'll also find that the descriptions of the drawing modes don't make much sense. And DrawMode 10, which is what we're using here, is called the Not Xor Pen mode. What does all this mean?

It's a little hard to explain. Most professional Windows programmers don't fully understand all the drawing modes, and may not need to understand how it works as long as you know it works. If you're interested, however, the reference on the DrawMode property will give you all of the information you need. It will be here, waiting for you, if you ever need to learn more about DrawMode.

REFERENCE

DrawMode Property

The DrawMode property allows you to control how Visual Basic draws colored lines (and shapes) on the screen. It works somewhat like using water colors and oil paints. With oil paints, you can paint one color over another color, and the new color will completely replace the old color. But water colors don't work the same way: when you paint a water color over an existing color, the two colors blend together where they overlap to give you a third color.

Visual Basic has two drawing options similar to the painting examples in addition to 14 other drawing modes. One of the nice things about computers is that they give you much more freedom than you might have in the physical world. But it takes a little while to understand all the nuances and meanings. You won't need to understand most of the material in this sidebar. You're going to be using only two modes here: 10 and 13. But later, when you're ready to experiment, you'll find it a useful reference, because much of this information isn't documented well anywhere else.

Understanding all the DrawMode values takes quite a bit of work, and we weren't able to find a good explanation in any of the books we looked at (including Microsoft's Windows programming reference manuals). Following is a comprehensive description of each of the 16 modes supported by Visual Basic.

Three groups of modes (Mask, Inverse, and Merge) are particularly difficult, so we'll say a few words about them. But first, the following table points out the modes most commonly used and gives you an idea of what they do.

Most Commonly Used DrawMode Modes

TYPE OF DRAWMODE	DRAWMODE NUMBERS
Combining light	15
Draw over (replace old color)	13 (the default)
Erasable draw	10, 7, or 6

Figure 8.14 shows a color wheel for the additive colors (using light rather than paint). The inverse of any color on this wheel is the color on the opposite side of the circle. Note that bright colors are turned into dark colors when they're inverted.

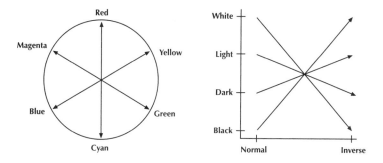

Figure 8.14 *The left side shows which colors are the inverse of other colors. The right side shows how the brightness of a color changes when you invert it.*

The Merge and Mask groups use color information from the pen and from each pixel currently on the screen where the shape will be drawn. Colors in Windows have three components: red, green, and blue. The Merge modes work with one pixel at a time and calculate each color component (red, green, and blue) by adding the pen color and the color of the pixel being drawn over. For example, if you draw a bright red pixel (RGB = 255, 0, 0) over a bright blue pixel (RGB = 0, 0, 255), you get a bright magenta pixel (RGB = 255, 0, 255). Drawing a green pixel on top of a bright magenta pixel gives you a white pixel. The Merge modes are analogous to the creation of anew color of light by combining two lights of different colors.

In the Mask modes, either the pen or the current pixel color (or its inverse) is used as a mask. A *mask*, in this case, limits the amount of red, green, and blue in the final pixel drawn on the screen. For example, if the mask color is (127, 127, 0), the red and green components of the final pixel will be limited to 127 or less, and the blue component will be 0. For example, if we use a mask of (127, 127, 0) to mask bright magenta (255, 0, 255), you'll get a light red pixel (127, 0, 0).

The following table lists the `DrawMode` values.

DrawMode Values

MODE VALUE	MODE NAME	DESCRIPTION
1	Black	Always draw in black. This ignores the pen color, and it draws over anything currently on the screen.
2	Inverse of Merge	Windows merges the pen and pixel colors and then draws the inverse of this on the screen.
3	Mask Screen using Inverse of the Pen	This mode masks the colors on the screen, using the inverse of the pen color as a mask.
4	Inverse Pen Color	Draws using a color that's the inverse of the pen color.
5	Mask the Inverse Screen	Inverts the colors on the screen and then masks them by using the pen color.
6	Invert Screen	In this mode, anything you "draw" will simply invert the colors on the screen. In other words, this mode ignores the pen color and just changes what's on the screen.
7	Xor Draw	Use this mode when you need to draw lines that you can erase by drawing them again. This mode will keep the correct color for lines you draw against a black background. Use mode 10 for a white background.

DrawMode Values (continued0)

MODE VALUE	MODE NAME	DESCRIPTION
8	Inverse of Mask Screen	This mode displays the inverse of the colors displayed by mode 9. It uses the pen color to mask the screen color, and then it inverts this color.
9	Mask Screen	Windows breaks the pen and pixel colors into red, green, and blue components, and then "clips" the red, green, and blue components so that they're no larger than the RGB components of the pen. For example, if you mask a white pixel (RGB = 255, 255, 255) using a dark blue pen (RGB = 0, 0, 127), you get a dark blue pixel on the screen.
10	Inverse Xor Draw	Use this mode when you want to draw lines that you can erase by drawing them again. This mode will keep the correct color for lines you draw against a white background. Use mode 7 for a black background.
11	Transparent	Doesn't draw anything. You'll probably never need to use this mode.
12	Merge Screen and Inverse of Pen	Merges the inverse of the pen color with the screen colors. To draw any pixel, Windows first inverts the pen color; then it adds together (individually) the red, green, and blue components of these two colors. Windows does this for each pixel being drawn over.
13	Pen Color (default)	Draws using the pen color. It draws over anything currently being shown.
14	Merge Pen and Inverse of Screen	Merges the pen with the inverse of the screen colors. To draw any pixel, Windows first inverts the pixel being drawn over, and then adds together (individually) the red, green, and blue components of these two colors. Windows does this for each pixel being drawn over.

DrawMode Values (continued)

MODE VALUE	MODE NAME	DESCRIPTION
15	Merge Pen and Screen	Merges the color of the pen with what's currently on the screen. For each pixel drawn, Windows adds together each color component (red, green, and blue) of the pen color and the pixel being drawn over. For example, if you draw a bright red pixel (RGB = 255, 0, 0) over a bright blue pixel (RGB = 0, 0, 255), you get a bright magenta pixel (255, 0, 255). Drawing a green pixel on top of a bright magenta pixel gives you a white pixel. (If any component adds up to a number greater than 255, it's set to 255.)
16	White	Always draw in white This ignores the pen color, and it draws over anything currently on the screen.

You will use `DrawMode = 10` to display an erasable second hand, so you need to figure out how to use this drawing mode. First, we'll describe the process in simple English. Then we'll try to describe it in a way that makes it easy to write this program. For the second way, we'll be using something called *pseudocode*, which combines a programming language and English.

First, the English description. You need to draw the second hand. Then, when you get the next `Tick_Timer` event, you need to erase the last second hand you drew and then draw a new second hand. It sounds simple enough, but this is only the first step in solving the problem. There are a number of special conditions, known as *boundary conditions*, to look at. Here, you'll try to identify the places where you might have to do something different. In other words, you want to find the boundaries of the problem.

For example, the very first `Tick_Timer` event you get after your program starts is slightly different from all the others. You want to erase the last line you drew before drawing the new second hand, but the first time you get a `Tick_Timer` event you haven't yet drawn a line. Because there's nothing to erase, you'll want to handle this case a little differently. This is the type of thing to look for when you're looking for boundary conditions.

There are other boundary conditions that you'll find later. But for now, the initial call to `Tick_Timer` is the only boundary condition you'll need to worry about.

Now let's rewrite our simple description of how to draw an erasable second hand, this time in more detail, using pseudocode. The solution will look like the following:

```
Tick_Timer()

    If previous line Then

        Erase the previous second hand

    End If

    Draw the new second hand.
```

As you can see, this is a cross between Basic code and English. We're using the Basic **If..Then** command, but for the condition and the statements we're using an English-language description. This powerful technique lets you express your ideas in a way that's much easier to turn into a program.

PSEUDOCODE: THE TOOL OF PROS

Pseudocode is a powerful tool for writing complex programs. Many professional programmers and professors use pseudocode to express their ideas before they start to write programs. There aren't any hard-and-fast rules about how to express ideas in pseudocode. The idea is to use *control structures* (such as **If..Then**) but use English descriptions for other statements and even for the conditions that will appear in the **If..Then** statements.

When you're writing pseudocode, you need to avoid getting bogged down in detail. Write as simple a description as you can and fill in the details later. If you're working with a complex idea, you'll probably find yourself rewriting your pseudocode several times, adding a little more detail each time.

When you have an idea of what you're going to do, it's time to turn it into real code. Before we show you our solution, try writing a solution yourself. We'll give you a couple of hints. You'll need to keep track of the location of the last second hand so that you can erase it. The obvious solution is to save this information in form-level variables. See whether you can write this new `Tick_Timer` event handler yourself.

Now for our solution. First, we've created two variables—`lastX` and `lastY`—to keep track of the endpoint of the second hand. Because the second hands always start at (0, 0), this is all the information needed to keep track of the last second hand. Put these two definitions into the (**General**) area of your control:

```
Private lastX As Integer       ' Endpoint of last second hand
Private lastY As Integer
```

Next, you need a way to let `Tick_Timer` know when there isn't a previous second hand for it to erase. You could do this if there were a way to set `lastX` to a special value before your program starts running. We've chosen to use 999, because X for the second hand ranges between minus 10 and 10, so it can never reach 999.

How can you set `lastX` to 999 before each control starts running? You can use another event handler, called `UserControl_Initialize`, that's called only when each instance of a user control is first executed. In other words, it's called only when the instance of the control is first initialized.

Use the left combo box to select **UserControl** and then select **Initialize** from the right combo box. Then enter the following code into the event handler:

```
Private Sub UserControl_Initialize()
   lastX = 999             ' No previous second hand
End Sub
```

Finally, you need to modify `Tick_Timer` so that it will erase the old second hand and remember the location of the new second hand. `Tick_Timer` is getting rather long, so instead of showing you the entire event handler, we'll show you only the changes for the following lines, starting with the **Scale** command (which you won't change):

```
   pct_Clock.Scale (-16, 16)-(16, -16)    ' Set scale for clock icon
   pct_Clock.DrawMode = 10                ' Set for erasable drawing
```

```
red = RGB(255, 0, 0)          ' Define red color

x = 10 * Sin(sec * pi / 30)   ' Calculate end of second hand
y = 10 * Cos(sec * pi / 30)
If lastX <> 999 Then          ' Erase any old second hand
    pct_Clock.Line (0, 0)-(lastX, lastY), red
End If
pct_Clock.Line (0, 0)-(x, y), red     ' Draw the new second hand

lastX = x                     ' Save end point of new hand
lastY = y
End Sub
```

Most of this new code should be fairly clear. We've pulled one small trick to cut down on any flicker in the second hand. You'll notice that you're now calculating the new x and y position before you erase the previous second hand. This approach allows the two **Line** commands to be as close together as possible. The closer together they are, the less time there will be during which no second hand appears on the screen. Trigonometric functions, such as **Sin** and **Cos**, tend to be slow.

You might want to experiment with this. If you move the three lines that erase the previous second hand (starting with `If lastX <> 999`) up two lines so that they're before the x and y calculations, you'll notice that the second hand flickers slightly each time it's moved. The way we wrote them previously, you won't see a flicker. Such small differences separate a good program from an excellent program.

Drawing the Hour and Minute Hands

You're almost finished writing your first user control. At this point you have only a couple of things left to add. First, you need to draw the hour and minute hands.

We still have a slight problem: sometimes the old second hand stays behind. This happens now because the x and y variables are floating-point numbers, whereas `lastX` and `lastY` are of type Integer. So it's possible for `lastX` to be different from the previous x as a result of rounding. You can fix this problem by defining x and y as `Integer` in `Tick_Timer`. Or you can redefine `lastX` and `lastY` so that they're of type Variant. Either solution will work.

As to adding the hour and minute hands, you'll see the new version of `Tick_Timer` shortly. You'll need to add the variable `lastHour` to the (**General**) section of your form, and there are a couple of other things we'll comment on. First, you'll notice a line that calculates a variable h. This line creates a fractional hour that includes the minute information, which allows the hour hand to move every minute. A real clock changes the position of the hour hand every minute so that it will fall between two of the hour marks at 30 minutes past the hour.

You'll also notice that we've carefully specified the drawing mode as erasable mode (10) for the second hands and nonerasable mode (13) for the hour and minute hands. This technique allows you to have an hour and minute hand so that the hour hand doesn't erase part of the minute hand. See what we mean, remove the line that sets `DrawMode` to 13.

Finally, we set `lastX` to 999 when the hour or minute changes. Whenever the hour or minute changes, the clock face is erased, so there won't be a previous second hand in such cases. The rest of this program should be familiar.

The final clock program has a single `Timer` control added to the form, called **Timer1**, with the name **Tick**. The property for the form is **Icon**, with the setting **Clock.ico**.

The following definitions are in the (**General**) part of your control:

```
Private lastMinute As Integer     ' Last minute shown on clock
Private lastHour As Integer        ' Last hour shown on clock

Private lastX As Integer           ' Endpoint of last second hand
Private lastY As Integer

Private Sub UserControl_Initialize()
  lastX = 999            ' No previous second hand
End Sub

Private Sub Tick_Timer ()
  Const pi = 3.141592653         ' Define the value of pi
```

```
Dim t                            ' The time information
Dim x As Integer                 ' Use same type as lastX
Dim y As Integer

t = Now                          ' Get the current time
sec = Second(t)                  ' Get seconds, 0..59
min = Minute(t)                  ' Get the current minute, 0..59
hr = Hour(t)                     ' Get hours, 0..23


pct_Clock.Scale (-16, 16)-(16, -16)      ' Set scale for clock icon
'
' If the hour or minute has changed, update the caption,
' then remove all the hands and redraw them
'
If min <> lastMinute Or hr <> lastHour Then
    lbl_Time.Caption = Format$(t, "h:mm AM/PM")
    lastMinute = min             ' Remember new current minute
    lastHour = hr
    pct_Clock.Cls                        ' Clear all clock hands
    lastX = 999                  ' No previous second hand

    pct_Clock.DrawWidth = 2              ' Draw 2-pixel lines
    pct_Clock.DrawMode = 13              ' Draw nonerasable lines

    h = hr + min / 60            ' Decimal hour, for hour hand
    x = 5 * Sin(h * pi / 6)      ' Endpoint of hour hand
    y = 5 * Cos(h * pi / 6)
    pct_Clock.Line (0, 0)-(x, y)         ' Draw the hour hand

    x = 8 * Sin(min * pi / 30)   ' Endpoint of minute hand
    y = 8 * Cos(min * pi / 30)
    pct_Clock.Line (0, 0)-(x, y)
```

```
    pct_Clock.DrawWidth = 1                    ' Set back to 1-pixel lines
End If


pct_Clock.DrawMode = 10                      ' Set for erasable drawing
red = RGB(255, 0, 0)              ' Define red color


x = 10 * Sin(sec * pi / 30)       ' Calculate end of second hand
y = 10 * Cos(sec * pi / 30)
If lastX <> 999 Then              ' Erase any old second hand
   pct_Clock.Line (0, 0)-(lastX, lastY), red
End If
pct_Clock.Line (0, 0)-(x, y), red        ' Draw the new second hand


lastX = x                         ' Save endpoint of new hand
lastY = y
End Sub
```

Congratulations! You've created a reusable clock control. We'll even use it in a project later in this book. When you run the program, you should see both instances of the clock running on the main form. Later we'll also enhance the control so that it has custom properties exposed, just as other controls do.

RELATED TOOLS

- Format$. This powerful command can be used to format many types of numbers. For example, if you want to display money information, such as displaying 2.3 as $2.30 (with a dollar sign and two decimal places), this is the command for you. You'll find details in the *Language Reference Manual.*

- Time and date functions. There are a number of time and date functions we haven't used in this chapter that you might find useful:

   TimeSerial. Calculates a Date value given the hour, minute, and second.

   TimeValue. Converts a string (such as "12:34PM") into a Date value.

`Date$`. Returns the current date in a string.

`DateSerial`. Calculates a Date value given a year, month, and day.

`DateValue`. Converts a string (such as "3/6/92") to a Date value.

`Day`. Returns the day of the month (1..31) from a Date value.

`Weekday`. Returns the day of the week, between 1 (Sunday) and 7 (Saturday), from a Date value.

`Month`. Returns the month (1..12) from a Date value.

`Year`. Returns the year part of a Date value (1753..2078).

- Trigonometric functions. In this chapter you learned about the **Sin** (sine) and **Cos** (cosine) functions. Visual Basic also provides the **Tan** (tangent) and **Atn** (arc-tangent) functions.

- Scale-related properties. When you set a custom scale, you can use the `ScaleWidth` and `ScaleHeight` properties to get the current width (in drawing units) and height of your form. You can also get the coordinates of the left and top edges using `ScaleLeft` and `ScaleTop`.

SUMMARY

You covered much ground in this chapter, and you should have a solid understanding of the construction of custom controls. In Chapter 9, we'll start all over again with a new program. This program, however, will be larger, so you'll get a chance to learn how to write large programs. You'll probably want to modify this useful program to suit your own needs.

We've covered the following topics in this chapter:

- Designing a control. You learned more about designing a control, implementing solutions using stepwise refinement, and planning ahead. It's always a good idea to think about what you want your program to look like and how you want it to work before you start programming. If you can break it into separate controls, they will become part of your toolbox for the creation of future programs. You also learned about using pseudocode to design programs. Pseudocode, used to quickly sketch the structure of a program, is a cross between English and Basic.

- Drawing inside icons. You can draw inside an icon just as easily as you can draw inside a form. You can also change the caption of a minimized program by setting the Caption property to any string.

- Creating multiple instances on a form. You can use a user control that you've designed just as you can use any other control. Multiple instances of the control can be placed on the form at the same time and executed concurrently (such as two clocks).

- Timers. You learned how to create a timer object and how to write code in the Timer event that will run at millisecond intervals. The timer interval is set by selecting the timer object on the form and then setting the Timer property using the Properties window.

- Reading the time. You can use the Time$ function to get a string that shows the current time in 24-hour format. You can also use the Format$ (now, "h:mm AM/PM") to display a string with the time in 12-hour format. The functions Hour, Minute, and Second will break a Date value, returned by the Now function, into the hour, minute, and second parts of the time.

- UserControl_Initialize. You can set up variables and initialize routines in the UserControl_Initialize event handler, which runs once when each instance of your control first loads (and before it appears on the screen).

- Const keyword. The Const keyword allows you to define constants in your programs. Like variables, constants have a name, but they have a single value and can't be changed.

- Color. The **RGB** function allows you to draw lines using any color. You provide a red, green, and blue component, and each component can be between 0 and 255 (0 is no color, and 255 is full color). RGB(0, 0, 0) is black, and RGB (255, 255, 255) is white.

- DrawMode. Setting DrawMode to 10 allows you to draw erasable lines. The normal drawing mode (13) writes nonerasable lines.

CHAPTER 9

Designing and Building Programs

- How to design programs
- Designing user interfaces
- Building programs

In this chapter you'll start designing a complete Visual Basic application, called Address Book, that will be robust enough for daily use. You'll see first-hand how programmers go about designing and building real programs. You'll also learn new techniques that you'll find useful in writing your own programs.

First, we'll spend some time talking about designing programs. As you'll see, there are a number of approaches you can take. We'll take just one approach in this book—the one that works best for us.

After this discussion of philosophy and approaches, we'll get down to the work of designing the address book. This program lets you keep track of names and addresses and print them out. Because we'll build this program for the next few chapters, you'll be able to change anything you don't like or add features you think are missing.

HOW TO DESIGN PROGRAMS

In the past chapters we have begun building a program and typing in the code with a little planning. Programs that will be used for broader purposes than the ones we've built usually require more emphasis on design before creation begins. There are two extremes in the world of programming: the completed-specification people and the code-as-you go people. Most programs are written using a process that fall between these poles.

The completed-specification proponents believe that programmers should write very detailed specifications before they write a single line of code or spend any time at the computer. This process takes a great deal of time, but its proponents argue that the time spent up front is saved later in the project.

The code-as-you-go theory is that programming is an incremental process that constantly evolves and that programmers should start writing something as soon as they can. We'll spend a few paragraphs explaining these approaches in more detail, and then we'll present the approach we use, which is the one that we'll discuss in the next few chapters.

We should mention that there is no one correct method for writing programs, although you may encounter people who believe there is one correct approach. Each person has his or her own approach. If you're working for someone else, you may have to use the approach he or she favors, rather than use your own. By understanding the different approaches, you'll be able to use different techniques even if you have to follow the "one correct approach" to software design.

Detailed Specifications

With the detailed specifications system, you design the program in detail before you touch the computer or write any code. This technique allows you to work out all the complicated interactions in a program before you've worked yourself into a hole. If you start writing the program without such a plan, you may discover that you've headed off in the wrong direction, so it's important to think things through first.

This method is often found in professional environments, where managers strictly track the progress of development. The amount of detail in design specifications may vary considerably, but they usually contain a description of the problems the program should solve and how it should solve them. Specs also may contain drawings of the various screens in your program. Highly detailed specifications contain a list of all the modules (and sometimes even subroutines and functions) that the program will contain. Also included are descriptions of each module and routine and the conventions to be used to call them.

Programming as Evolution

In the other approach, you need only the idea for a program before you start to code. You start writing something as soon as possible and modify the design as you go along. In a sense, this approach is evolutionary. The design will be very fluid.

This technique is most popular among self-taught programmers. It emphasizes the creative part of programming, because new ideas are incorporated as they are invented. The program evolves as new features are added, pieces are debugged, and the focus of the program changes. This method is much less systematic than the detailed-specification approach, and it is much more difficult to project a completion date or predict what the program will look like when it is complete.

To many managers, this approach is scary. They won't know when the program will be completed or what it will actually do until it's finished. Many times, programmers keep adding clever new features and never complete the application. If you're working on a program for your own use or if you're building the next great application all by yourself, this may be a good approach.

In-Between Approaches

In between these two basic approaches lie many variations. Visual Basic makes it easier to favor the evolutionary approach. Programs and features can be designed and implemented quickly. Typically, though, a Visual Basic application moves from one approach to another as it progresses from conception to completion. When the project is started, a general concept of its function is defined and a prototype is built. Features and code are added ad hoc until the program begins to look like a viable project.

At this point, a detailed specification may be created, along with a plan for completion. The level of detail depends on a number of factors, including the number of programmers working on the program, the number of other people involved in the project, the philosophy of the managers, and so on.

For most commercial projects, the ideal design specification is about five pages long. If it is much longer than that, few people will refer to it. This document usually lists features that should be in the finished program, with a one- or two-paragraph description of each feature. The specification should also describe the general philosophy of the program and explain how the features should work together. The specification can then become a working document used during development to keep developers on task to meet the project's objective.

The Approach We'll Use

We believe that if you go too far in writing specifications, you'll lock yourself into a design that may not work well. We've discovered that you often don't know the real problems you're trying to solve until you've tried some of your ideas. At times we've had a clear idea of "the best way" to solve a problem, only to discover that the solution had its own problems when implemented. If we had been compelled to keep the original approach, we would have ended up with a program that wasn't very easy to use and wasn't very reliable. The moral of the story is that you often learn the real problems that you're trying to solve only after you've done a few experiments.

DESIGNING THE USER INTERFACE

Every program—particularly Visual Basic programs—has a user interface. It's the part of the program that users see on the screen, and the part that responds to key presses and mouse clicks. It's often the most important part of the program, and its quality will determine whether or not someone will use the program effectively. People seldom refer to manuals (usually as a last resort when they have exhausted other possibilities), so the more effective the user interface, the more your program will be used.

Given Visual Basic's ability to create a substantial prototype complete with forms and controls, starting with the user interface design is often the best idea for program implementation. Often you'll find that you must try your ideas before you discover what they feel like. You may discover that other people have problems using your design. If this happens, try to figure out why and then try some other ideas. Leaving the interface until the end won't give you time to experiment.

If you work on the interface first, you can design the rest of the program to fit the interface. But if you design the interface last, you're forced to design it to fit the rest of the program, and that isn't a very good solution.

User interface design is a complicated topic, and entire books have been devoted to it. Because Visual Basic makes programs easy to design, the Visual Basic community has been cursed with many programs that have dreadful user interfaces. This situation is terrible for both the programmer and the users. The users find the program so difficult to navigate that they either give up or dread touching the application. For the programmer who has spent many hours creating and debugging the application, its failure is a great disappointment.

Therefore, it's a good idea to take a little time to make your program conform to a design that people will feel comfortable with. We'll discuss four tenets that will guide you in the right direction: copy other programs, be consistent, keep the user informed, and consider process flow. Copy the design of programs that your users already understand. Be consistent with your user interface so that controls and processes operate as users expect. Keep users informed of the progress of a lengthy or failure-prone operation. Finally, make sure that the most common operations are simplified so that the program has a good process flow.

Copy Other Programs

This recommendation is listed first because it is the most valuable. If you duplicate the user interface of programs that your users are already familiar with, you are far ahead of the game. Most programmers want to invent a new model through which the user works with the application. Unless others have told you that your ideas would make the program easier to use, resist this temptation.

Most likely, your new ideas are only slightly better than the ones currently in use. For this slight improvement, you require many users to relearn how to interact with the program, and many of them will simply refuse. If all your users work with WordPerfect every day, use it as the model for your user interface. All the programs included in the Microsoft Office suite (Word, Excel, PowerPoint, Access, and Outlook) use an almost identical user interface, so it is hard to go wrong mimicking these applications.

If you want to use an innovation of your own, make it an addition rather than a substitute for the feature. If you provide users with a traditional way as well as your better way, they can choose the approach they prefer.

Be Consistent

One of the worst user interface flubs we have seen is the mixed use of menus in the same application. The menu bar consists of menu items—such as File, Edit, Tools, and Exit—running along the top of the window. Clicking on any of the menu items brings up a list of options, as with any standard menu. The exception is **Exit**. When you click on this item in the menu bar, instead of dropping down a menu, the item acts as a button and quits the program. The exception created by this inconsistency can upset and frustrate users. People are creatures of habit, and they expect things to be consistent.

You should always make elements of your user interface consistent. If clicking on an item in the menu bar usually drops down a list of menu options, then it should *always* drop down a list of menu options. We could describe numerous cases in which this rule is broken, but each one is a special case. Make your program consistent within itself as well as with other programs that users understand.

When users approach an application, they have certain expectations of how things should work, just as in the real world. Turning a knob on a door opens the door. When we operate a faucet in a sink, we expect water to come out. An application should work the same way. When the **Exit** command is selected, all professional programs ask you whether you want to save changes you have made. If a user selects **Exit** on your program and the program quits, dumping the changes made, the user will probably be unhappy.

Programs should be internally consistent and consistent with other programs used by your intended audience. Applications that ignore this recommendation create a great deal of frustration and anxiety among users, who often are not entirely comfortable with using a new program anyway.

Keep the User Informed

Most users will forgive a program that takes a long time to complete an operation as long as they are not left in the dark about what the program is doing. Your programs should use status bars, information boxes, progress bars, and appropriate cursors to keep users up-to-date on what is taking place.

The most important consideration is usually the time it takes to complete an action. If less than a second passes before control is returned, probably no information is necessary (except perhaps a note that the operation is complete). A process that takes a minute probably calls for a box that says something like "Processing is occurring, please wait..." A wait of more than a minute almost requires a progress bar or progress text that updates regularly and tells the user, "Item #38 of 209 has been processed." Without these indications, the user feels helpless. Has the program crashed? Is it caught in an endless loop? What is it doing?

A progress indicator is also useful when failures occur often. Most programs that use a modem indicate progress with text such as "Dialing...", "Activating Modem...", and "Connecting...". If a failure occurs, the user has a good idea of where to begin looking. An attempt that fails at the dialing stage, for example, can be checked for a dial tone, correctly configured modem, or another user on the line.

Rarely are users overwhelmed with progress reports. They take additional time to implement, and often a programmer must second-guess where users will need progress information. The time, however, is well spent in both peace of mind for the user and troubleshooting information for you. Imagine trying to correct the previous modem problem if it lacked any progress indication and simply stated, "Hooking to remote computer."

Consider Process Flow

Process flow is the most subtle, most difficult, and often most frustrating aspect of user interface design. Process flow relates to what a user must do to complete a process within a program.

For example, a simple process might include clicking on an item to select it and then pressing the **Del** key to eliminate it. A more complicated version of this function might require users to pull down a menu to select the **Select Object** option. The cursor changes so that the user can select the item. Then the menu option **Delete Objects** is shown. The user now selects the **Delete Single Object** option and clicks on the **OK** button. Another dialog box appears that asks, "Are you sure you want to delete that object(s)?" Clicking on the **OK** button finally eliminates the object.

The first process took two simple steps: a click and a key press. The second process accomplishes the same action in six complicated steps. Now imagine that you must delete 20 objects a day using the second method. It would be annoying and time-consuming, wouldn't it?

Analysis of process flow entails considering the most common operations your users will perform and minimizing the number of steps those actions require. Tab order, for example, is a simple problem that's common to many programs. In the address book that we will construct, will users enter a full address for most people they store in the book? Probably not. Far more common is to enter the name and then the phone number. An address is entered afterward if at all.

Pressing the **Tab** key moves the text cursor from one text box to the next. If the name text box comes first, followed by the address boxes (address1 and 2, city, state, and ZIP) and then the phone number, the user must press the **Tab** key six times before the text cursor advances to the phone number box. If we change the tab order so that the phone number is listed second, however, only one tab press is required.

Consider the process flow for all the major operations that your program executes. Does a window cover up a button that is needed often? Could a function key activate an option that usually requires many actions? Be careful not to oversimplify so that the user cannot figure out how to complete an operation without the manual. Paying attention to process flow can vastly increase the efficiency of users when they must use a function daily.

Now that you have a good idea of the primary tenets of user interface design, let's begin applying them by creating the address book. Let's start by thinking about the user interface—what it should look like and how people will interact with it.

The Initial Design

One final comment before we start to design the Address Book program: whenever you create a design for a program, you should consider the design to be preliminary. You should allow yourself the freedom to change the design as you learn more about your program by building it.

Let's take a look at what we want the Address Book program to do and how we want it to work. When we design a program, the step is to come up with a short list of features we want in the program. In a sense, this list is a set of objectives for the finished program. We also come up with initial ideas for the user interface, usually sketches drawn on paper or quickly created on a Visual Basic form.

A simple program such as an address book may not seem to need very many features. After all, you just want to keep a list of names and addresses. But computer programs aren't as simple as the paper analogies we're accustomed to. A paper address book has a number of features built-in.

First, a typical address book has a number of pages that are divided into sections corresponding to the letters of the alphabet. We all know from experience that these sections are based on last name. Each page is also divided into sections, usually with ruled lines in each address along with some boxes for phone numbers. All these elements are, in a sense, features.

Now let's look at how we'll transfer these ideas to the computer. But first, a word of warning: computers work with information very differently than we do. Things that work well on paper may not be the best solutions when we try to implement them in a computer program.

For example, it doesn't make sense to implement individual pages—each one holding a number of addresses—that you have to flip through on the screen. It makes more sense to use your computer's ability to search for and find names. So instead of flipping pages looking for a name, you could type the name of the person you're looking for. The computer would then search for that name and display the address and phone numbers.

Writing a Feature List

We'll create a new design that exploits the computer's abilities. We'll begin by writing down a list of features we want in this program. First, we'll talk you through the thinking process we followed to come up with the list. Then we'll present the final list.

When you're writing a feature list, you'll often need to include things that may seem obvious. Even though they're obvious to you, someone else might not think about doing it in the same way. For example, it's clear that we need to be able to type in names and addresses. But it isn't clear how this information should be entered. Most address book programs we've worked with have a number of text boxes marked **First Name**, **Middle Initial**, **Last Name**, **Address Line 1**, **Address Line 2**, **City**, **State**, and **ZIP Code**. Figure 9.1 shows an example of what this will look like in our address book program.

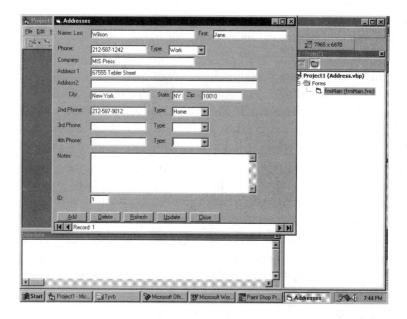

Figure 9.1 *Most address book programs require that you enter an address into separate fields.*

You might wonder why you have to enter the parts of addresses in text boxes instead of simply typing the information into a single box. By dividing addresses into separate text boxes (known as *fields*), you make it possible for the database to perform a number of functions, such as sorting by last name, printing address labels grouped by ZIP code (which gives you lower rates for bulk mail), listing people in a certain city, and so on.

In other words, the choice of a data entry form such as the one shown in Figure 9.1 has more to do with how a program is written than with how users interact with it. This example is one of the many you will discover in which function dictates form. By splitting the pieces of information into different boxes, you can manipulate and search the information in much more power-ful ways. Therefore, the user interface must look more like a form than a blank word processing document. A form enforces standard input of infor-mation.

In addition to the address, we'll want to be able to type in phone numbers of different kinds. We've chosen to allow as many as four phone numbers. Each phone number can be of a different type, such as fax, home, office, and car. We also like to be able to write notes to keep track of information such as birthdays, follow-up dates, or the purpose of a call.

For the address list to be really useful, however, you need to be able to use these names and addresses after you've typed them. There are several ways you can do this. First, you might want to print the address list so that you can find certain names. You'll need these names to be in alphabetical order, so you'll need a way to sort the names. If you're working with your computer rather than a printed list, you'll need to be able to type a name (first or last name or company name) and have your computer search for it, a much eas-ier operation than searching through a printed list.

Now that we've thought through the feature list, we can write it down. The following is the list we used when we designed the address book program for this book. This sketch points us in the direction we want to go, leaving many details unspecified.

- Name and address. You'll use input text boxes to enter the first name, last name, middle initial, first address line, and so on in separate fields.
- Phone numbers (up to four). You'll also want to keep track of the type of each number, such as fax, home, office, and car.
- Notes. You should be able to write notes along with a name and address so that you can record facts such as spouse's or children's names.
- Printing. You'll want to be able to print the address list so that you can take it in your briefcase.
- Searching. You should be able to search for any person by name or company name. For this feature, you'll search the entire address infor-mation.
- Sorting. This may seem obvious: you'll want to sort the names in alpha-betical order. As you'll see, this feature will take quite a bit of work.

Drawing the Screens

When we have a preliminary feature list put together, we will draw sketches of the screens. We also tend to change, remove, and add features as we gain experience using the program. Often your best ideas will appear only after you've started to build a program, and they are usually triggered by something that happens when you're using what you've built so far. That's what happens to us when we're creating new programs.

For example, Figure 9.2 shows a prototype of the screen. We constructed it by simply drawing controls on a form. None of the text boxes actually stores information yet. However, by creating this "dummy" form, we can begin to see what is missing or what should be removed. This prototype can also be used to demonstrate the program to the people who will be using it. They might tell you right away that they need, say, a third address line. You can make that change before development has begun.

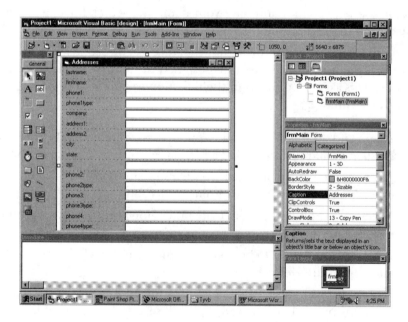

Figure 9.2 *The prototype screen of the Address Book program we'll build in the next few chapters.*

The final version of the address book will look different from this screen. However, most of the changes are rather small, and you'll see them appear as we build the program. A prototype gives you a good idea of what the program will look like and how it will function when it's complete. It's also rewarding to see your idea come to life.

BUILDING PROGRAMS

Building a program proceeds through several stages of maturity, and a testing methodology is usually followed to make sure that the program is refined and tested. These stages, such as alpha and beta testing, help define when a program is ready for testing by different types of users. By using the add, test, and redesign methodology, a programmer can reduce the time needed for these stages and improve the quality of the project.

Alpha Testing and Beta Testing

In the beginning stages of program testing, an application usually has so many problems, or *bugs*, that it cannot be used in a day-to-day environment. You will probably be shocked when you write a program, test it to make sure it works correctly, and then watch as it breaks immediately when used by someone else.

The program passes your testing because, as the designer, you know exactly how the program is used. Your user may not know, for example, that you shouldn't press **Del** while in save mode or that numbers greater than 100 shouldn't be entered into the calculation field. A bug that you never knew existed becomes instantly apparent. In the world of programming, therefore, people have divided testing into stages that tell approximately how reliable a program is for everyday use.

In a typical programming project, a team of programmers writes code to implement all the features in the program. When the key features are implemented, the software goes into a testing phase called alpha testing. In alpha testing, most of the features are implemented, but many of them aren't working correctly.

Alpha testing is done primarily by the developers of the program. A few other people who are close to the development may receive copies of the program so that they can instantly report program bugs or request a particular feature. At this stage, the program has too many bugs and too few error-trapping routines to make it useful to end users. The idea is that the program will be far enough along that you can start to work with it and identify any problems with the design.

During the next stage of testing, *beta testing*, most of the features should be working correctly, but the program may have many bugs that keep it from working reliably. These bugs might include incompatibility with a particular piece of hardware or an error that occurs when a number of functions are executed in a particular order. Beta testing is usually done by people outside the company or organization.

If you're doing personal programming such as building a checkbook program, your alpha testers might be members of your family. They will forgive you if data is lost or the program crashes repeatedly (after all, they love you). For beta testing, you might give the program to your friends or place it on the Internet or other online service and solicit feedback. People can then test your program on a variety of systems and under varying conditions, providing you with the information you need to improve it.

The last phase of development is a mad scurry to eradicate all the remaining bugs in the program. At the completion of this stage, the program has been tested enough so that it can be deployed in the workplace, used for system-critical applications, or sold on the market. The final copy made before the program is shipped, called the *gold master*, is created when no more changes will be made before the program is distributed. At this stage all the major bugs have been eliminated and the program is deemed usable by the general public.

There is no absolute division between alpha testing and beta testing. Some individuals and companies release programs into beta testing that have scores of bugs. Programmers must decide for themselves when a program is ready for others to begin using it.

THE ORIGIN OF THE TERM *BUG*

One of the first modern-day computers was the Harvard Mark I, built in the early 1940s. One hot day in the summer of 1945, the Mark I computer mysteriously failed. After a careful search, the programmers found the remains of a moth blocking an electrical relay inside the machine's circuitry. They extracted the insect with a pair of tweezers and taped it into the logbook that they kept of their work on the Mark I for the U.S. Navy. Grace Hopper (who found the bug) recalled, "From then on, when the officer came in to ask if we were accomplishing anything, we told him we were 'debugging' the computer."

The term stuck, and today a *bug* is some type of failure in a computer program. Programmers *debug* programs by looking for the problem and fixing it. A program that has many problems in design or reliability is said to be a buggy program.

Add, Test, Redesign

When we're building a program, we start by implementing some core features. As each feature is implemented, we carefully test each one so that we'll have a debugged and reliable program when we finish the first part. This initial program has too few features to be useful, but it will allow us to start using the program as quickly as possible.

Then we start to add other features. Each time we add a feature, we test it to make sure that it usually works correctly and that it "feels" right. In other words, we start usability testing very early in the development. The earlier you start such testing, the easier it is to change your mind about how you want your program to work.

Often, we'll partially implement a feature so that we can get a sense of how it will feel and work. This is before we've invested much time handling all the special cases that will make the feature general-purpose and reliable. By doing our testing early, we can easily make major changes in the design without affecting the final schedule.

Even if you're not going to let others use your program immediately, start asking them what they think as soon as possible. By asking potential users to try out the interface early, you can make changes and incorporate suggestions before it takes significant work to change a feature that would have been easy to redesign earlier.

What Is Good Design?

There is no single answer to this question. In many ways, good design is a matter of consensus. If a design is accepted by many people, it is most likely effective. This means that it's important that you test your designs on other people. Unless your program is designed for other programmers, you should test it with real users—people who don't have programming experience, but who would use the program you're writing.

When you test your programs on users, you'll probably be frustrated. They won't understand how to use it the way you do, and they'll make mistakes. When they make mistakes, don't correct them. If you explain the right way to do things, you're not really testing your program; you're simply teaching someone how to use it.

So when a user has problems with your program, resist the urge to teach. Instead, ask questions so that you can understand the source of the problem. It may be hard to admit that the design you worked so hard on may have flaws, but if you open your mind you can learn a lot. Then you'll be able to think about how to improve the design to make the program easier to learn and use. Remember that any design, no matter how good, can be improved.

There are several ways to learn good design. One way is to work with as many different Windows programs as you can so that you can learn from other programmers. Microsoft programs are often considered to be the de facto standard for user interface design, but even Microsoft doesn't always do a good job. But the company spends a lot of time and effort on testing and redesigning the programs in usability labs, so you'll probably learn a lot from its programs.

Another good source of information is books. There are many books about user interface design and about program design in general. Our own favorites are listed here.

- Norman, Donald A. *The Design of Everyday Things.* New York: Basic Books, 1988. If you read only one book from this list, read this one. It will open your eyes to the problems that people have with common, everyday designs. It will give you insight into how to build designs that get around these problems.

- Heckel, Paul. *The Elements of Friendly Software Design.* Second edition. Alameda, CA: Sybex, 1991. This useful book can help you gain a better understanding of the things you should think about when you're designing user interfaces.

- Laurel, Brenda. *The Art of Human-Computer Interface Design.* Reading, MA: Addison-Wesley, 1990. This excellent book is a collection of papers and articles published on user interface design. It has much more information about graphical environments (such as Macintosh and

Windows) than the preceding two books, and it covers far more ground.

- Brooks, Frederick P. Jr. *The Mythical Man-Month.* Reading, MA: Addison-Wesley, 1975. Anyone developing computer software should read this book. You'll learn a lot about why it's difficult to use classic management techniques with software projects.

- Microsoft Corp. *Microsoft Windows User Interface Style Guide.* Seattle, WA: Microsoft.

SUMMARY

This chapter has been more philosophical than other chapters in the book, but it's good to know more about designing programs. The following is a quick review of the material in this chapter:

- Specification. You'll probably want to write some type of design specification for any programs you write except very small ones. Such documents range from a page or two to 100 pages (although we believe there is such a thing as a spec with too much detail).

- User interfaces. Learning how to design good user interfaces is important, and not everyone can become an expert at it. You can't become an expert in a vacuum, so talk with other people and see how they interact with your programs. Ask questions, and don't succumb to the temptation to explain to your testers how to use the program. You should also read some books such as the ones we listed in this chapter.

- The four tenets of good user interface design: copy other programs, be consistent, keep the user informed, and consider process flow. Copy the design of programs that your users already understand. Be consistent so that controls and processes operate as the user expects. Keep the user informed of the progress of a lengthy or failure-prone operation. Finally, make sure that the most common operations are simplified so that the program has a good process flow.

- Building programs. Just as there are many opinions on how a program should be designed, so, too, are there many opinions on how programs should be built once they are designed. We tend to view a program as organic. You help a program grow by adding features and simplifying the user experience. It is an evolutionary process rather than a straight forward coding task.

- Testing. It's important that you test your programs. We'll have much more to say about this in Chapter 11, where you'll get down to the work of building the Address Book program. There is an art to testing programs, and it begins with being skeptical about whether your program really works correctly.

- Address Book design. We spent some time in this chapter writing a short design specification for the Address Book program you'll be building in the next few chapters.

CHAPTER 10

Accessing Data: Visual Data Manager

- What is a database?
- What is an index?
- Designing the address book database
- Entering so sample addresses

In this chapter you'll use the Visual Data Manager (included with Visual Basic) to create a database for the Address Book application. A *database* is a file that is specifically structured for quick access of information. In a program such as Address Book, the structure of the database will define the capabilities of the program. If the data is stored in a way that makes it easy for the program to manipulate, the application can be powerful and full-featured. If the database is not constructed correctly, the program's capabilities will be limited.

Until you decide how you want the data stored in the database, you won't be able to finalize the property settings for the form. For example, you know that your database will contain people's names and addresses, but until you decide how to break down the information for each person (by name, by company, by address, and so on), you won't know how to place it as controls on your form.

Experimenting with the placement of controls can help you to make these database decisions, but you will not be able to work with the data until you have created the database. We have already set up the database structure for the new Address Book application, so you can simply create it.

NOTE   The data control in Visual Basic 5 uses the file format of Microsoft Access 97 databases. You can use Access 97 to create your database for use in Visual Basic. Additionally, Visual Basic can read and write databases stored in other formats—such as Access versions 1.0, 1.1, and 2.0—as well as with the following external databases: dBASE, Paradox, FoxPro, and Btrieve.

WHAT IS A DATABASE

What if you don't have Microsoft Access or any of the other compatible database programs? No problem! You can use Visual Basic's Visual Data Manager to create a database. Visual Data Manager uses the same database engine used by Microsoft Access, so the Access database format is native to Visual Basic. But before you jump right in to the Visual Data Manager program, let's define a few terms.

A database is a collection of information (data) stored in a particular file format so that the information is easy to search, add, edit, and sort. Visual Basic has become a popular programming environment largely because of its ability to quickly and easily access databases. Whether you want to store addresses, accounting information, cooking recipes, geological data, or the list of items in a collection, or you want to organize any other information, you can use a database.

The structure of a database is hierarchical. A database is made up of one or more *tables*, which are used to separate types of information. For example, if you were creating a database for a company, you would need at least two tables: one to track the addresses of customers and another to hold financial transactions. Such a database could be named **MyBusiness.MDB** and contain a table named Customers and another table named Transactions (see Figure 10.1).

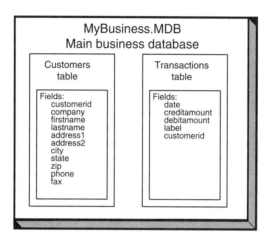

Figure 10.1 *Sample business database.*

Each table within a database is divided into *fields*, which store the individual information that can be searched or sorted. For example, if you wanted to find all the people who live on Oak Tree Lane, you would tell the database to search the address fields (**address1** and **address2**).

The fields define the structure of the database, and the actual information is stored in individual *records*. For example, we could create a record in our address book for John Smith and another one for Jane Wilson. The **firstname** field of John Smith's record would contain **John**. The **firstname** field of Jane Wilson's record would contain **Jane**. The fields of a database are a structural template of how the information will be stored for each record.

Typically, there are two ways to view a database. One way, in fields and records form, is shown in Figure 10.2. This is the format traditionally used for data entry. Our Address Book form will look something like the screen in Figure 10.2.

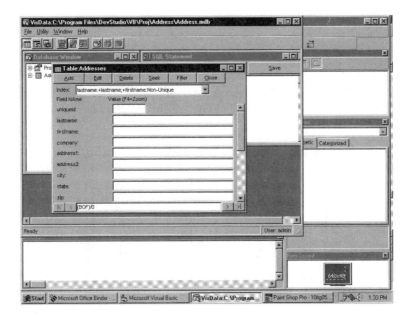

Figure 10.2 *Fields and records view of a database.*

Database tables can also be viewed in columns and rows, just like tables in a word processing document. Columns are usually referred to as fields, and each row is a record. In the Address Book sample application, each row or record will represent a person, and you'll have columns or fields for name, address, phone numbers, and other information. Figure 10.3 shows an example database when viewed as a series of rows and columns.

Like most other things in Visual Basic, databases are actually objects; you have database objects, table objects, field objects, and even index objects. Just as you access control objects on a form, you can manipulate database objects. In the Address Book application, we'll access the database objects only a little. Using the Data Access Objects (DAO) to manipulate the database is a robust and complicated object model and hence beyond the scope of this book. However, we'll include a brief summary of some of the more common objects in the model.

A database object has properties that define such things as the Name of the database, the Connect string used to open the database, the CollatingOrder indicating the sort method to be used, whether the database is Updatable, and whether it supports Transactions.

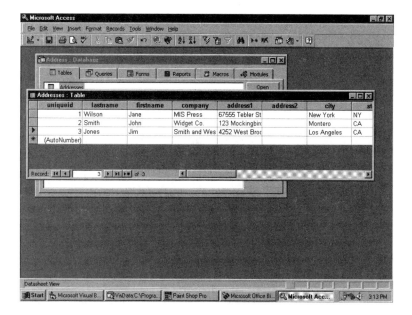

Figure 10.3 *Example database records.*

Each database object also has a collection of table definitions (TableDef objects) that define the fields and indexes of each table—one TableDef for each table in the database. TableDef properties include Name, DateCreated, LastUpdated, and Updatable.

Each TableDef, in turn, maintains a collection of field objects to define each field—one field object for each field or column in a table. And (surprise!) field objects have properties, too, including Name, data Type, and maximum Size.

Another part of the TableDef object is its collection of indexes. Four of the Index properties will be most important to you at this time: the index Name, the field or Fields that make up the index, whether the value in the index must be Unique for each record (thereby prohibiting duplicates), and whether the index in question is the Primary index for the table.

Many of the properties we've mentioned are not available at design time, and some of them you will not need to set, instead accepting the default settings. For example, not only is the CollatingOrder property of a database object not available at design time, but it is also set by the language argument when the database is originally created. You can look up the valid setting for each of these properties in the *Microsoft Visual Basic Language Reference*. If you check out the descriptions of these properties, you'll also find that some of them—for example, the Connect property—apply to more than one object (both the Database and TableDef objects have a Connect property).

Indexes

Searching for a particular piece of information can be a slow process. If there are 10,000 records in a table, the computer might have to search through 9000 of them before it located the right one. To solve this problem, database engineers invented something known as an *index*. In many ways, a database index is similar to an index in the back of a book. Instead of storing a page number reference for each entry, however, a database index stores a record number.

To understand indexes, consider how the data would be stored in a database. We have our address database and want to add a new record, say for example Joe Johnson. If we try to insert Joe Johnson in alphabetical order in the table, we must find where in the alphabet his record needs to be inserted and then move all the records that follow his down one space to make room. This process would be slow, especially if you have 10,000 records in the file.

Even if you did such an insertion for each record, what if you need the database sorted by ZIP code? Sorting the entire database takes a long time. The solution is to allow the creation of one or more indexes. An index points to a particular record, wherever it is in the database. When a new record is added, it is simply added to the end of the database file; the indexes are modified, and that takes very little time.

In Figure 10.4, you can see that the records in the table on the left (D, F, J, and so on) are not sorted in any way. They are simply numbered based on the order in which they were added. The index file, however, points to the various records in the desired sorted order. The figure shows the table sorted alphabetically when searched through the index, but the actual order in the table remains unchanged.

When you create an index, Visual Basic creates an *internal pointer*. Instead of reading entire records to find information, the pointers reference the chosen key field(s). You can also use indexes for sorting records and checking for duplicates. Once the index is created, the rest of the process is transparent to you. The database objects automatically maintain the indexes for you.

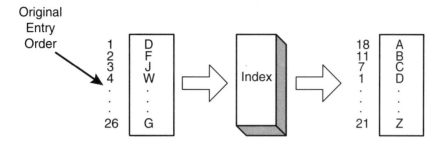

Figure 10.4 *An index to a table.*

PLANNING YOUR DATABASE

The first step is to decide which tables and fields you'll need in your database. The Address Book program uses only one table, Addresses. We've prepared a complete field listing, along with the type and size settings for the Addresses table (see Table 10.1). Like variables, fields have types. In the next section you'll use this listing to create your table fields.

Table 10.1 Fields for the Address Table

FIELD NAME	FIELD TYPE	FIELD SIZE
uniqueid	Long	—
lastname	Text	40
firstname	Text	15
company	Text	30
address1	Text	35
address2	Text	35
city	Text	15
state	Text	2
zip	Text	10
phone1	Text	20
phone1type	Text	5
phone2	Text	20

Table 10.1 Fields for the Address Table (continued)

FIELD NAME	FIELD TYPE	FIELD SIZE
phone2type	Text	5
phone3	Text	20
phone3type	Text	5
phone4	Text	20
phone4type	Text	5
notes	Memo	—

USING THE VISUAL DATA MANAGER

Now you're ready to create the Address Book database. If you haven't done so yet, start Visual Basic. Then select **Visual Data Manager** from the Add-Ins menu. When you select this option, a dialog box (shown in Figure 10.5) will appear that asks about a system security file. We won't worry about security for this application, simply click **No**.

The blank Visual Data Manager application window will appear. Select **New** from the File menu and select **Microsoft Access > Version 3.0 MDB**. When the New Database dialog box appears, create a new folder in the PROJ folder you've created previously. Name this folder **Address**. Then type in the database filename **ADDRESS.MDB** (the extension must be **.MDB**) and click **Save**. The Database: ADDRESS.MDB window appears, as shown in Figure 10.6.

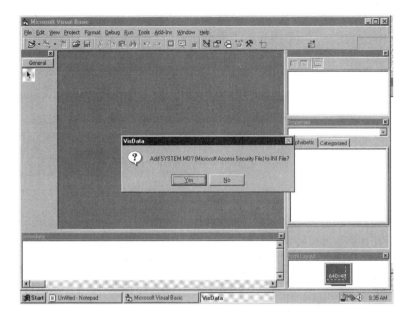

Figure 10.5 *Click **No** on the System Security dialog box.*

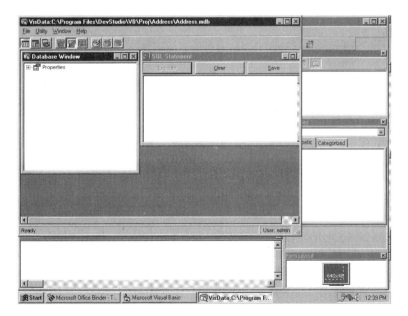

Figure 10.6 *Visual Data Manager Database window.*

The main portion of the Database window is empty, because you have not yet created any tables. The ADDRESS database needs only one table, which we'll call Addresses. Click the right mouse button within the Database window and select the **New Table** option. When the dialog box appears, enter the table name in the **Table Name** text box, as shown in Figure 10.7.

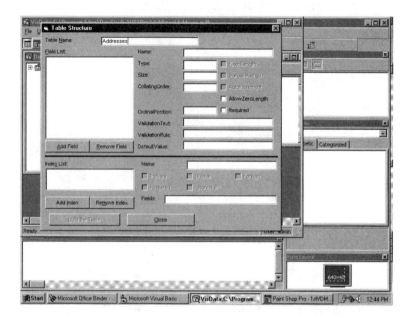

Figure 10.7 *New table dialog box.*

Now click the **Add Field** button. The window that is shown will be used to add all the fields we need for the address book. Let's start by adding the first field, **uniqueid** (see Table 10.1). Type **uniqueid** into the **Name** text box. Each record in a database should have a unique identification number (also known as a primary key). The database objects allow you to set a type to automatically increment the ID with each record added, so this field will be the unique identification for this table.

We need to select the type of field. Click on the **Type** combo box and select **Long**. This means that the field will be a Long Integer, the required type for an automatically incrementing field. Click the **AutoIncrField** check box. Finally, click **OK**. You might see the window in the background that shows the field that was added. If you cannot see the background window, but want to see that the field was added, click the **Close** button to return to the table creation window. You can now see the new field. Then click the **Add Field** button to return to the Add Field window.

Now we'll add our first text field, in this case, **lastname**. Enter **lastname** into the **Name** field. You can see that the type is already selected to **Text**, the default. We want this to be a text field, so you can leave that setting alone. In the **Size** box, enter **40**. This allows 40 characters to be entered into the **lastname** field. If you think that you will have last names in your address book longer than 40 characters, feel free to increase the size of this field. Click **OK** to enter the field into the table.

Follow this same process for all the other fields listed in Table 10.1. When this task is completed, close the Add Field window. Your table creation window should look like the window shown in Figure 10.8.

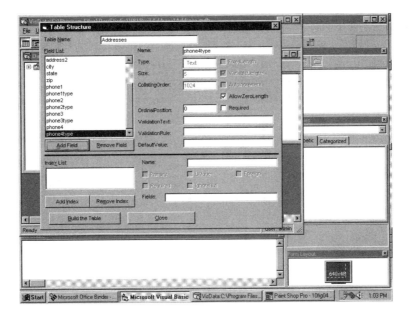

Figure 10.8 *The Table Structure window with all the fields entered.*

To finish the table creation, click **Build the Table** button. You should see the Addresses table entry now in the Database window. Fantastic! You've just created your first database table. Now let's add an index.

ADDING AN INDEX

Now that the table definitions are complete, you can select the appropriate fields to create the indexes. Right-click on the **Addresses** table and select the **Design** option from the menu. The same Table Structure window will appear that you saw before. Click the **Add Index** button; a window will appear that is titled Add Index to Addresses. We'll create three indexes: one for the **lastname** field, one for the **company** field, and one for the **uniqueid** field. Let's give the indexes the same names as the fields that will be indexed.

In our example, the index names happen to be the same as the field names. When the index is made of only a single field, this arrangement is often simpler. However, it is not a requirement. You can name your indexes anything you want.

N O T E

Enter **lastname** in the **Name** box in the window. In the list box labeled **Available Fields**, click on the **lastname** field. You should see this field entered into the **Indexed Fields** text box. We would like this index to sort by both last name and first name. In that way, Abe Smith would appear in a list before John Smith. Click on the **firstname** field, and it should appear in the **Indexed Fields** text box after the **lastname** field, separated by a semicolon.

When defining an index, you can combine as many fields as you like, assuming that the names of the fields (including +, -, and ;characters that separate field names) do not add up to more than 254 characters. Memo and Binary object fields, however, cannot be used in an index. You can create as many indexes as you want, but you can have only one primary index per table.

N O T E

Before we create this index, uncheck both the **Primary** and the **Unique** check boxes. The **Primary** check box indicates that this is the index for the primary key, which is our **uniqueid** field. The **Unique** check box indicates that there will be no duplicates in these fields. Because there may be more than one John Smith, we don't want the index to require unique entries. Click the **OK** button, and the index will be added to the database.

We create an index for the **company** field in the same way. Enter **company** into the **Name** text box and click on the **company** field. Make sure that both the **Primary** and the **Unique** check boxes are unchecked (remember that **Unique** is the way to prohibit duplicate entries). Click **OK** to create the **company** index.

Finally, let's create the index that will set the **uniqueid** field as the primary key. Type **uniqueid** into the **Name** field. Select **uniqueid** from the **Available Fields** list box. This time, make sure that both the **Unique** and the **Primary** boxes are checked. Click **OK** to add the primary key index. Click **Close** to close this window.

The Table Structure window should now show all three indexes in the list box labeled **Index List**. We're finished adding the indexes, so click the **Close** button in this window.

The table structure is complete. Next, we'll enter some data into the table so that when we create the application we will see immediately how the data is entered.

USING THE VISUAL DATA MANAGER TO ENTER DATA

Before you move on to creating the form, you'll take advantage of one more Visual Data Manager function. You'll use the Visual Data Manager to enter some into the Addresses table. Right-click on the **Addresses** table again, but this time select **Open**. You will see a window similar to the one shown in Figure 10.9. At the moment, the database is empty. At the bottom of the window, you'll see **EOF/0**, which means it's at the end of the file and there are zero records in the table. Now that the table is open, you can add, edit, or delete records as indicated by the buttons in this window. You can also use **Seek** to search for records, and **Filter** to create a filter for the data.

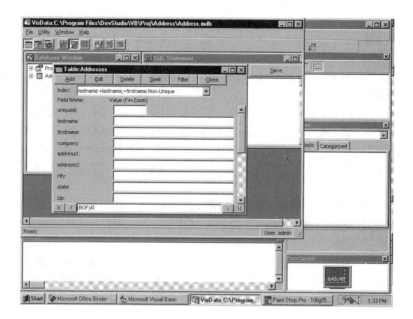

Figure 10.9 *Visual Data Manager window for Addresses table data entry.*

To add a record, click **Add** and then fill in the fields. Leave the **uniqueid** field blank, because the database objects will automatically fill that field with the automatic incrementing. You can add your own data and create three records (such as John Smith, Jim Jones, and Jane Wilson) with names, addresses, phone numbers, and so on. You can use the **Tab** key to move from field to field, or use your mouse and the scroll bar. As you might guess by looking at the table, it is not required that you fill in all the fields.

When you have filled in all the data for the first record, click **Update** to save the first record and clear the fields for the next set of values. Click **Add** again to add the next record. Continue until you have created at least three records so that the table has some sample data to use when we build the new project.

You can move through the database using the left and right arrow buttons at the bottom of the window. If you spot any mistakes, press the **Edit** button, type in the correction, and press **Update**. When you've entered all the data from the table, the database is ready to go.

You've completed all the essential parts of the database. In Chapter 11, we will use this database to create the primary form for the Address Book.

SUMMARY

This chapter has introduced you to the structure and creation of databases. Databases are the mainstay of most computing, because the computer's ability to store and search information is unparalleled. The following is a quick review of the material in this chapter:

- Databases, tables, and fields. A database holds information in a structured way for quick access. Each database can have one or more tables. Each table is defined by its fields, which determine the size and type of each piece of data. Fields are also known as columns when a database is represented as a spreadsheet.

- Records. Information is actually stored in records. There is one record for each entry (in our address book, a record will hold all the information for one person). Records are also known as rows when a database is represented as a spreadsheet.

- Indexes. Like a book index, a database index provides a pointer reference. A database index is a list of pointers to individual records. Indexes are used to speed searches and sorts.

- Data entry. The Visual Data Manager not only allows you to construct a database file but also allows you to enter data into tables.

CHAPTER 11

Building the Address Book Interface

- Creating a data-aware form
- Using the data control
- Setting Data category properties
- Controlling tab order
- Implementing cut, copy, and paste
- Setting up combo boxes

In this chapter, you'll start building the Address Book program we designed in Chapter 9. As you'll recall, we sketched a design for Address Book and wrote down a short list of features for the program. In this chapter you'll work mainly on the user interface.

You'll start by creating a form to match the fields of the database. Then you will add controls to the form that allow you to add a new record, delete a record, and so on. When you have all the controls, you'll expand Address Book by adding some code. You'll continue this process in the next few chapters by bringing more and more of Address Book to life.

USING THE DATA FORM DESIGNER

The Visual Data Manager has a built-in tool called the Data Form Designer. It automatically constructs a form that contains text boxes and labels from your database and adds the form to a currently open project. We'll use the Data Form Designer to create the main form for the Address Book. This arrangement will save you a great deal of the work it would take to individually construct a form with each field.

When we left off in Chapter 10, you still had your database file open in the Visual Data Manager. You'll need to create a new project to develop the Address Book application. Therefore, close the Visual Data Manager by selecting **Exit** from the File menu. This will return you to the main Visual Basic application.

Select the **New Project** option on the File menu. Click **OK** to select a standard **EXE** file. A blank Form1 should be shown in the form window. We'll remove this form from the project after we have added a form with all the fields from our database.

Open the Visual Data Manager window again (the selection is under the Add-Ins menu). A blank Visual Data Manager window should appear. The most recently accessed files automatically appear on the File menu in the same way that recent documents appear in Word's File menu. Pull down the File menu and select the **Address.MDB** file.

To create our form, select the **Data Form Designer** option under the Utility menu. We'll name the form it creates **Main**, so type that into the **Form Name** text box. From the **RecordSource** combo box, select our table **Addresses**. The **Available Fields** box will automatically fill with all the fields from the table, and the dialog box will look like the one shown in Figure 11.1.

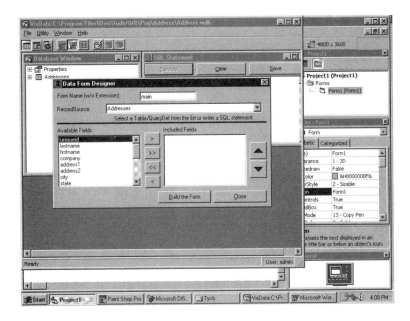

Figure 11.1 *The Data Form Designer with the form name property set and the record source pointing to your data file.*

We want to include all these fields on the form, so click on the button labeled **>>**. All the fields will now appear in the **Included Fields** list box. The up and down arrows to the right of this box are used to change the order of the selected field. The **uniqueid** field should be selected. We want to move this field to the bottom of the list so that it appears last on the form. Click the down arrow until the field is at the bottom of the list. In Chapter 9, we said that you should make your application so that the most common operations require the fewest number of steps. Most of the time when using the Address Book, you will want to enter a person's name and phone number first. If you have the rest of the information, you would fill it in later. Let's move the **phone1** and the **phone1type** fields up so that they appear directly under the first name field. You will have to move them one at a time. When you've completed moving these fields, the Data Form Designer should look like the one shown in Figure 11.2. We're all set to have the Data Form Designer create our new form.

Click **Build the Form**, and the Designer will add the form to your project. You can close the Designer window and exit the Visual Data Manager, because we are finished with it for the moment. Upon returning to Visual Basic, you will see the form that the Data Form Designer constructed for you. It should look like the form shown in Figure 11.3.

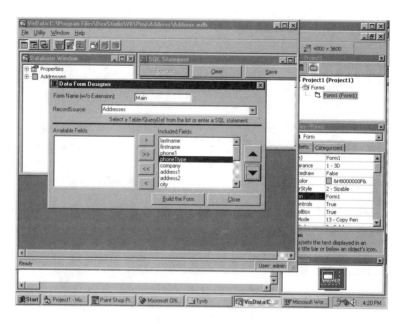

Figure 11.2 *The* **uniqueid** *field has been moved to the end of the list, and the* **phone1** *and* **phone1type** *fields are moved right under the name fields.*

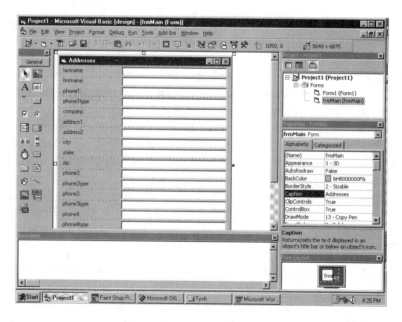

Figure 11.3 *The main form constructed by the Designer includes all the fields that you selected.*

We could run this form right now except that the original Form1 is still in our project, and it is the first form that executes when the project is run. Select the **Project1 properties** option under the Project menu. This option will display the dialog box that allows you to set many of the preferences for your project. You'll notice that the **Startup Object** combo box currently says **Form1**. Change the **Startup Object** to **frmMain**, which is the form just created by the Data Form Designer. Click **OK** to accept the change.

We are now ready to remove the original Form1. Use the right mouse button and click on the Form1 form in the Project - Project1 window. From the pop-up menu, select **Remove Form1**. The form will disappear from the project.

You're almost ready to run the application, but first let's save the project and the main form. Select **Save Project** under the File menu. In Chapter 10, you created a folder named Address in the PROJ folder. Go to that folder now. The default filename of **frmMain.frm** is fine, so click the **Save** button. Change the name of the project to **Address.vbp** and click **Save**. Your project is now safely stored to the hard drive.

If you execute the application now (by pressing **F5**), your form will instantly appear. The data you entered into the records in chapter 10 will show in the appropriate fields. You can use the navigation bar at the bottom to move forward or backward through the records. You can even use the **Add** or **Delete** button to add or remove records.

How the Data Control Works

Now that you have seen the form working, let's take a look at the magic behind the scenes. We could have constructed this form entirely by hand. The Data Form Designer simply automated the placement of the controls and the setting of the properties. Now we'll look at what was actually done on the form so that you can enhance or augment the form.

Lets first look at the data control. The bar along the bottom of the form (with the arrows to the right and left) that you used to navigate between records is one type of data control. It's the only one on our form.

Data controls are used in conjunction with other controls to display, add, modify, and delete data from a database. To make the connection between a form and a database, you place a data control in the form and set its properties to identify the name of the database and table that you want to access. If your form contains data from more than one table, you will need to use more than one data control—one for each table.

To see the properties of the data control, select it on the form and look at the Properties window on the right side of the screen. The Properties window has two tabs: **Alphabetic** and **Categorized**. Until this point, we've been using the **Alphabetic** tab. With data-related controls, it is often easier to use the **Categorized** tab. If you click on this tab and scroll down to the **Data** category, you'll see all the properties that directly relate to the database access of the control. Your properties window should look like the one shown in Figure 11.4.

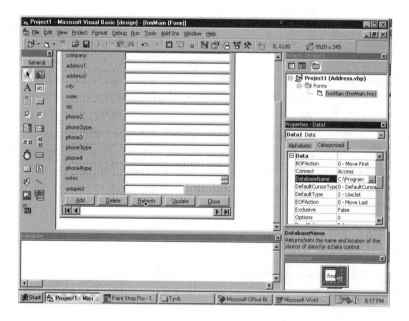

Figure 11.4 *The Properties window with the data control selected lets you examine the properties that relate to the Data category.*

Placing the data control on the form creates a gateway to the database you want to access. Then other controls, such as the text boxes on this form, can be attached to the data control. When controls are attached to a data control, they are said to be *bound* to the control.

Some programmers allow the data control to remain visible on the form and take advantage of its simple built-in functionality. Other programmers prefer to make the data control invisible (setting its `Visible` property to `False`), using instead their own command buttons and menus. Like most controls, the data control is fully programmable, so all of its functions can be duplicated in code.

Making the control invisible gives the programmer far greater flexibility not only with the visual interface but also in writing code that does more than the data control's built-in functions would do alone. However, programming the data control takes a fair amount of skill. In Chapter 12, we will use programming to select the sort and to search the database. At that point you will be introduced to the type of coding required for manipulating the control. For now, let's look at the most important properties of the control.

As you might have guessed, the `DatabaseName` property identifies the name of the database. If you examine the `RecordSource` property, you will see that the Addresses table is listed. The `RecordSource` property always identifies which table in the database is to be managed by this data control.

The data control's `Name` property is also important, because it will identify the data control to each of the other bound controls, making them *data-aware*. Note that the control's Name is **Data1** and is listed under the **Misc** category in the Properties window.

Setting the `RecordSource` property for a data control is an option only when Visual Basic can open the data file referred to in the `DatabaseName` property. This means that you must set the `DatabaseName` property first.

N O T E

What Are Data-Aware Controls?

The term *binding* refers to making a connection between the data control (in this case, **Data1**) and the other controls on the form. This connection will tell each control where to find the data. In other words, each of the other controls will look to the data control for the name of the database, table, and field where the corresponding data is stored.

This isn't as complex as it may sound. To see a bound control, click on any of the text boxes on the form. Now look at the **Data** category in the properties of this control. You'll see only two properties in the category: `DataField` and `DataSource`. The `DataField` property points to the field that is accessed by data shown in this text box. If you selected the text box for the last name, the `DataField` property reads **lastname**.

And what is listed in the `DataSource` field? Why, **Data1**, of course. This data-aware text control is bound to **Data1**, the data control at the bottom of the form. If you wanted to place a new bound text box on the form, you would draw the control, set the `DataSource` to point at a data control, and select a field from the pop-down menu for the `DataField` property. After the `DataSource` has been set for a bound control, the `DataField` automatically loads all the possible fields from the selected database into a combo box list.

NOTE You're free to make your controls any size you want and place them wherever you want on your form. Address Book will work correctly no matter where the controls are or how large they are. So feel free to redesign the look of Address Book.

Modifying the Form

Now that you understand how the data control works and how all the bound controls are pointed at the necessary fields, let's modify the form to make it more attractive. We'll resize most of the controls so that they fit on the form. Modify your form so that it looks approximately like the one shown in Figure 11.5. To resize the form itself, click on an empty area of the form that contains no controls. The six blue squares should appear around the border. Click and drag the squares to reshape the form to the new size.

Notice that we have also changed the captions of most of the labels. The Data Form Designer creates captions that merely duplicate the field names. They are just labels, however, so changing them does not effect the application's performance in any way. For example, we changed the `Caption` property of **lastname** to read **Name: Last**. By putting the **firstname** bound text box on the same line, we make things more apparent to the user.

There are two ways that you can set the location and size of a control. First, you can use the information shown on the right side of the toolbar (see Figure 11.5). When you drag controls around on the form and resize them, the toolbar tells you the size of the control and the location of its upper-left corner.

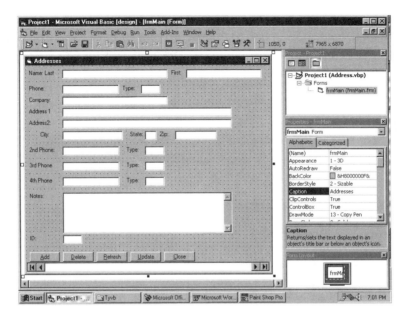

Figure 11.5 *Reformatted main form.*

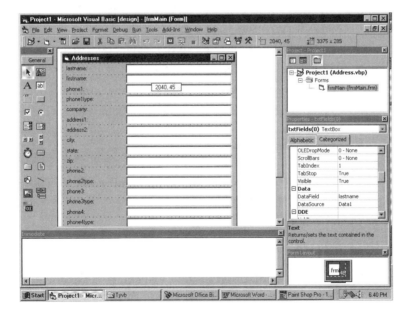

Figure 11.6 *The toolbar showing the Top, Left, Width, and Height values for the selected object txtAddress.*

The other option is to directly set the `Top`, `Left`, `Width`, and `Height` properties of a control. Doing so will change the size and location of a control to match the numbers you type in. Both methods work well, so which one you choose depends on your preference.

SHORTCUT

You can use a number of useful keyboard shortcuts to help you navigate the Properties bar. (They are documented in the online help, but because they're hard to find we've summarized them in the following table):

Keyboard Shortcuts in the Properties Window

SHORTCUT	DESCRIPTION
Ctrl+Shiftalpha	Select property. Select the property that starts with the letter **alpha** in the Properties window. Pressing **Ctrl+Shiftalpha** again selects the next property that starts with the same letter.
alpha	Change setting. Typing any character when the form is active will change the value in the Settings box. For settings such as Caption, pressing a key inserts that character and activates the Properties window. If the Settings box is a combo box, typing a letter selects the first option that starts with the letter (or number) you typed.
Esc	Cancel changes. Cancels changes you've made to the setting.
Enter	Accept setting. Accepts the changes in the Settings.
F4, Alt +	Drop combo box. Pulls down the active combo box. If the Settings box has a ... button at the end, pressing one of these keys is the same as pressing the ... button.

Once you've completed the new look of the form, we will add a few controls that make the Address Book more functional.

BRINGING ADDRESS BOOK TO LIFE

You now have an Address Book program that you can run. Go ahead and run the program and experiment with typing text into the text fields. You'll notice you can type multiple lines of text into the **Notes** text box, and you can use the **Enter** key to start new lines in this text box. On the other hand, Visual Basic beeps whenever you press **Enter** inside one of the phone number text boxes.

Controlling the Tab Order

Now try using the **Tab** key to move among the different controls. Each time you press the **Tab** key, a different control in your program will receive the focus. The control with the current focus is the control that responds to keys you press. In other words, the *focus* refers to which control has the keyboard's focus of attention. When a text box has the focus, anything you type will appear inside that text box. When a command button has the focus, pressing the **Spacebar** has the same effect as clicking on that control with the mouse button.

Not all controls are capable of receiving the focus from the keyboard. Labels, for example, can respond to mouse clicks but not to keyboard events, so labels will never receive the current focus. The controls in Address Book that can receive the focus are the text boxes, the combo boxes, and the command buttons.

Each time you press the **Tab** key, Visual Basic uses a property called `TabIndex` to determine which control should receive the focus next. Whenever you create new controls on a form, Visual Basic assigns `TabIndex` values to each one, starting with 0 and counting up. The Data Form Designer automatically assigns the tab order in the order the fields appear on the form. If you decide you want to change the tab order, you change the `TabIndex` property for each control.

REFERENCE

TabIndex Property
Visual Basic uses the `TabIndex` property to determine which control will receive the focus next when you press the **Tab** key. Here's how it works. Every time you press the **Tab** key, Visual Basic looks at the value of `TabIndex` for the control that currently has the focus; then it scans the controls looking for the next highest `TabIndex` number. If this new control can accept the keyboard focus, Visual Basic moves the focus to this control. Otherwise, it looks for the next higher `TabIndex` value until it finds a control with a higher `TabIndex` value.

When there are no more controls with higher `TabIndex` values, Visual Basic starts over again with 0 and looks for the first control with a `TabIndex` of 0 or higher that can accept keyboard input.

When you first load a form, the control with the lowest `TabIndex` (usually 0) that can accept keyboard input will receive the focus.

Here's how to set up a tab order. Click on the control you want to receive the focus when your program first starts. Set its `TabIndex` property to 0, and then click on the next control and set its `TabIndex` property to 1, and so on. Visual Basic will automatically adjust all the other `TabIndex` values if a control already has the `TabIndex` value you assign to a control.

Setting Up the Combo Boxes

The combo boxes you'll use here are called *drop-down lists,* because whenever you click on the down-pointing arrow you'll see a list of options. We'll replace the bound text boxes for the phone type so that we have a number of available options.

The phone combo boxes will have the following options: Home, Office, FAX, Direct, and Car. Figure 11.7 shows what the phone combo boxes will look like when the list is dropped down. All six possibilities are in this combo box, in the order we wrote them previously. You can put these entries in any order: we chose the order that made the most sense to us. But you may decide, for example, that you want the Office, Direct, and fax numbers to appear before the Home number. It's entirely up to you.

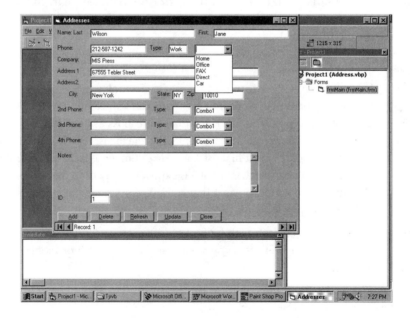

Figure 11.7 *The cboType combo boxes will look like this when you click on the down-pointing arrow.*

First, let's add the combo boxes to the form. We don't want to delete the old text boxes until we know that the new combo boxes work. Select the **ComboBox** control from the control toolbox on the left of your screen. Now draw a single combo box to the right of the first **Type** text box. Change the (**Name**) property of the control to **cboType**. With the combo box still selected, select the **Copy** option on the Edit menu. This action will copy the current combo box into the clipboard. Now select **Paste** under the Edit menu.

Before the control is pasted onto the form, Visual Basic checks the form to make sure that it does not contain controls with identical names. We just copied the control from the form, so when we paste the control it finds an identical one already there. You will see a message box that asks whether you want to create a control array. You may remember that we created a control array for the different line-thickness menu items for the Sketch program. This is the same type of array.

A control array will work fine for what we need, so click the **Yes** button. The combo box will appear in the upper-left corner of the form. Move it down to the right of the second phone type field. Paste two more times and move these combo boxes into place next to the third and fourth **Type** boxes. Your form will look like the one in Figure 11.8. Now you'll add the code to provide the combo boxes with the appropriate lists.

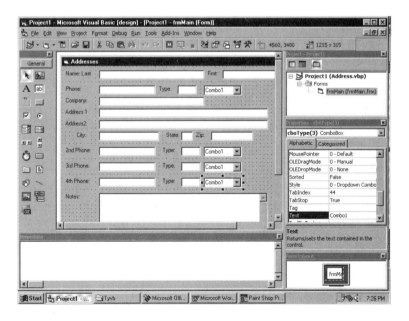

Figure 11.8 *The main form with the four new combo boxes in place to the right of the **Type** text boxes.*

Let's look at how to create this list in a combo box. Each combo box has a list of items you can select from. But when Visual Basic first creates a combo box (when it first loads a form), there are no entries in this list. The programmer must add these items to the list.

When do you add items to the list? In this case, the items will never change, so you can load them into the list whenever your form is loaded into memory. The Form_Load event is called by Visual Basic every time a form is loaded. This is the best place to write code that will fill in the combo box's list.

Combo boxes, like any other object in Visual Basic, have a number of methods you can use to control them. One method, AddItem, adds a single item to your combo box. For example, if you have a combo box called myCombo and you want it to have two choices—**Red** and **Green**—you can write the following code to add the two items to the combo box's drop-down list:

```
myCombo.AddItem "Red"

myCombo.AddItem "Green"
```

REFERENCE

The AddItem Method

The AddItem method allows you to add items to a combo box's list of possibilities (which you'll see when you click on the down-pointing arrow). This code adds the item in item$ to the control (which can be a combo box or a list box, which you haven't used yet):

```
control.AddItem item$ [, index%]
```

The optional parameter, index%, allows you to control where the item will be added in the list. Without this parameter, Visual Basic always adds the item to the end of your list.

You use the RemoveItem method to remove items.

Initializing the cboType Combo Boxes

The Address Book program has four combo boxes you need to initialize using AddItem, and each combo box needs to have six items added to it. The code looks something like this:

```
cboType(0).AddItem "Home"

cboType(0).AddItem "Office"

cboType(0).AddItem "FAX"

cboType(0).AddItem "Direct"

cboType(0).AddItem "Car"

cboType(0).AddItem ""

cboType(1).AddItem "Home"

cboType(1).AddItem "Office"
        .

        .

        .
```

The problem with this approach is that you need a total of 24 lines of code to add six items to each of the four combo boxes. That's a lot of code! Fortunately, you can use the **For..Next** command to reduce these 24 lines of code to eight:

```
Private Sub Form_Load ()

  For i = 0 to 3

    cboType(i).AddItem "Home"

    cboType(i).AddItem "Work"

    cboType(i).AddItem "Fax"

    cboType(i).AddItem "Beep"

    cboType(i).AddItem "Car"

    cboType(i).AddItem "Work2"

  Next i

End Sub
```

Add this code to the Form_Load event handler in your form and run Address Book. You should now have four combo boxes, each with a list of these six items.

It's a good idea to save your program before you run it in case your computer should crash (it happens) when you're running your program. It can be frustrating to lose work, even if it's only five minutes' worth. One way to save your project is to press **Alt+F V**. An even easier way is to set **Save Before Run** (an environment Option accessed from the Tools menu) to **Save, Don't Prompt**. The save will be automatic and require no further action on your part. If you prefer, you can choose **Save, Prompt** to give you the option of bypassing the save.

There is one small problem: the combo boxes don't access the proper database field even though they now have the correct list of items. You must change the data properties to bind the control to the data control. Click on the combo box for the first phone type field. Go to the Properties window and select the **DataSource** property. You will see a combo box down arrow in the field. If you click on the arrow, a list of all the data controls on the form will be shown. In this case, the only control on the form is **Data1**, so select it.

Now if you click on the **DataField** control, you get a list of all the fields that are accessible from the data control. Select **phone1type** for this first combo box. Now set these two properties for each of the other three combo boxes (for fields phone2type, phone3type and phone4type). When you're finished, run the program. You should now be able to select any of these options from the combo boxes, and clicking **Update** will write the data into the database.

Stop the program and delete the text boxes that were created to hold the phone type fields. Move the combo boxes so that they take the place of the text boxes. Your program should look like Figure 11.9. Address Book is looking more and more like a real program.

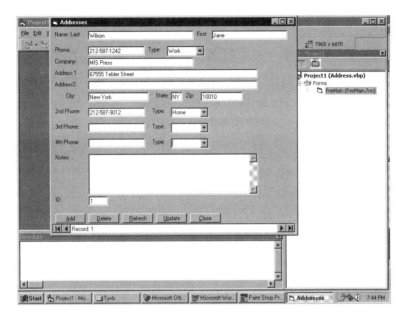

Figure 11.9 *Your version of Address Book should now look like this. Notice that the combo boxes show the correct titles.*

CREATING THE MENU BAR

Now that your form has all the controls it needs, we'll create the menu bar. Table 11.1 shows all the menus, items, and control names for the menu. The accelerator is a short-cut key combination to access that item. Add this menu to your program the same way you did in Chapter 6 for the Sketch program.

Table 11.1 Address Book Menu Items

CAPTION	CTLNAME	SHORTCUT
&File	menFile	
&Print...	miPrint	Ctrl+P
P&rint Setup...	miPrintSetup	
-	miFileLine	
E&xit	miExit	

Table 11.1 Address Book Menu Items (continued)

CAPTION	CTLNAME	SHORTCUT
&Edit	menEdit	
&Undo	miUndo	Ctrl+Z
-		miEditLine1
Cu&t	miCut	Ctrl+X
&Copy	miCopy	Ctrl+C
&Paste	miPaste	Ctrl+V
-		miEditLine2
&Find...	miFind	Ctrl+F
&Address	menAddress	
&New	miNew	Ctrl+N
&Delete		miDelete
-		miAddressLine1
Ne&xt	miNext	F4
&Previous	miPrevious	F3

Adding Code to Menu Items

Data controls have built-in functionality for moving forward and backward through the database. This functionality includes moving one record at a time and the ability to jump directly to the first or last record in the database. Also, whenever you use the data control to move forward or backward, any changes made to the current record will be saved.

In the Address Book program, you have two ways to navigate. You can click on the >> button to move forward and the << button to move back one record, or you can use the **Next** and **Previous** items from the Address menu. The code for the miNext, miPrevious, miNew, and miDelete click event subroutines is as follows:

```
Private Sub miNext_Click()

  ' Make sure we're not at the end of the file

    If Not Data1.Recordset.EOF Then
```

```
        Data1.Recordset.MoveNext
    Else
       Beep
    End If
End Sub

Private Sub miPrevious_Click()
  ' Make sure we're not at the beginning of file
  If Not Data1.Recordset.BOF Then
      Data1.Recordset.MovePrevious
  Else
      Beep
  End If
End Sub

Private Sub miNew_Click()
  Data1.Recordset.AddNew
End Sub

Private Sub miDelete_Click()
  Data1.Recordset.Delete
  If Not Data1.Recordset.EOF Then
      Data1.Recordset.MoveNext
  End If
End Sub
```

You use the data control name with the RecordSet property (representing the table name) and the MoveNext or MovePrevious method:

```
Data1.RecordSet.MoveNext
Data1.RecordSet.MovePrevious
```

You might wonder what would happen if you wanted to move to the next record but you were already looking at the last record in the table. If you were using the standard data control, you'd click on the forward arrow and nothing would appear to happen.

Our `miNext` routine checks to see whether you have reached the end of file (EOF). The `miPrevious` routine checks whether you are at the beginning of file (BOF). If you are already at the end of file when you choose to move next, the **Beep** command is invoked. The same thing occurs if you try to move before the first record of the database.

Add the following code to bring the **Exit** menu item to life:

```
Sub miExit_Click ()
    Unload address
End Sub
```

NOTE   You'll find the code for the other three menu items (**Find, Print** and **Print Setup**), in Chapter 12.

CUT, COPY, PASTE, AND UNDO CODE

All commercial applications support **Cut, Copy, Paste,** and **Undo** items on the Edit menu. However, many in-house programs do not include these options because programmers don't know how to implement them. As you'll see here, it is easy to add an Edit menu to any program that uses text box controls. Add the following code to the four event handlers for the Edit menu:

```
Private Sub miUndo_Click()
    SendKeys "%{Backspace}" ' Send Alt+Backspace
End Sub


Private Sub miCut_Click()
    SendKeys "+{DELETE}"    ' Send Shift+Del
End Sub
```

```
Private Sub miCopy_Click()

    SendKeys "^{INSERT}"    ' Send Ctrl+Ins
End Sub


Private Sub miPaste_Click()

    SendKeys "+{INSERT}"    ' Send Shift+Ins
End Sub
```

Here's how these subroutines work. Visual Basic has a **SendKeys** command that sends keystrokes to the control that has the current keyboard focus. To allow you to send special characters, such as **Alt+Backspace**, this command uses special characters: % for **Alt**, + for **Shift**, and ^ for **Ctrl**. Also, any characters between the curly braces {}, such as {BACKSPACE}, refer to a key, and **SendKeys** will send this keystroke rather than the text inside the braces.

All text boxes support the keyboard combinations as follows:

COMMAND	KEYSTROKES
Undo	Alt+Backspace
Cut	Shift+Del
Copy	Ctrl+Ins
Paste	Shift+Ins

The code need only send these keystrokes to the edit boxes.

The Address Book application is beginning to look polished. Try running it and navigate using the menu items. Add a new record or delete one. When we add the enhancements of Chapter 12, the application will be impressive.

RELATED TOOLS

- RemoveItem. The RemoveItem method allows you to remove items from combo or list boxes that you added with AddItem.
- ListCount. You can use the ListCount property (read-only and available only at run time) to get the number of items in a combo box's drop-down list.

- `MinButton`. This property allows you to control whether your form has a **Minimize** button (it also controls whether the control menu has a **Minimize** item).

- `ControlBox`. You can remove the control menu (and box) entirely by setting this property to `False`.

- Font properties. There are a number of font properties, whose names start with `Font`, that you can use to control the appearance of characters in text boxes, combo boxes, labels, and many other controls.

- `TabStop`. If you don't want the **Tab** key to be able to move to one of your controls (such as the cboType combo boxes), you can set `TabStop` to `False`. This property is called `TabStop` because it controls whether the focus can stop on a control when you press the **Tab** key.

SUMMARY

You should now have enough understanding of programming. We will continue to enhance the appication we've created in the next chapter.

The following is what you've learned in this chapter:

- Drawing controls. The toolbar provides size readouts that you can use to set the size of your controls. You can also set the `Height`, `Width`, `Left`, and `Top` properties using the Properties window.

- Text boxes. The text box control allows you to create text-entry sections in your forms. These text boxes can be limited to a single line of text, or you can allow multiple lines by setting the `MultiLine` property to `True`. You can also use the `ScrollBars` property to add scroll bars to any text box.

- Data controls. Data controls are used to access a database and point to a particular table. If more than one table needs to be accessed, multiple data controls must be present on the form.

- Bound controls. Controls such as text boxes, check boxes, combo boxes, and so on. that are linked to a data control and a particular field in the database.

- Labels. These controls are useful whenever you want some text on your form that you don't need to be able to edit. You can use labels for static labels and for information readouts.

- Command buttons. Visual Basic makes it easy to add command buttons to your programs.

- Combo boxes. These are the controls that you spent the most time on in this chapter. You learned how to add items to the lists attached to combo boxes using the `AddItem` method, and you learned how to select an item in a combo box using the `ListIndex` property.

- Tab order. The `TabIndex` property allows you to determine which control will receive the keyboard focus when you press the **Tab** key. Visual Basic looks for the control with the next-highest `TabIndex` that can accept keyboard input and sets the focus to that control. **Shift+Tab** moves the focus backward through the same list.

- `AddItem` method and `ListIndex` property. The `AddItem` method allows you to add items to a list box's drop-down list. You can use the `ListIndex` property to select one of these items into the list box, but only at run time. The `ListIndex` property can't be set until you run your program.

CHAPTER 12

Searching, Printing, and Sorting

- Searching for strings
- Printing the address book
- Sorting addresses

In this chapter, you'll learn how to manipulate the database using program code to control the data control. In Chapter 11, we did very little of this, instead using the MoveNext and MovePrevious methods. In this chapter we will use the methods of the data control more extensively. We will use the RecordSet object that is part of the data control to perform searches, print all the records in the database, and sort the database.

SEARCHING

Using the forward and backward arrows to browse a database and locate records is fine if the number of records is small. When the number of records grows, you will want to use a **Find** function. The **Find** item in the Edit menu will allow you to search through the names for any text. For example, you can search for the word *Smith* to find the following person:

Joe M. Smith

Great Software Company

238 Somewhere Lane

Imaginary, CI 12345-6789

We'll add code that allows the Address Book program to search for any string that appears inside the last name, first name, or notes field of the address records. If it finds the string, it will display that address record; otherwise, it will beep. We have chosen these three fields to be searched, but the routine can easily be expanded to include other fields.

Searching the database isn't very difficult. After all, most of the power inherent in a database is focused on its ability to locate information quickly. The database objects in Visual Basic include all the methods to perform such a search.

You'll need to implement a couple of other things before your searches can be executed. First, when you select **Find** from the Edit menu, you'll need to display a dialog box to accept a search string, such as the one shown in Figure 12.1. You are probably familiar with Find dialog boxes, because they are common in word processors.

To create this dialog box, create a new form using the **Add Form** item from the Project menu. In the dialog box that appears, select **Form**. Next, add a text box and two command buttons. We've created what's called a *modal* form (no resizable borders, no minimize or maximize buttons, no control menu, and a 3-D look) by setting the properties shown in Table 12.1.

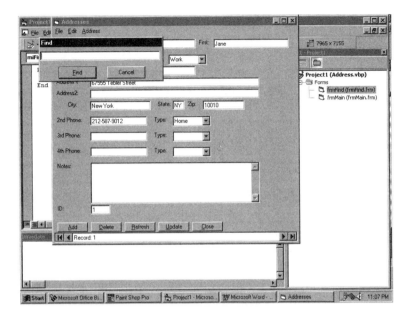

Figure 12.1 Address Book's Find dialog box.

Table 12.1 Properties for a Modal Dialog Box

PROPERTY	SETTING
BorderStyle	3 - Fixed Dialog
ControlBox	False
Caption	Find
Name	frmFind

N O T E

You might have thought that the Common Dialog custom control on the toolbox would do the trick here. After all, Find is a common function. Unfortunately, the Common Dialog custom control includes only **Open**, **Save As**, **Print**, **Color**, and **Font**. (The third-party custom control files from Crescent Software Inc. and MicroHelp Inc. support additional functions such as Find and Search-and-Replace.)

Set the **(Name)** property of the text box to **txtFind**, the **Cancel** button to **cmdCancel**, and the **Find** button to **cmdFind**. Make sure you delete the **Text1** message from the **Text** property so that the text box is empty the first time the form is shown. Also, set the **Default** property to **True** for the **Find** button, and the **Cancel** property to **True** for the **Cancel** button. This arrangement gives you the alternative of pressing **Enter** to execute the **Find** function and pressing **Esc** to cancel the dialog box.

You might want to make one more adjustment before we proceed. Recall our discussion of the tab order in Chapter 11. When the **Find** form is first shown, you want the cursor to appear automatically in the **txtFind** control. The easiest way to ensure this is to set the **TabIndex** property of this control to **0**. That will make it the first control with the focus when the form is shown.

Now that you have two forms in your project, you may wonder how to use the new form that you've added. So far, we've used only one form in each of our projects. It turns out that you need to load a form into memory and then show the form. Loading the form triggers an event called Form_Load, which you've already used in other programs, but it doesn't actually cause a form to become visible on the screen. You display a dialog box using the Show method, which will load a form if it isn't already loaded into memory:

```
frmFind.Show        ' Load and display dialog box
```

When you display this dialog box, you'll probably need to make it a modal dialog box. Modal dialog boxes always stay in front of the main window until you click **Find** or **Cancel**. To display this dialog box as a modal dialog box, you use the Show method of a form followed by a 1:

```
frmFind.Show 1      ' Display modal dialog box
```

Putting a 1 after Show tells Visual Basic that you want the form displayed as a modal dialog box, so the subroutine that calls Show won't continue to run until the new form is no longer visible on the screen. (You can hide a form using the Hide method.) Add this code to the **Find** menu item event code:

```
Private Sub miFind_Click()
    frmFind.Show 1      ' Display modal dialog box
End Sub
```

Don't run the program yet. Selecting **Find** will show the Find dialog box, but we haven't activated the buttons to cancel it and there is no close box on the window. Let's put that code in the program now. In the Click event handler for the **Cancel** button, we'll want to set the **Text** field of the text box to an empty string: "" so a user cancel will clear the search text box. In the Click event handler for each buttons, hide the form as follows:

```
Private Sub cmdFind_Click ()
  Hide                    ' Return to Address Book
End Sub


Private Sub cmdCancel_Click ()
  txtFind.Text = ""       ' Indicate cancel
  Hide                    ' Return to Address Book
End Sub
```

Now try running the application. When you select the **Find** option, the Find dialog box will be shown. Clicking either **Find** or **Cancel** should hide the Find window.

We haven't yet written the code to do the searches. You will use the FindNext method of the data control to find a record. You'll use a search string that includes the Like keyword with a search string pattern, making it possible to do searches that are not case-sensitive. First, however, we'll add a method to the frmFind form. Called GetString(), this method will return the string the user entered in the text box. By creating this new function (method) as a Public function instead of a Private function, you will be able to call it from any other form.

To create a new procedure, open the code window for the frmFind form and select **Add Procedure** from the Tools menu. In the resulting dialog box, type **GetString** and then click **Function** before you press **Enter**. Notice that **Public** is already selected at the bottom of this window; see Figure 12.2. You have the choice of making any new function either Public or Private; Private functions can be called only by code inside the same form or module as the function you're calling.

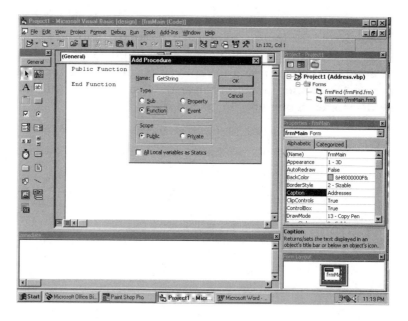

Figure 12.2 *This dialog box allows you to define new subroutines and functions.*

Move to the general declarations section of the form (remember how we used the left and right combo boxes to get there in Chapter 2). Enter the following code to define a string to hold the search string:

```
Dim findStr$                    ' Keep track of last
                                ' string
```

Now add the extra line in the cmdFind button code to save the text to the new string:

```
Private Sub cmdFind_Click()
    findStr$ = txtFind.Text    ' Remember the search
                               ' string
    Hide                       ' Return to GetString
End Sub
```

To the `Form_Load` event, add the code to set the text box to the last searched text and select it from beginning to end:

```
Private Sub Form_Load()
    txtFind.Text = findStr$      ' Show previous search
                                 ' string
    txtFind.SelStart = 0         ' Select entire string
    txtFind.SelLength = 32767
End Sub
```

The code for the `GetString` method displays the Find dialog box in modal form, sets the function itself to return the text in the text box control, and then unloads itself:

```
Public Function GetString() As String
    Show 1                      ' Show as modal dialog
    GetString = txtFind.Text    ' Get the final string
    Unload Me                   ' Can now remove from
                                ' memory
End Function
```

Once you have the function `GetString` defined in this form, using the form is simple even if you don't know anything about loading or unloading forms. To call a function defined inside a form, change the code in the **Find** menu item event:

```
Private Sub miFind_Click()
    searchStr$ = frmFind.GetString()
    If searchStr$ = "" Then
        ' The find dialog box was canceled
    Else
        ' Do the find...
```

```
        Beep
    End If
End Sub
```

As far as your code is concerned, you're calling a single function that belongs to the frmFind form; the `GetString` function takes care of all the details of displaying and unloading the form from memory. Using public functions, as we've done here, allows for simpler, cleaner programs.

Now let's add the code to perform the search. The search begins with the `miFind_Click` subroutine. Here, you'll create some variables, place a bookmark on the current record, display the Find dialog box, and then create a query string. For each of the fields we will search, we'll add an asterisk to the beginning and end of the search string to create a pattern. A *pattern* is a string that contains wildcard characters—in this case the *—representing any characters.

A *search string* defines the field that you're looking for and the string that should match it. For example, if you wanted to search for a name that had *son* somewhere in it (you can't remember whether the person's name was Johnson or Levinson), you could do so easily. The query string to search the **lastname** field would look like this:

```
queryStr$ = "lastname like '*son*' "
```

The first part of the string selects the field **lastname**. The `like` keyword searches for the specified text but ignores the case (for example, it would find the last name Sonner). Notice that the search string is surrounded by apostrophes ('). In Visual Basic, an apostrophe indicates a comment, but in a search string it tells the search engine to look for a string. If we were searching numeric fields, we wouldn't use the apostrophes. Finally, the `*son*` makes Visual Basic search for the string *son* anywhere within the **lastname** field. If we instead used the search string `*son`, it would find only last names that ended in *son*.

After the user enters the text, the search begins. If the search is successful, the found record is retrieved and displayed. If the search is not successful and no matches were found, the bookmark is used to return to whatever record was current before the search.

The syntax for the `FindNext` method is `Data1.RecordSet.FindNext cri-teria`, where `Data1` is the name of the data control and `criteria` is the name of the variable containing the search string. In the Address Book program, `criteria` turns out to be a variable called `searchStr` that uses the `Like` opera-tor to compare two string expressions—in this case, comparing the string inside the specified field with the pattern made by adding the asterisk to the string entered in the Find dialog box. The following is the full code listing for the `miFind_Click` subroutine.

N O T E

The string expression in the call to the `FindFirst` method is actually a snip-pet of SQL code. In this case, it is the part of SQL known as the WHERE clause (without the word WHERE actually in the string). If you search for the string `Smith`, for example, the string that `miFind_Click` builds to search the **Address** field looks like this:

```
lastname LIKE 'Smith'
```

This searches for a record that has the word *Smith* (or SMITH, SmItH, and so on) in the **lastname** field. There are other forms you can use for other types of searches. You can find more information in Visual Basic's online help. From the Help menu, select **Search For Help On** and enter **where**. Press **Enter**. Then in the lower list box, click on **WHERE Clause (SQL Only)** and click the **Go To** button.

Enter this code in the menu event for the **Find** option. Make sure that you have created the frmFind dialog box, because this routine calls the public `GetString` method to show the dialogbox and retrieve the search string.

```
Private Sub miFind_Click()
    ' This subroutine displays the Find dialog box and
    ' then looks for a record that contains the text you
    ' typed in.
    '
    Dim searchStr$, varBookmark, result

    ' Get the find string from the frmFind dialog
```

```
searchStr$ = frmFind.GetString()

If searchStr$ = "" Then

    ' The find dialog box was canceled, do nothing

Else

    Screen.MousePointer = 11   ' Set to hour glass cursor

    ' Use the Data1.Recordset object for all (.) references

    With Data1.Recordset

        ' Set bookmark, so if no record is found, can return to cur-
rent record

        varBookmark = .Bookmark


        ' Set up query to search three fields: lastname, firstname,
and notes

        queryStr = "lastname like '*" & searchStr & "*' or firstname
like '*" & searchStr & "*' or notes like '*" & searchStr & "*'"

        ' Execute query

        .FindNext queryStr

        ' If no match, start at the beginning of database

        If .NoMatch Then

            .FindFirst queryStr

        End If


        ' No record found

        If .NoMatch Then

            MsgBox "No record found.", vbExclamation, "Not found"

            ' Return to original record

            .Bookmark = varBookmark

        End If

    End With

    Screen.MousePointer = 0 ' Restore mouse pointer to default

End If

End Sub
```

Now execute the application. You should be able to find any text string located in the **lastname**, **firstname**, or **notes** field. The code that defines the querystr uses the or command to search for multiple fields. You can easily modify the field to search additional fields such as **company**.

Now that you have achieved some skill in Visual Basic programming, we suggest you make an addition to the program: a **Find Next** option. To create the routine to find the next occurrence of the search string, you create a variable in the general declarations section to hold the string. You can use the code for the find routine once you have removed the extra code that gets a new search string with the frmFind. Try it! You should be able to enhance the application with such an addition.

SORTING THE DATABASE

Wouldn't it be nice if the Address Book automatically sorted the records into alphabetical order when it executed? We added the index to the **lastname** field so that this function would not only be easy to implement, but also fast to execute. We simply need to add the correct statement to the Form_Load event:

```
Data1.RecordSource = "SELECT * FROM Addresses ORDER BY lastname"
```

This code tells the data control that we want to select from the Addresses table all the fields (hence the *) to be affected by this sorting, and we want to sort them by the **lastname** field. This code is written in a language called SQL, which stands for Structured Query Language and is pronounced "sequel." SQL is important in world of relational databases. By the use of SQL, Visual Basic's Access engine provides a great deal of power. If you plan to do a lot of database work with Visual Basic, we strongly recommend that you learn more about Microsoft Access and SQL.

The preceding SQL code is placed in the RecordSource property. Normally, a simple table name appears in the RecordSource property, because nothing needs to be done to present the records. By adding this statement, we filter the incoming data into alphabetic order by the **lastname** field. You can change this statement to sort by another field, such as the **company** field, if you desire.

In most cases, a short bit of SQL code will be much faster (sometimes 10 times or more faster) than the same code written in Visual Basic using the database commands and methods.

You already know that moving from one record to another forces an automatic save or in Visual Basic terms, an update, if any of the data has been changed. If you were using the standard data control alone, you would not need to write any code, because this functionality is built-in. The Address Book program takes advantage of this automatic function. That's why you do not need to write code to save the current record before adding a new one.

However, if you need to change some of the text from your program (as we will in Chapter 13), you need a way to tell the data control to update the database. The database also needs to be re-sorted (because the new record was added). To re-sort the database after a record has been added, you could use code such as this:

```
Data1.RecordSource = "SELECT * FROM Addresses ORDER BY lastname"
Data1.Refresh
```

New records are initially added at the end of the database rather than in alphabetic order. The records won't be put into alphabetic order until we tell the data control that we want to update, or *refresh*, the view of the database. Because of the SELECT statement you attached to the data control in Form_Load, Refresh is the method used for sorting the database:

```
Data1.Refresh
```

We won't use this method in this chapter, but if you would like to add code to the **Update** button, you might include this command to make it re-sort the records. Additionally, to update records through the program, you need to use the Update method of the data control. When we add the Clock control to the application in Chapter 13, we will update records automatically. The Update method is used with the name of the data control and the RecordSet property:

```
Data1.RecordSet.Update
```

You now have an address book that is sorted by last name when executed. What if you wanted to print this alphabetic list? Once again, you will use the RecordSet object to access all the individual records stored in your database.

PRINTING ADDRESSES

Printing the address book doesn't take much work, but we'll use a few new concepts and techniques. You'll notice from the menu you created earlier that there are two menu items to support: **Print** and **Print Setup**. The **Print** menu item allows you to print all the addresses in your address book, and most Windows programs show a standard Print dialog box that lets you confirm your choice before the printing starts. The Print Setup dialog box, on the other hand, allows you to specify a different printer or switch between portrait and landscape modes.

Both the **Print** and the **Print Setup** functions in Address Book use a set of dialog boxes provided by a control called the Common Dialog control, which is not automatically included in the Visual Basic toolbox. To use this Visual Basic OCX, you'll need to add it to the toolbox by selecting the **Components** item from the Project menu. In the Custom Controls dialog box, check the item **Microsoft Common Dialog Control**. A new control will appear on the toolbar. If you move the mouse over a control in the toolbar and pause, a small yellow window (a tooltip) will appear with a name in it. The control you want will display the name **CommonDialog**.

We want to add this control to the main Address Book form. Make sure that this form is showing and double-click the **Common Dialog** control to make it appear on the form. Don't worry where it is placed. Like the Timer control we used in the Clock program, the Common Dialog control does not show up when the program is running. By default, the first Common Dialog control placed on a form is named **CommonDialog1**.

Implementing the Print and Print Setup dialog boxes is simple. The only tricky part is setting the correct flags before you call the ShowPrinter method. Fortunately, Visual Basic predefines all the constants that you'll need.

The actual work of printing records takes a little work, but it's not difficult. Each address consists of a series of fields, so they must be combined in the correct order. The output from the Print routines looks something like this:

Joe M. Smith

Great Software Company

238 Somewhere Lane

Imaginary, CI 12345-6789

Home: 251-231-2312

Work: 251-231-2313

We need to access the `Printer` object as we did with the Sketch program. Instead of drawing lines, this time we'll print text. You will use the **Print** command to send the text to the printer. As you were taught in Chapter 3, using the semicolon (;) between entries will put them together without a space separating them. Into the **Print** menu option, type the following code:

```
Private Sub miPrint_Click()
    Dim BeginPage, EndPage, NumCopies, i
    ' Set Cancel to True
    CommonDialog1.CancelError = True
    On Error GoTo ErrHandler
    ' Reset all flags
    CommonDialog1.Flags = 0
    ' Display the Print dialog box
    CommonDialog1.ShowPrinter
    ' Get user-selected values from the dialog box
    BeginPage = CommonDialog1.FromPage
    EndPage = CommonDialog1.ToPage
    NumCopies = CommonDialog1.Copies
    For i = 1 To NumCopies
        ' Print basic header
        Printer.Print "-- Address Book Print -- Printed: " & Date
        Printer.Print
        Data1.Recordset.MoveFirst
        Do Until Data1.Recordset.EOF
```

```
            ' Print Name as first line

            Printer.Print Data1.Recordset!firstname; " ";
Data1.Recordset!lastname

            ' Make sure there is text in the field before printing the
line

            If Data1.Recordset!company <> "" Then

                Printer.Print Data1.Recordset!company

            End If

            If Data1.Recordset!address1 <> "" Then

                Printer.Print Data1.Recordset!address1

                If Data1.Recordset!address2 <> "" Then

                    Printer.Print Data1.Recordset!address2

                End If

                Printer.Print Data1.Recordset!city; ",";
                Data1.Recordset!state; "   "; Data1.Recordset!zip

            End If

            If Data1.Recordset!phone1 <> "" Then

                Printer.Print Data1.Recordset!phone1type; ": ";
                Data1.Recordset!phone1

            End If

            If Data1.Recordset!phone2 <> "" Then

                Printer.Print Data1.Recordset!phone2type; ": ";
                Data1.Recordset!phone2

            End If

            If Data1.Recordset!phone3 <> "" Then

                Printer.Print Data1.Recordset!phone3type; ": ";
                Data1.Recordset!phone3

            End If

            If Data1.Recordset!phone4 <> "" Then

                Printer.Print Data1.Recordset!phone4type; ": ";
                Data1.Recordset!phone4

            End If
```

```
            ' Print separator between entries
            Printer.Print "_____"
            Printer.Print
            ' Move to the next record
            Data1.Recordset.MoveNext
        Loop
        ' End the document
        Printer.EndDoc
    Next i
    Exit Sub
ErrHandler:
    ' User pressed the Cancel button
    Exit Sub
End Sub
```

This code may seem complicated at first, but it isn't difficult to understand. It starts by activating the Common Dialog to show the Print dialog box (using the `ShowPrinter` method). If the user has clicked the **OK** button, the printing routine swings into action. First we must define a For..Next loop to print the number of copies selected by the user. The code inside this loop does the printing.

The first line is not surprising. It simply prints a header with the current date. The following line activates the `MoveFirst` method of the `RecordSet` object so that the current record pointer selects the first record in the database and we can print them all. We then create a loop to print all the records until the end of file is reached. The code ensuing may appear confusing. Here's the code to print the name line:

```
Printer.Print Data1.Recordset!firstname; " "; Data1.Recordset!lastname
```

You can see that the Printer object is used to print the line. What is the `Data1.Recordset!firstname` command? All fields available in the data control are accessible through the `RecordSet` object. The exclamation point (!) allows the specification of a field that the data is read from. The **Print** command leaves a single space (between first and last names) and then prints the entry in the **lastname** field of the current record.

The code that follows these routines prints all the other lines of the record. Notice that we use If…Then statements to ensure that there is text in these fields. No one would want a printout full of blank lines. If there is no entry in a field, it is not printed.

The **Print Setup** menu item is far simpler. You set a flag to show the Print Setup dialog box instead of the Print dialog box. In the **Print Setup** menu option, enter the following:

```
Private Sub miPrintSetup_Click()

    ' Make sure Cancel doesn't cause an error

    CommonDialog1.CancelError = False

    ' Set the flag to display the Print Setup dialog box

    CommonDialog1.Flags = cdlPDPrintSetup

    ' Display the Print Setup dialog box

    CommonDialog1.ShowPrinter

End Sub
```

Your Address Book application will now print all the necessary information from the database. We haven't included fancier items, such as page headers, footers, or page numbers. These additions are up to you. You should have a good understanding of how the printer works, so why don't you attempt some additions of your own? Start with something simple, such as adding the **Notes** field to the printout, which hasn't been included here.

SUMMARY

With understanding you've gained of programming and Visual Basic, you should now be able to start working on your own programs. In Chapter 13, we will make one more addition to the Address Book. Then we will call it complete, at least as far as this book is concerned. You can use the Address Book if you add a few extra features. Make it your own.

The following is what you've learned in this chapter:

- Searching. You now understand how to create a basic query, including the use of wildcard characters (*) and multifield searches. For our example, we searched the **Notes** field, which is not indexed. For the fastest search, be sure to search indexed fields.

- Public functions. The Public function you created, `GetString()`, allows you to access the frmFind dialog from any form with only a single line of code. By hiding all inner workings of the Find dialog box and providing a single point of entry, you used information hiding, an object-oriented programming technique mentioned in Chapter 4.

- Sorting. Using the simple `Order By` clause, you saw how to sort the data as it appeared on your form. Setting the `RecordSource` property to a SQL statement let you filter the records that were displayed by the data control.

- Printing. You've used the `Printer` object before, but this time you learned how to print text. You also learned how to access the data contained within the fields of a record through subroutine code.

CHAPTER 13

Adding the Clock User Control

- Creating a common control folder
- Adding drag support to the Clock control
- Adding drop support to the **Notes** field
- Updating the modified table

We've added a tremendous amount of functionality to the Address Book application, but most of the code is specific to this program. It would be difficult to reuse most of the parts we created. You may remember, however, that when we created the Clock user control we said it could be reused across any number of applications.

Let's add the Clock user control to the Address Book application. This will demonstrate how to build a collection of components that you can use time and again without reinventing the wheel. The debugging time you will save by using components is, by itself, significant.

We will also augment the features of the Clock control to demonstrate how a control that you've created can interact with a separate program. To implement this interaction, we'll add drag-and-drop support, thereby allowing the user to click on the clock and drag it into the **Notes** field. The time and date from the Clock control will then be automatically inserted at the end of the notes.

SET UP A CONTROLS FOLDER

Before we begin, let's create within the PROJ folder a new folder to hold all common controls. Whenever you create a new control, it can be saved in the Controls folder for use by other applications. You can also update a single control in the Controls folder, and those changes will be instantly reflected in all the projects that use the control.

We won't modify the original Clock user control. Instead, you'll make a duplicate of the control for placement in the new folder, leaving the current Clock project intact. If you later want to modify the original Clock application, you can simply open that project, remove the old user control, and add the central one stored in the new folder.

First, you need to create the new folder. As you can see in Figure 13.1, we've created a folder called Controls inside the Proj folder. We've used the Windows Explorer to create the folder, but you can use any method. After the folder is created, copy two files (**Clock.ctl** and **Clock.ctx**) from the Clock folder to this one.

Create the new folder by selecting the **Proj** folder and then using the **New > Folder** option on the File menu. Name the folder **Controls**. Using the **Copy** option in the Edit menu is perhaps the easiest way to copy the files to the new folder. Move to the Clock folder and select these two Clock user control files (**Clock.ctl** and **Clock.ctx**). Select the **Copy** menu option. This menu option copies an image of the files to the clipboard. When you paste from the clipboard, duplicates of the files are stored in the selected folder. Select the **Controls** folder and select the **Paste** option under the Edit menu. A copy of the files should appear in the new folder.

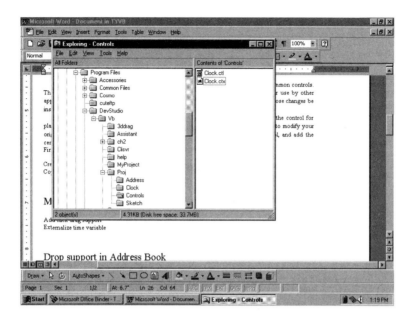

Figure 13.1 *Create a new folder called Controls and copy* ***Clock.ctx*** *and* ***Clock.ctl*** *into it.*

We are now ready to begin adding the Clock control to the Address Book project. Before we can implement drag-and-drop support, however, we must make some changes to the control.

MODIFICATION OF THE CLOCK CONTROL

Open Visual Basic and make sure that the Address Book project is open (you can use the **Recent** tab of the Open dialog box to find it quickly). In the area labeled **Project - Project 1** on the right side of the screen, you will see that the project contains the two current forms (frmMain and frmFind). The User Control folder will be shown in the project once we add the control.

Under the Project menu, select **Add User Control**. The Add User Control dialog box will appear, with the default tab selection set to **New**. We don't want to create a new user control but instead to add the current Clock control. Click on the **Existing** tab and navigate the folders until you can select the **Clock.ctl** control in the Controls folder.

You should now see the user control icon added to the bottom of the tool-box. Because the ctl_Clock control has been added, your Project window should look like the one in Figure 13.2. If the Clock control is not visible but the folder has a plus sign (+) to its left, click on the plus sign to expose the control.

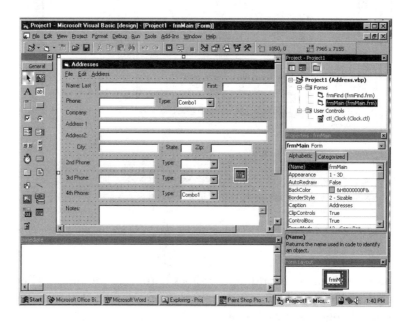

Figure 13.2 *The Project window shows both controls and the user control ctl_Clock.*

Let's begin our modification of the Clock control to add the features that will make it useful in the Address Book. For the control to provide information to outside objects, it must provide a Public variable. The Public variable will then be accessible to any other code or controls on the form in which it is inserted. A Public variable becomes a property of the user control. The process of making the variable public is called *exposing* a property.

We need to expose a property that will give the current time and date, which are regularly updated by the control. To support the dragging and dropping of this information, you'll need to expose a variable that we'll call the CurDateTime property. To begin the modification, double-click the **Clock** control in the Project window. The window that contains the control will appear in Visual Basic.

To add the property and the necessary commands, select the **Code** option under the View menu. You will be presented with a code window showing all your general declarations. All these variables are currently Private. Let's add a public `CurDateTime` property by using the following code:

```
Public CurDateTime
```

This variable is now exposed as a property of the object every time a clock control is added to a form. However, the variable itself does not contain any data. We must update this variable—using the Timer control that is active within the Clock control—so that the current time and date will always be available and accurate.

From the left combo box in the code window, select the **Tick** control. Recall that the Tick control is the Timer control that we added to the Clock; it activates every second to update the time display. We will augment the timer so that it also updates `CurDateTime` every minute.

You will see the code we previously (in Chapter 8) placed in the `Timer` event (`Timer` should appear in the right combo box). We'll add code to update the `CurDateTime` variable. In the current procedure you will see the commands that update the caption to show the current time. Directly below the line that sets the `Caption` property, place the following code:

```
CurDateTime = t
```

Earlier in this code, the variable `t` was set to equal the returned value of the function `Now`. The `Now` function returns the current date and time of the system. We now have set the `CurDateTime` property equal to the variable `t`. Every second when the Tick timer control is called, the `CurDateTime` variable will now be updated to show current values.

That's it! We're finished with our modifications to the Clock user control. Select the **Save Clock** option under the File menu to store the changes you've just made. Close the Clock control using the icon menu to the left of the File menu.

Make sure you close the `Clock` control, or else it will not appear in the toolbox palette for placement on your form. If you were to simply select the main form without closing the clock, this might be confusing.

N O T E

ADD DRAG SUPPORT TO THE CLOCK OBJECT

Now that you have made the necessary changes to the control, let's insert it into the Address Book form. The easiest way, which you've done before, is to double-click the icon for the **Clock** user control on the toolbox. The Clock control will be placed somewhere on the Address Book form. Drag the control into an empty area of the form so that your form looks approximately like the one in Figure 13.3.

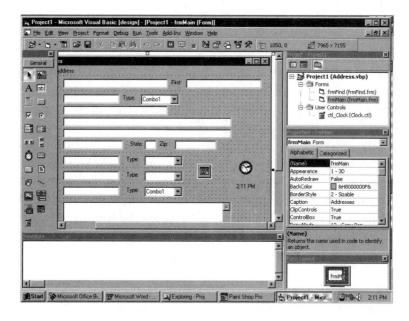

Figure 13.3 *The Address Book form with the Clock user control added.*

If you now executed the application, the clock would show the time on the form. However, we want to add the ability to drag and drop the current date and time into the **Notes** field. To accomplish this, we must make a change to a property of the instance of the Clock control placed on the form. We must also add some code to the text box to accept the information from the control when it is dropped on the text box control.

Click on the **Clock** object that you earlier placed on the main form. In the Properties window, you will see a property labeled **DragMode**. It will currently be set to the default value, which is **0 - vbManual**. The manual setting requires that you write the necessary code to activate the object-dragging method. We want Visual Basic to take care of this, so change the **Property** setting to **1 - vbAutomatic**.

The manual setting provides a great deal of flexibility if you need to accomplish special functions, but we don't need it here. Setting the **DragMode** property to **automatic** makes the control, when dragged, show its outline.

DragMode Property

There are a number of reasons that you would use the **vbManual** drag mode and not the automatic function as we have in this application. Let's look at two of them.

When the **DragMode** is set to **automatic**, every click on the control allows the control to be dragged. For our Clock control, we have no need to click on the clock to do anything else, but what if you had a list box control? The user would want to be able to select items in the list box as well as drag items from within the list box to other controls on the screen. With the automatic drag mode set, this option would be impossible.

The list box example brings up another reason to use the manual drag mode: to activate another control. With the Clock control, the outline of the entire control is shown when dragged. With a single field from a list box, it would be inappropriate to drag the outline of the entire list box. Instead, a program could copy the contents of a selected list item into a previously invisible label control and activate dragging for the label (by using the Drag method of the object). To users, it would appear as if they were dragging the single item that they selected.

Try running the program now (using the **F5** key). When you click on the **Clock** and hold down the button, the outline of the Clock control is dragged with your cursor. No matter where on the form you drop the control, however, nothing happens!

Because every object is different, the routine to accept the information of the dropped object must be written by hand. You might ask, "Why isn't support built-in so that an object can just be dropped onto another object and the information is transferred?" The answer is that different objects need to communicate different things. For example, what would happen if you dropped a text control full of characters on a picture control? The picture control would not understand the text. If the text contained within the text control were the name of a picture file, however, the picture control could display the file. This behavior could not easily be done automatically and would have to be programmed.

ADD DROP SUPPORT TO THE NOTES FIELD

Now that you've seen how the control dragging works, let's work on the drop portion. Stop the program from running by closing the window or selecting the **End** command from the Run menu.

We will modify the Notes text control to accept the information that is dropped into it by the Clock control. We need to add code in the DragDrop event to receive the information provided by the Clock.

However, there is one problem. The text box controls that were automatically created by the Data Form Designer in Chapter 11 where created on the form as a control array. When we made the combo boxes into a control array, all the events and procedures were held in common. Therefore, you weren't able to write code for a specific control from the ones in the array without checking the index number every time.

If we wrote a routine to accept the dropped information, it would allow the text to be dropped into all the text boxes unless we did specific filtering. We don't want to be able to drop the current time and date into just any field. If it were dropped onto the state field, which is only two characters wide, an error would occur.

On the other hand, filtering for the specific index number of the control would also be a bad idea for this project. What if more controls are added and the current controls get renumbered? Then our code would break, because it wouldn't reference the proper index of the **Notes** text box.

To solve this problem, we remove the **Notes** text box from the array. To accomplish this task, you'll change two properties: the **(Name)** property and the **Index** property. With the **Notes** text box selected, the **(Name)** property will be set to **txtFields**. In fact, the Properties window will be titled **txtFields(16)**. If the index number of your Notes control doesn't match 16, don't worry; we're going to change it anyway.

Change the (**Name**) property to **txtNotes**. The title of the window should now read **txtNotes(16)**. You can see that changing the name without eliminating the **Index** property has just created another control array, this one named **txtNotes**. Move to the **Index** property, and it will read **16**. Delete this number and leave the property blank. The title on the Property window should now be **txtNotes**.

DRAGICON PROPERTY

You may have noticed another drag property known as DragIcon. This property allows you to select an icon that will be shown when the object is dragged instead of the control's outline. This property is useful when the outline of the object is particularly large.

Now the Notes control has been removed from the control array. Double-click on the **Notes** text box, and you will be presented with the code window. The left combo box will say **txtNotes**. The right combo box will show the **Change** event, because it is the default event for this type of control. Change the right combo box to the **DragDrop** event selection.

The code for the DragDrop event, which is activated when a control is dropped on this control, will now appear in the window. Add the following code:

```
Private Sub txtNotes_DragDrop(Source As Control, X As Single, Y As
Single)
    ' Edit the selected record
    Data1.Recordset.Edit
    ' Append the string of CurDateTime to the current notes
    txtNotes.Text = txtNotes.Text + Str(Source.CurDateTime)
    ' Write changes into the database
    Data1.Recordset.Update
End Sub
```

Because we are storing all the information in the database, we must set the current mode to edit before we make any changes. By accessing the

Recordset object, we call the Edit method to prepare the database for the changes that will be made.

For the txtNotes control, all the current text for that field is stored in the Text property. You can see that one of the parameters passed to the DragDrop event is the Source property. This property refers to the object that was dropped on the txtNotes control. Here, we are assuming that the only control that will be dropped is one of our clock controls. By using the reference Source.CurDateTime, we can retrieve the date and time stored in the control that was dropped.

The Str() function is used to convert the date and time available in the CurDateTime property to a string. We want to add the string to the end of any notes already in the **notes** field. Therefore, this string is appended to the current text stored in the Text property.

Now try executing the application. You should be able to drag the clock control onto the **Notes** text box and drop it. The time and date are added to the end of the current notes. This feature is particularly useful if you want to note the times you contacted this person.

You might wonder why we haven't appended the text to the database record itself. We could have done this just as easily. We would simply replace the line that modifies the txtNotes control with code to modify the field directly:

```
Data1.Recordset!notes = Data1.Recordset!notes + Str(Source.CurDateTime)
```

That wasn't hard at all, was it? Visual Basic has dramatically simplified the work that must be done to implement drag-and-drop interfaces when compared with other development systems. If you want to enhance this drag-and-drop support, you might add an icon to the DragIcon property.

The string that is added to the notes could also be improved. We used the Str() function to quickly convert the date and time to a string. You might want to format the inserted text by using the Format$() function.

SUMMARY

The Address Book is now complete. By building this application, you have learned a tremendous amount of information about program building.

You've learned how to construct a database, access it with the data control, save information, sort the database, search the database, and add drag-and-drop support. That's a significant accomplishment, wouldn't you say?

Through the creation of this and the other sample applications, we have used many of the standard controls (such as combo boxes and text boxes) but we have not covered all the controls included with Visual Basic. Chapter 14 provides information on the most common controls that are included with the development system.

You have created the complete Address Book program, at least as far as this book is concerned. Don't stop here, though. If you add a few extra feature, you can make it your own.

The following is what you've learned in this chapter:

- Controls folder. By placing all your reusable controls in a single folder, you create a common place to find them from many different projects. You also provide a centralized place where any revisions to the controls will be reflected in the projects that use them.

- Drag-and-drop support. Using the `DragDrop` event function, you can have a program accept data from an object that drops it. You can use the `Drag` method to manually activate the drag process.

- Exposed properties. By making a variable Public, you can transform a variable into a property of a control. Controls can therefore have specific exposed properties from which other controls can obtain information.

CHAPTER 14

Using Common Controls

- Intrinsic and ActiveX controls
- Common Dialog control
- Chart control
- Comm control
- Tabbed dialog control
- FlexGrid control
- Data Bound Grid control
- RichTextBox control

Throughout this book we have used various toolbox controls to create applications. We have not demonstrated many of Visual Basic's ActiveX controls, which can be used in your projects to great effect. This chapter will present some of these controls along with sample code that demonstrates how to use them.

By mixing and matching the appropriate controls, you can build a professional application quickly. To create graphs, you can use the Chart control. Most of the common dialog boxes you will need, including Open, Save, Print, Font, and Color, are encapsulated in the Common Dialog control. The TreeList control allows you to create hierarchical trees similar to the ones used by the Windows Explorer. Other controls, such as Option and Frame controls, give you enhanced user interface features.

USING INTRINSIC CONTROLS

Intrinsic controls don't need to be added to a project. They appear on every toolbox and are built into the system. The ActiveX controls, on the other hand, are added using the **Components** option under the Project menu.

We've used many of the intrinsic controls, such as command buttons and text boxes, in the projects we have created so far. Now we'll look at some other controls that you will find valuable. Frame controls allow you to subdivide a form into functional areas. Option buttons present a number of choices from which one choice can be made. The file system controls (DriveListBox, FileListBox, and PathListBox) let you implement a file selection.

Let's look at these controls before we move on to other ActiveX controls included with Visual Basic. You can easily identify controls by pausing the arrow cursor over a control in the toolbox and reading the tooltip that will appear.

Frames and Option Buttons

The Frame Control is one of the simplest controls. This useful control is essentially a container into which you can place other controls. The controls are then *grouped* with the frame and can subsequently be moved around the form as a single unit. Grouping controls is an excellent way to display categories of options that are related.

Option controls are the small round controls that include a caption to the right. By placing option buttons in a group, you let a user select one option from many. Let's create a form that incorporates Option controls and a Frame control and demonstrates how they work together.

Start a new project and select the **Frame** control. Draw a Frame control roughly the size shown in Figure 14.1. Select the frame that you just drew and then select the **Option** control from the toolbox. Draw an option button within the frame. If you select the frame on the form and move it, the option button should move with it. Draw two more option buttons within the frame. Then draw the final two option buttons outside the frame.

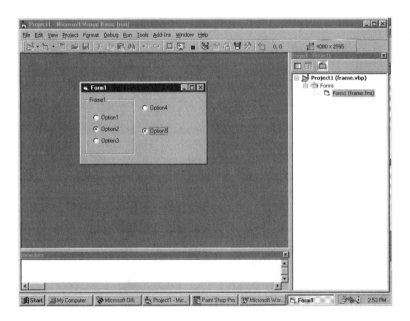

Figure 14.1 *Form with a Frame control containing three Option controls and two additional Option controls.*

Click on the first option button inside the frame. Set the **Value** property (which defaults to False) to **True**. Select the first option button that you drew outside the frame and set its **Value** property to **True**. Now run the application (by pressing **F5**).

The three option buttons within the Frame control are grouped so that only one of them may be selected at a time. Notice that the two option buttons outside the frame do not affect the ones within the frame; they affect only each other. You can change the `Caption` property on the frame to separate groups of controls according to function.

DriveListBox, FileListBox, PathListBox and PictureBox Controls

The file manipulation capabilities that are provided with Visual Basic are substantial. To provide a user interface for these features, Microsoft has included all the controls necessary to make file-related forms. You could even create your own Open file dialog box.

The DriveListBox, FileListBox, and PathListBox controls can be coordinated to select any file on a hard disk. They work like traditional list box controls, but include specialized functions to provide disk access without programming. Let's create a project that uses these controls. Figure 14.2 shows the final project running.

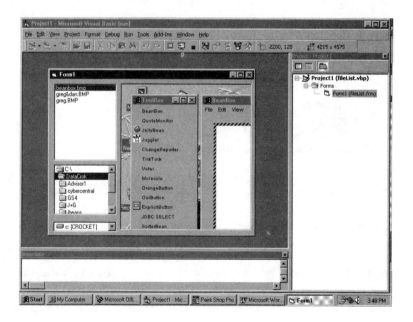

Figure 14.2 Running form with the DriveList ZBox, FieldList Box, and PathList Box used to display a bitmap.

The FileListBox (File1) is on top, with the `PathListBox` underneath and the DriveListBox at the bottom of the window. On the right is a `PictureBox` control that will be used to display a file that the user double-clicks in the FileListBox. Draw all the necessary controls on the form.

We want the FileListBox to show only BMP files. Therefore, change the **Pattern** property from its default of ***.*** to ***.bmp**. Now add the following code to the appropriate controls:

```
Private Sub Dir1_Change()
    ' Coordinate a change in directory with FileListBox
    File1.Path = Dir1.Path
End Sub


Private Sub Drive1_Change()
    ' Coordinate DirListBox with drive change
    Dir1.Path = Drive1.Drive
End Sub


Private Sub File1_DblClick()
    ' Load picture that the user double-clicked
    Picture1.Picture = LoadPicture(File1.Path & "\" & File1.filename)
End Sub
```

Whenever the PathListBox or DriveListBox changes, the change is immediately reflected in the content of the other two list boxes. When the user double-clicks on a bitmap, we use the `LoadPicture` function to load the bitmap into the `Picture` property of the PictureBox control.

USING THE COMMON DIALOG CONTROL

You will probably add the Common Dialog control to nearly all your projects. We used the Common Dialog control in Chapter 12 to add the Print and Print Setup dialog boxes. This control supports seven of the most common dialog boxes: open, save, print, print setup, font, help, and color palette. We will create a form that displays all these dialog boxes (see Figure 14.3).

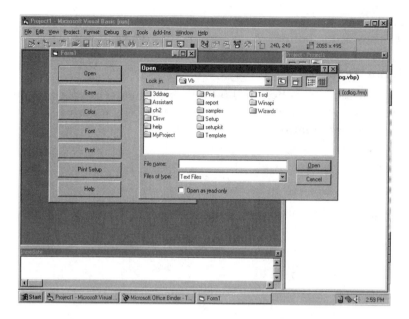

Figure 14.3 *Seven buttons are used for the common dialog boxes*
*(the **Open** button has been clicked).*

Create a new project and add the component **Microsoft Common Dialog Control** (using the Components window selected under the Project menu). Add seven buttons, one for each type of common dialog. Now enter the following code into each of the appropriate buttons.

```
Private Sub cmdColor_Click()
    ' Show the dialog box with an initial color and show the full dialog
    box
    ' To use two flag parameters, simply add them together
    CommonDialog1.Flags = cdCClFullOpen + cdlCCRGBInit
    ' Set currently selected color to blue
    CommonDialog1.Color = RGB(0, 0, 255)
    CommonDialog1.ShowColor
    ' Place color selected by user in variable
    returnedColor = CommonDialog1.Color
```

```
End Sub

Private Sub cmdFont_Click()
    ' Set flags to show both printer and screen fonts
    ' Alternatively, use the flag cdlCFPrinterFonts or cdlCFScreenFonts
      to show a specific set
    CommonDialog1.Flags = cdlCFBoth
    CommonDialog1.ShowFont
    ' Display selected font
    MsgBox "Font Name: " & CommonDialog1.FontName & " Font Size: " &
    CommonDialog1.FontSize, vbInformation, "Selected Font"
End Sub

Private Sub cmdHelp_Click()
    ' Show the Visual Basic help file
    CommonDialog1.HelpFile = "VB.HLP"
    ' Display the contents of the file
    CommonDialog1.HelpCommand = cdlHelpContents
    CommonDialog1.ShowHelp
End Sub

Private Sub cmdOpen_Click()
    ' Clear current filename
    CommonDialog1.filename = ""
    ' Show only text files to open
    CommonDialog1.Filter = "Text Files|*.txt|All Files|*.*"
    CommonDialog1.ShowOpen
    ' Check to make sure user selected a file
    If CommonDialog1.filename <> "" Then
        MsgBox "File: " & CommonDialog1.filename, vbInformation,
        "Selected file"
    End If
```

```
End Sub


Private Sub cmdPrint_Click()
    ' Clear current flags
    CommonDialog1.Flags = 0
    CommonDialog1.ShowPrinter
End Sub


Private Sub cmdPrintSetup_Click()
    ' Show print setup dialog box
    CommonDialog1.Flags = cdlPDPrintSetup
    CommonDialog1.ShowPrinter
End Sub


Private Sub cmdSave_Click()
    ' Set default save filename
    CommonDialog1.filename = "Doc1.txt"
    ' Save as text file
    CommonDialog1.Filter = "Text Files|*.txt"
    CommonDialog1.ShowSave
End Sub
```

You need not learn very much to use the Common Dialog control effectively. The code is commented extensively to explain factors that are unique to each control. For example, if the proper flags are not set, the Font dialog will return a "No Fonts Installed" error. Be sure to set the Flags field of each control to make sure all the parameters are correct for the dialog box you want to use. You can include multiple parameters in the Flags property simply by adding them together. All of the flag options are explained in the Visual Basic Online help.

CREATING BAR CHARTS WITH THE CHART CONTROL

If you are creating business or home applications that require graphing (fitness and biorhythm programs commonly need this feature), the Chart control included with Visual Basic provides powerful graphing capabilities. Although not as full-featured as the graph capability supplied in Excel, the Chart control should give you most of the functionality you need.

Create a new project and add the component **Microsoft Chart Control**. Draw the control on a form. When you first insert the control on the form, it will automatically show a sample form based on the current property and will create bars based on random data. The RandomFill property is, by default, set to True, and that generates the data.

The default chart type in the **chartType** property is set to **1 - VtCh2DchartTypeBar**. Let's make our chart a little fancier. Change the type to **0 - VtCh3DchartTypeBar**, the new 3-D chart type. Also, set the **ShowLegend** property to **True**.

Next, add a command button to add data and legend information to the graph. Enter the following code into the Click event of the command button:

```
Private Sub Command1_Click()
    ' All dot commands will address the MSChart1 object
    With Form1.MSChart1
        ' Set Legend properties.
        .Legend.Location.LocationType = VtChLocationTypeRight
        .Legend.TextLayout.HorzAlignment = VtHorizontalAlignmentRight
        ' Right justify

        ' Set number of columns to 6
        .ColumnCount = 6
        ' Set rows to 3
        .RowCount = 3
        ' Create a loop to cycle through all columns
        For Column = 1 To 6
            ' Select current column
            .Column = Column
            ' Set label of selected column
            .ColumnLabel = "M" & Column
            ' Cycle through rows
```

```
            For Row = 1 To 3

                ' Set currently selected row

                .Row = Row

                ' Set data for currently selected col and row

                .Data = (Row * 5) + (Column * 2)

            Next Row

        Next Column

    End With

End Sub
```

When you click the button, the data will be added and the new chart will be displayed (Figure 14.4). This sample displays three rows and six columns of data. You can easily modify the control to display any data that can be entered programatically or retrieved from a data source.

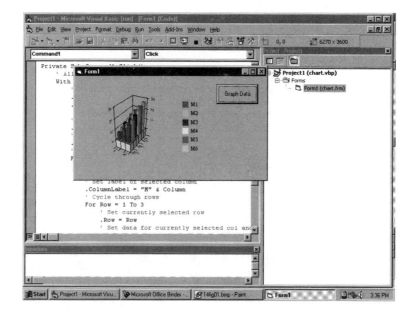

Figure 14.4 The Chart object after the command button has been clicked.

ACCESSING A MODEM WITH THE COMM CONTROL

Many custom applications, especially those created by hobbyists, need to access the serial, or comm, ports. The Comm control gives you complete control over all the parameters that regulate the ports, including buffer size, parity, speed, transmission control, and others.

We have included a sample that queries the COM1 port for a Hayes-compatible modem. To use this sample, create a new project. Add the **Microsoft Comm Control** component to the project. You will see a control with a phone sitting atop a modem. Double-click the icon in the toolbox or draw it on the form. Its exact location is not important, because, like the Timer control, it doesn't appear during run time.

Add a command button to activate the modem check. Enter the following code into the Click event of the button:

```
Private Sub Command1_Click()
    ' Create variable to hold buffered characters
    Dim myBuffer$
    ' Create timer variables
    Dim WaitTime As Single, StartTime As Single, FinalTime As Single
    ' Set variable for amount of time in seconds to wait before abort
    WaitTime = 30
    With MSComm1
        ' Set comm port to 1
        .CommPort = 1
        ' Set modem parameters: 9600 baud, no parity, 8 bits, 1 stop bit
        .Settings = "9600,N,8,1"
        ' Set control to automatically read entire buffer
        .Inputlen = 0
        ' Open COM1 port
        .PortOpen = True
        ' Send the AT (attention) command to the modem followed by
        ' a carriage return (ascii 13)
```

```
        .Output = "AT" + Chr$(13)

        ' Use timer function to get number of secs since midnight

        StartTime = Timer    ' Set start time.

        ' Loop until modem returns response or time expires

        Do While (.InBufferCount < 2) And (Timer < StartTime + WaitTime)

            ' Set caption of command button to show how many seconds
              have passed

            Command1.Caption = Str(Int(Timer - StartTime))

            ' Let system refresh any events

            DoEvents

        Loop

        If .InBufferCount < 2 Then

            MsgBox "No input returned", vbCritical, "Modem not respond-
            ing"

        Else

            'Read input buffer. Should be standard "OK" response

            myBuffer$ = .input

            ' Display returned characters

            MsgBox myBuffer$, vbInformation, "Returned characters"

        End If

        ' Close COM1

        .PortOpen = False

    End With

End Sub
```

This code attempts to contact the modem using the industry standard
Attention (**AT**) command. It then waits for either a return response (**OK**) or
aborts after the number of seconds defined in the `WaitTime` variable. If the
modem has responded, the text of the response is displayed in a message box.

USING THE DATA BOUND GRID CONTROL

In the Address Book application, we displayed all the data as individual records. In other cases, you may want to display data using the spreadsheet style, in which each record is a row and each field is a column. The Grid control allows you to support this style of data interaction simply and easily.

Let's view the data from the Address Book application using the Data Bound Grid control. Once you have pointed the grid at the Address Book database, the form will display the data as shown in Figure 14.5. Data shown in the control can be modified as if one record were displayed at a time.

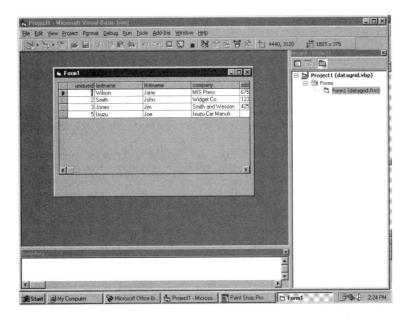

Figure 14.5 The Data Bound Grid displaying the data from the **Address.MDB** database.

Start a new project. Add the **Microsoft Data Bound Grid Control** component to the project. Draw a grid on the form that is about the size shown in the figure. Also, draw a data control at the bottom of the form. The Grid control must be attached to the data through the data control. However, we don't want the user to see this control on the form. Select the data control (**Data1**) and set the **Visible** property to **False**.

Now select the **Databasename** property of the data control and locate the **Address.MDB** file. Set the **Databasename** property to point to this file. Now set the **RecordSource** property to point to the **Addresses** table.

Once the database access has been configured, attaching the grid is simple. Use the DataSource control to select **Data1**. That's it! If you run this application, all your data should appear in the Grid control. Updates are automatically handled by the Data1 control.

USING THE FLEXGRID CONTROL

The FlexGrid control can be used for much more than displaying a database. It need not be attached to a database but instead can be used as a list box or combo box to display information. Because it can easily create multiple columns, it can display information quickly and easily (such as the simple entries shown in Figure 14.6).

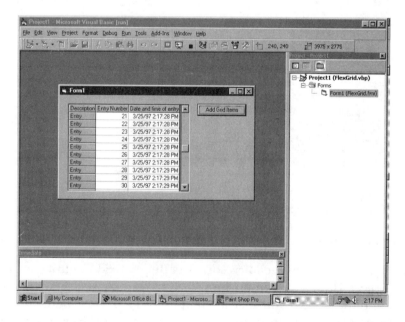

Figure 14.6 *The FlexGrid control filled with 50 simple entries.*

Create a new project and add the **Microsoft FlexGrid** control. Draw a FlexGrid control on the form approximately the size of the one shown in the figure. Add a command button to add data to the grid. Enter the following code into the command button `Click` event:

```
Private Sub cmdAddGridItems_Click()
    ' Declare variables
    Dim Entry$, I

    ' Clear any current data
    MSFlexGrid1.Clear
    ' Set grid to 3 columns width
    MSFlexGrid1.Cols = 3
    ' Set # of rows to 1
    MSFlexGrid1.Rows = 1
    ' FormatString will define 1st row column headings
    MSFlexGrid1.FormatString = "Description|Entry Number|Date and time
                            of entry"
    'Insert 50 rows
    For I = 1 To 50
        ' Create Entry$ with all 3 col entries separated by a tab (ASCII
          9) character
        Entry$ = "Entry " & Chr(9) & I & Chr(9) & Now
        ' Add row to grid
        MSFlexGrid1.AddItem Entry$
    Next I
End Sub
```

When the command button is clicked, 50 line items are added to the grid. Notice that the top row and the left column appear in a different color (gray). The top row is specified by the `FixedRows` property, and the left column by the `FixedCols` property. These Fixed cells have special properties (such as allowing full column or row selections) but also can be set to 0 for a homogenous grid.

RichTextBox Control

The traditional text box control is ideal for typical text entry. It's quick, small, and simple. However, what if you want to allow the user to enter text with varying fonts and sizes? What if users need to apply boldface to a piece of text? The RichTextBox control supplies this ability. We have created an example of using this control (see Figure 14.7) to enter multiple fonts, sizes, and styles of text.

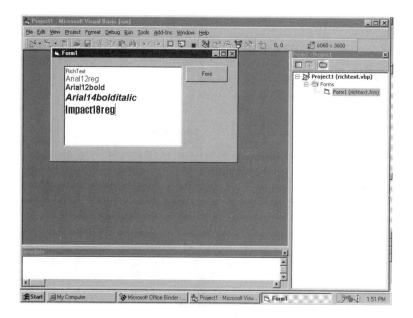

Figure 14.7 *A RichTextBox with text entered using multiple fonts.*

Create a new project and add both the **Microsoft RichTextBox** and the **Microsoft Common Dialog** controls. We will use the Font dialog box from the Common Dialog controls to allow the selection of a font. Add a RichTextBox control, the Common Dialog control (which will be invisible at run time), and a command button. To the `Click` event of the command button, add the following code:

```
Private Sub cmd_Font_Click()
    ' Show both printer and screen fonts
```

```
CommonDialog1.Flags = cdlCFBoth
' Show the Font common dialog
CommonDialog1.ShowFont
' Set the selected text in the RichText control to those selected by
the user
RichTextBox1.SelFontName = CommonDialog1.FontName
RichTextBox1.SelFontSize = CommonDialog1.FontSize
RichTextBox1.SelBold = CommonDialog1.FontBold
RichTextBox1.SelItalic = CommonDialog1.FontItalic
' Return focus to RichTextBox
RichTextBox1.SetFocus
```
End Sub

If you run the form, you can enter any text you want into the RichTextBox. Clicking on the **Font** command button will allow you to select fonts and styles. If no particular text is selected, it will change the style at the current cursor location. When text is selected, the style will change for this text.

TABBED DIALOG CONTROL

It often happens that you need to fit more information on the screen than space will allow. Additionally, some parts of a window may need to be grouped but frames are not appropriate. The Tab control is a fantastic tool for maximizing screen space. You have probably seen tabs in Options dialog boxes in one of the Office applications. We can easily add a Tab control to a form to implement a similar application (see Figure 14.8).

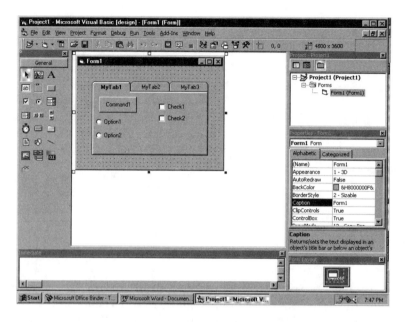

Figure 14.8 *The Tab control helps you use screen space more efficiently.*

Begin a new project and add the **Microsoft Tabbed Dialog** control. Draw a tabbed control on the form. It should automatically be selected. In the Properties window, select the **(Custom)** option to show the Custom properties dialog box. Here you can give the tabs appropriate new captions.

Freely draw any control on the tab where you want it to appear. As with the Frame control, if you add a control to a particular tab, it becomes a child of that tab. The control is then grouped with the tab control.

WINDOWS COMMON CONTROLS

Windows also supplies common controls, which use features that are built into the Windows 32-bit system. If you add **Microsoft Windows Common Controls** to the components of the project, the eight common controls icons (TabStrip, Toolbar, StatusBar, ProgressBar, TreeView, ListView, ImageList, and Slider) will appear in the toolbox. Any of these controls can then be used by your project.

Progress Bar

In Chapter 9, we extolled the virtues of keeping the user informed by using progress bars. The Windows Progress bar common control makes adding status bars incredibly simple (see Figure 14.9). They can easily be placed in a window and do not require a call to the DoEvents procedure to update their display (the setting captions require to display new information).

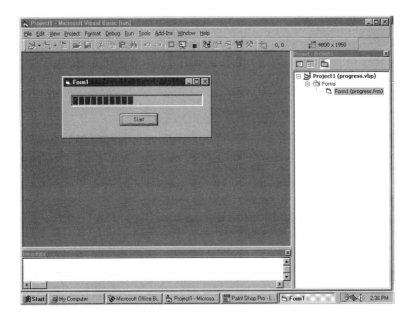

Figure 14.9 *The Progress Bar control keeps users informed.*

Start a new project and add the necessary components. Now add a Progress Bar control and a command button to the form. To the Click event of the command button, add the following code:

```
Private Sub cmdStart_Click()
    ' Set minimum and maximum values for progress
    ProgressBar1.Min = 1
    ProgressBar1.Max = 5000
    ' Loop 5000 times
    For i = 1 To 5000
```

```
        ' Set current value to loop value so progress will show status
        ProgressBar1.Value = i
    Next i
    ' Tell user routine is complete
    MsgBox "Done", vbInformation, "Complete."
End Sub
```

This code creates a simple loop that counts from 1 to 5000, updating the
progress bar along the way. If your computer is very fast, you might want to
increase this amount. If it's very slow, you might decrease it. Be sure to change
both the number specified by the loop and the Max property so that the bar
accurately reflects the loop's progress.

TreeView Control

Organizing information can sometimes be difficult in a standard list box or
combo box, especially if you need to categorize it. The TreeView control
allows you to place information into an outline format similar to the one
you're accustomed to in the Windows Explorer. Figure 14.10 shows the example that we are going to build.

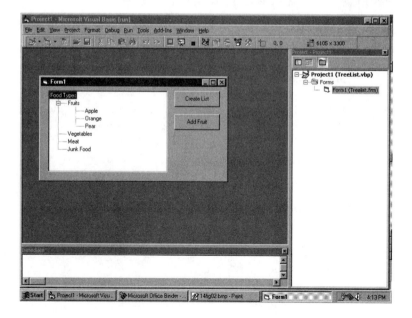

Figure 14.10 A TreeView control.

Let's begin by starting a new project. Add the Windows Common Controls to the project. Now add a TreeView control to the form as well as two command buttons. Add the following code to the command buttons:

```
Private Sub cmdCreateList_Click()
    ' Create dummy node for the creation of new nodes
    Dim nodX As Node
    ' Create original root node and set key = "R"
    Set nodX = TreeView1.Nodes.Add(, , "R", "Food Types")
    ' Add nodes as tvwChild nodes under the node with the "R" key
    Set nodX = TreeView1.Nodes.Add("R", tvwChild, "Ft", "Fruits")
    Set nodX = TreeView1.Nodes.Add("R", tvwChild, "Vg", "Vegetables")
    Set nodX = TreeView1.Nodes.Add("R", tvwChild, "Mt", "Meat")
    Set nodX = TreeView1.Nodes.Add("R", tvwChild, "Jk", "Junk Food")
    nodX.EnsureVisible
End Sub


Private Sub cmdAddFruit_Click()
    ' Create dummy node for the creation of new nodes
    Dim nodX As Node
    ' Add nodes underneath the Fruits item (key: Ft)
    Set nodX = TreeView1.Nodes.Add("Ft", tvwChild, "Ap", "Apple")
    Set nodX = TreeView1.Nodes.Add("Ft", tvwChild, "Or", "Orange")
    Set nodX = TreeView1.Nodes.Add("Ft", tvwChild, "Pr", "Pear")
End Sub
```

The TreeView control makes is simple to add items. Each item inserted into the tree can be given a key. When you need to insert a new item under this item in the hierarchy, simply specify this key as the parent.

SUMMARY

You have now created several projects using some of the controls included with Visual Basic. It is important to realize the power of building programs with this method. You can use the controls included with Visual Basic or purchase the controls you need. This flexibility can save you a tremendous amount of time and energy in bringing your applications to life.

The following is what you've learned in this chapter:

- Intrinsic controls. Intrinsic controls are included with Visual Basic. They need no extra installation and are included in every Visual Basic project. The ones you've used in this chapter include the Frame control, the Option buttons control, and the file management controls.

- ActiveX controls. ActiveX controls include all the other controls we reviewed. These controls are added to a project by using the **Components** option under the Project menu.

- Windows Common Controls. Although controls such as the Chart control need to be installed on the systems that will use your applications, Windows Common Controls are built into 32-bit Windows and Windows NT.

CHAPTER 15

Overview of Advanced Techniques

- Creating installation disks
- Using OLE automation
- Custom controls
- DLLs and Windows functions

In this chapter, we'll give you a quick overview of advanced techniques that you can use in the Visual Basic programs you write. We will cover several categories: creating installation disks, using OLE automation to control external programs and dynamic link libraries (DLLs) and Windows API functions. We'll describe each category briefly and then demonstrate how you can put these techniques to use in your own projects.

You can use Visual Basic without using these advanced techniques. Our purpose here is to provide an overview of some of the more advanced functions available to you as your skill level increases. This chapter provides a stepping-stone for topics that will lead you into intermediate and advanced program creation.

CREATING INSTALLATION DISKS

When you create a Visual Basic application, it requires many files to run on another machine. Additionally, any ActiveX controls that are used by your program must be registered with the Windows system. To aid you in creating installation disks for your program, Microsoft has included an Application Setup Wizard. You select a Visual Basic project, and the Setup Wizard determines which files need to be included.

Let's use the Application Setup Wizard to create installation disks for the Address Book application. Start the Application Setup Wizard by selecting it from the Visual Basic group in the Start menu. The introduction screen of the wizard will be displayed. Click **Next** to advance to the first step.

Use the **Browse** button to select **Address.VBP**. It will automatically recompile as an **EXE**, ensuring that the most recent version of the application is being used. Click **Next** to allow the wizard to recompile the **EXE** and check the condition of the project.

In the next step, you select how the application will be distributed. Three options are presented: floppy disk, single directory, or disk directories. The floppy disk option is most appropriate when you need to make a single set of installation disks. The single directory option is useful when the application will be installed over the network. For the Address Book program, choose the disk directories option, which writes the individual disk images into separate directories. You can make as many installation disks as necessary, and the individual disk directories can also be installed over a network.

Click **Next** to select the directory to hold the install images. The default directory is \Windows\Temp\SWSetup. This directory is fine for our purposes, so click **Next** to continue.

The Data Access selection is now displayed. If you are using the default database access (using the DAO), as we have in the Address Book application, you can leave all these boxes unchecked. For other projects, if you access another type of database, such as a FoxPro DBF, you will need to include the drivers for it. The last item on the list is the Jet 2.x driver. This driver is needed if you will be accessing older, 16-bit Visual Basic databases or Access 2.0 files. For our address book, we need only the default drivers, so click **Next**.

No ActiveX controls are used in the Address Book application, so you can again click **Next**. The Confirm Dependencies screen will show the files that are common to your application. Notice that the last file listed, **COMDLG32.OCX**, is needed to display the Common Dialog boxes such as Print and Save. Click **Next** to check all the necessary project references, and then continue to the File Summary screen.

The File Summary screen (shown in Figure 15.1) is the next-to-last screen. Shown in the list box are all the files that are needed for a complete installation of your application. At this point you often need to add a few files. For example, most applications include a **ReadMe.TXT**, which is not added to the Visual Basic project. Also, any necessary clip art, audio files, help files, or tutorials can be added to the list. Generally, there is no need to remove files that the Setup Wizard has selected. Visual Basic selects all the files you will need for the application to function, and removal of some of them may render your application unable to execute.

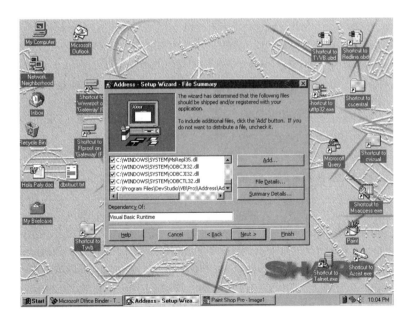

Figure 15.1 *The File Summary screen of the Setup Wizard shows all the files needed for the Address Book application.*

For the Address Book, we need to add our **MDB** file as a starting point for users' address books. Click the **Add** button and select **Address.MDB** in the Address folder. Adding this file to the project will install it with the application. Then click **Next** to enter the final screen.

The final screen allows you to save the template of this installation setup. If you believe you will be updating the Address Book and will need to make future installations, save the template. This option is particularly useful if you have added many files in the previous step. When you make modifications to Address Book, you can simply load the template with all the setup you have done and quickly create the necessary installation.

Click **Finish** to begin the creation of the disk install images. The wizard will display a progress indication as it creates the necessary files. All the files needed by your application are compressed and added to the install file. When the installer is run, the files are uncompressed onto the hard disk of the user's machine.

When the Setup Wizard has completed the installer, look in the SWSetup folder. You will see three folders, one for each disk image that needs to be created. If you're concerned that three disks is too many for such a small program, don't worry. These three disks include all the core files for Visual Basic distribution. As your programs expand and add numerous features, the number of installation disks will not grow substantially. The core files take most of the space; the program itself takes very little space.

If you place the files in each of the folders on individual disks, you will be ready to install. Just run **Setup.EXE** (stored on the first disk) to begin the process. Now you can easily give copies of your application to anyone who wants it.

Using OLE Automation

Did you know that you can control the Excel application from Visual Basic? Or Word, PowerPoint, Access, Outlook, Visio, or Internet Explorer? Imagine being able to automatically create an Excel spreadsheet from calculations done in your Visual Basic application. How about creating a PowerPoint presentation from data stored in a database? Even adding or retrieving contact information from Outlook and presenting it to the user of your program? You can do all this and more using a control process known as OLE automation.

OLE automation is one part of the OLE technology built into Microsoft Windows. OLE automation allows a program, through an application's object model, to control another application. You can use the object model of Excel to add spreadsheets, change numbers in cells, execute macros, change fonts, or almost anything that you normally do in Excel.

You have seen how you can use Visual Basic to access the functions of other programs, and you can also allow control of your own program. Although this topic is beyond the scope of this book, a Visual Basic application can be turned into an OLE automation server. You can expose particular functions that other programs can call (such as Excel using Visual Basic for Applications, or VBA). For example, suppose you created an application that did a series of calculations based on numbers passed to it. It might be valuable for people who program Excel to be able to call these routines. By creating an automation server, you could allow a VBA program to call functions in your program and retrieve results.

Using this technology linked with the remote automation server technology, the application need not be running on the user's machine. Remote automation allows OLE automation servers to be accessed over the network. Therefore, an Excel program could call a function on a main server machine. All the processing would occur on the server, and the results could simply be passed back to the original machine (known as the *client*).

OLE automation, for all its power, is fairly simple to use. Let's make a simple example that creates an Excel file and saves it to the hard disk, all without leaving Visual Basic. Note that you must have Excel currently installed on your machine. Start Visual Basic and create a new project. Place a command button on the form. Enter the following code into the Click event of the button:

```
Private Sub Command1_Click()
    ' Create object variables
    Dim xl As Object, AppXL As Object
    Dim ws As Object

    ' Display hourglass cursor
    Screen.MousePointer = 11
    ' Create instance of Excel object
    Set AppXL = CreateObject("Excel.Application")
```

```
' Set pointer to Application object in Excel object model
Set xl = AppXL.Application
' Add a new workbook (Excel file)
xl.Workbooks.Add
' Add a sheet to the Worksheets collection
xl.Worksheets.Add
' Set pointer to the active sheet
Set ws = xl.ActiveSheet
With ws
    ' Set the name of the sheet
    .Name = "MIS"
    ' Set the values of a few cells
    .Range("A5").Value = "Book Rating:"
    .Range("B5").Value = 654.85
    .Range("A6").Value = "Author Rating:"
    .Range("B6").Value = 171.92
End With
' Save Workbook
xl.ActiveWorkbook.SaveAs "C:\MISTest.xls"
' Close workbook
xl.ActiveWorkbook.Close
' Release instance of Excel
Set ws = Nothing
Set xl = Nothing
Set AppXL = Nothing
' Return cursor to normal
Screen.MousePointer = 0
End Sub
```

When the command button is pressed, this code loads an instance of the Excel object and creates a new workbook file. It then enters four values into cells of the spreadsheet. The workbook is then saved as **MISTest.xls** to the root directory of your C drive. You can now execute Excel and look at the file that was created.

Although a thorough explanation of this code is beyond the scope of this book, we will show you a way to examine some of the objects available in Excel. The set of objects contained in a program is called an *object model*. Using a utility called the Object Browser, which is included with Visual Basic and all the VBA programs, you can examine the object models of any applications registered for OLE automation capabilities.

Let's take a look at the Excel object model using the Object Browser. With Excel loaded, press **Alt+F11** to show the VBA editor (access is also possible through the Macro submenu on the Tools menu). Now select the **Object Browser** option on the View menu (or press **F2**).

The Object Browser window will appear. Click on the combo box that displays **All Libraries** and select the **Excel** option. The window will now look like the one shown in Figure 15.2. On the left you can see all the Excel classes (remember that classes are like blueprints for creating object instances), and the right pane shows all the *members* of the class. Members can include properties and methods of the object.

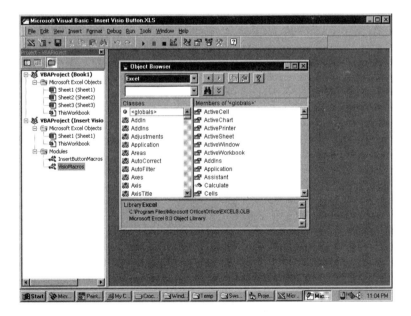

Figure 15.2 *The Object Browser window showing the Excel object model.*

By using the objects shown in the Object Browser, you can see the object model, which allows you to manipulate the entire Excel application. The Object Browser is also an excellent reference if you need to find a member; it includes complete searching capabilities. With the Object Browser, the full power offered by OLE automation becomes apparent.

CUSTOM CONTROLS

OLE automation provides just one way to harness the functionality of outside resources. Adding control components to your program can be one of the best ways to enhance it. A number of commercial add-on packages for Visual Basic include *custom controls*, which appear in Visual Basic's toolbox when you add a special file to your project. These files have the extension **OCX** (see Appendix A for more information).

Visual Basic 5 has the ability to use ActiveX controls (previously known as OLE custom controls). The power available through ActiveX controls is substantial. Controls can be purchased from reliable third parties and shipped with your application. In Chapter 16, you will learn how to build an ActiveX control.

To add a custom control file to your project, select the **Components** item from the Project menu and check the box of the name of the appropriate ActiveX file. After you add an ActiveX file, additional control icons will appear in Visual Basic's toolbox, as you saw when you added the Common Dialog control to the Address Book application.

DLLs AND WINDOWS FUNCTIONS

The Windows system is the foundation code of the entire Windows environment. Calls to procedures in the Windows system are actually calls to the Windows API (application programming interface). The Windows API provides hundreds of functions and subroutines that programs can call to create windows, menus, and controls, to do drawing, and so on. Any Windows program calls a number of these functions and subroutines. Visual Basic programs you write call these subroutines and functions indirectly. For example, Visual Basic's **Line** command is converted into a call to the Windows API **LineTo** command, which draws lines inside a window.

All these Windows API functions are provided through a mechanism known as a dynamic link library (DLL), a code library that's loaded into memory and connected to your program on demand. Windows comes with a number of DLLs to provide all the subroutines and functions Windows programs can call.

One powerful feature of Visual Basic is the ability to call almost any DLL function or subroutine in Windows DLLs and in other DLLs that you or someone else might write. Visual Basic provides only a subset of the total functions of the Windows API. Using the DLLs, you can make direct calls to any functions not included in Visual Basic.

The Declare Statement

To call a routine inside a DLL, the first step is to define the function or subroutine. You do this by using the `Declare` statement, which defines several pieces of information. The basic syntax for `Declare` is as follows:

```
Declare Sub subName Lib libName$ [Alias aliasName] ([argument list])
```

This statement defines the subroutine called `subName` located in the DLL called `libName$`. You need not include the extension for the DLL, only its filename.

The following code defines a function called `functionName` located in the DLL called `libName$`, which returns a value of `type`. Again, you don't need to include the extension for the DLL.

```
Declare Function functionName Lib libName$
        [Alias aliasName] ([argument list]) [As type]
```

In the following sections, you'll find a number of examples of how to use and declare Windows functions and subroutines. We'll show a brief example of `Polyline`, a function normally unavailable in Visual Basic. `Polyline` allows the creation of polygon shapes.

Translating between Types in C and Visual Basic

Whenever you're working with Windows API calls or with other DLLs, the documentation will probably be written for C programmers and will use a number of terms and abbreviations you may not be familiar with. Let's take a look at a simple example. Here's how the Windows `Polyline` function is defined in the Microsoft Windows programmer's manuals:

```
BOOL Polyline(hdc, lppt, cPoints)

HDC hdc;            /* handle of device context */
POINT FAR* lppt;   /* address of array with points */
int cPoints;       /* number of points in array */
```

What does all this mean? The names in all uppercase letters, such as BOOL, are C's version of types. For example, BOOL is a Boolean type, which means it is an Integer that returns either 1 or 0 (True or False); HDC and POINT are also types. The lowercase int is also a type that is exactly the same as Visual Basic's Integer type.

Because there can be so many different types in C and Windows, we've put together two tables that show how to translate between C types and Visual Basic's types. Tables 15.1 and 15.2 provide much of the information you'll need. See the **WIN32API.TXT** using the API Text Viewer application included with VB5.0 for definitions of all the functions and subroutines available in Windows.

Table 15.1 Translating between C and Visual Basic Types

WINDOWS NAMES	C	VISUAL BASIC
BOOL	int	ByVal ... As Boolean
BYTE	int	ByVal ... As Byte
WORD	int	ByVal ... As Integer
DWORD	long	ByVal ... As Long
LPSTR	char FAR*	ByVal ... As String
BOOL FAR*	int FAR*	... As Boolean
BYTE FAR*	int FAR*	... As Byte
WORD FAR*	int FAR*	... As Integer
DWORD FAR*	long FAR*	... As Long

The Intel microprocessor treats bytes as words when you pass them to subroutines.

Table 15.2 Other Types of Variables and Some Rules on How to Convert from Some Windows Types to Visual Basic's Types

WINDOWS	VISUAL BASIC	COMMENTS
Hxxxxx	ByVal … As Integer	Any type of handle is an Integer.
ATOM	ByVal … As Integer	
struct	ByVal … STRUCT	A user-defined type created with the Type statement.

Note the following:

- To pass both a string and a NULL pointer to a subroutine, define that parameter As Any. You can pass a NULL pointer by passing the value 0&.
- Define all strings as ByVal when you pass them to DLLs. Visual Basic will automatically convert them to C strings before calling the DLL, and it converts C strings back to Visual Basic strings when the DLL finishes.
- Regarding arrays, pass the first element in the range that you need to pass. For example, if you have an array of points called points, you could send part of this array to a DLL, starting with the fifth element, by using points(4) as the "value" you pass to the DLL.

The Polyline declaration looks like this:

```
Declare Function Polyline Lib "gdi32" Alias "Polyline" (ByVal hdc As
Long, lpPoint As POINTAPI, ByVal nCount As Long) As Long
```

As long as the variables are adapted to their C counterparts, this function can be called as you would call a normal Visual Basic function. All the necessary information for Windows API calls is included in the WinAPI folder in your Visual Basic folder. The necessary declarations and constants are included in the **Win32api.txt** file in this folder.

When you're ready to start using Windows API calls on your own, you'll find a number of examples and information in the *Visual Basic Programmer's Guide*. A number of books also have excellent examples of using the Windows API calls.

The Windows API allows complete control over the printer, access to direct screen display routines, network protocols, and a slew of other advanced functions. The API functions are not used extensively in Visual Basic programs, because Visual Basic provides the necessary functions for 98 percent of the routines you will need to access. However, the `Declare` statement will allow you to reach into the Windows system when you cannot otherwise access something that you need to use. The important thing to realize about the Windows API is that there is no limit to what you can do in Visual Basic.

Summary

In this chapter you have created installation disks, used OLE automation, and briefly examined the Windows API. The information provided here is not necessary to use Visual Basic, but it will become more important as you advance in development. Chapter 16 will introduce you to creating your own ActiveX controls in Visual Basic—controls that can be used in other programs or on the Internet. You can even use OLE automation to manipulate your controls inserted into other programs.

The following is what you've learned in this chapter:

- Creating installation disks. Using the Application Setup Wizard, we created three setup disks for the Address Book application. The wizard automatically searches your project and finds all the dependent files and controls necessary for full installation. At the File Summary stage, you can add any necessary files such as a database, read me files, audio files, or other files not contained within the project.

- Using OLE automation. Through OLE automation you can control many programs, including any of the Office applications. You used OLE automation to create a new spreadsheet in Excel, insert new values, and save the sheet without leaving Visual Basic. OLE automation can even be used to control remote objects across a network.

- The Object Browser. Using the Object Browser, you can look at the object models of any of the registered OLE automation applications available on the computer. The Object Browser shows all the members (methods and properties) of a registered application.

■ Windows API and DLLs. The Windows API contains all the functions available to any Windows program. Visual Basic provides only a subset of the total functions, but you can use the `Declare` statement to directly access the remainder of the routines. For the Windows API, all the routines are stored in DLLs. Using C or C++, you can create your own DLLs.

CHAPTER 16

Building an ActiveX Control

- Creating an ActiveX control
- Adding the control to an Excel spreadsheet
- Calling an ActiveX method from VBA code
- Packaging the ActiveX control for use on the Internet

In Visual Basic 5, Microsoft added the ability to create ActiveX controls. An ActiveX control is like the Clock user control that we created earlier. Unlike a user control that can be inserted only into a Visual Basic project, an ActiveX control can be placed in any application that accepts controls. Such applications include the Microsoft Office suite and numerous third-party applications, including Lotus Notes, Visio, and so on.

ActiveX controls can be used not only within programs but also over the Internet or in an intranet. If a user installs your control on his or her system, that control can be accessed from within a Web page. You can create an ActiveX control that contains your most useful routines, and that control can then be used by any ActiveX-aware environment.

In this chapter, we will construct an ActiveX control that can be used in a number of applications. You'll insert the control into an Excel spreadsheet and then use the control in a Web page. Although we will demonstrate inserting it into Excel, any of the Office applications can be used as easily.

ACTIVEX AND OLE CONTROLS

Microsoft originally created Visual Basic extensions (controls) to allow routines and objects to be used in multiple projects. Known mostly by their file extension (VBX), these controls were so useful that the first market for reusable controls appeared. VBXs flooded the market, providing functions for everything from 3-D rendering to accounting. The market was limited, however, because VBXs could be used only in Visual Basic. This limitation made them inaccessible to C, C++, or other applications programmers.

Then Microsoft extended the specification so that controls could be used in any program that was an acceptable container. Microsoft created a new set of technologies known as object linking and embedding (OLE). OLE did much more than allow controls to be used in programming environments. OLE included OLE controls (OCXs), OLE automation (which you used in Chapter 15), and OLE object linking and embedding. OLE has become extremely popular for building business applications.

As the OLE controls were becoming established, a new technology growth sector exploded: the Internet. To move into this emerging market, Microsoft modified some of the OLE technology to work on the Web. It also invented new tools to use this technology. The OCX model was extended, and controls formerly known as OCXs became ActiveX controls, which can be used both within applications and across the Internet.

Microsoft also created VBScript (a subset of the Visual Basic language), which can be used within the HTML code of Web pages. VBScript can be used to activate and manipulate ActiveX controls. We will use VBScript later in the chapter to insert our ActiveX control into a Web page.

BUILDING AN ACTIVEX CONTROL

The process of building an ActiveX control is nearly identical to the one we used in creating the Clock control. One exception is the attention you must pay to the location where the control will be deployed. If you are sending the control across the Internet, you must concern yourself with two issues: the size of the control and the number of other controls that it uses.

In Chapter 14, we compared intrinsic controls (those controls built into Visual Basic) with ActiveX controls (which must be activated separately). When you create an ActiveX control, if you use other ActiveX controls, you must include them during the installation of your control. However, any intrinsic controls you use are automatically included in the system. To keep our ActiveX control simple, we will use only the intrinsic controls.

Our control will have a visual and a nonvisual component. As we will demonstrate, you may not always want to have a visible control. If you wanted to include calculation routines in a control, for example, you might not need to display anything. Such a control could be used in a spreadsheet without any visible component.

Let's get started. Execute the Visual Basic environment. Create a new project, but instead of selecting a standard **EXE** as we have in the past, select the **ActiveX Control** option. Visual Basic will create a project that looks identical to an **EXE** in most respects. However, the original form will lack the border that is traditionally on a form.

On the control, draw a command button. Set the **Name** property to **cmdMessage** and the **Caption** property to **Message**. Use the resizing boxes to shrink the control to fit around the command button. Your project should look like the one shown in Figure 16.1.

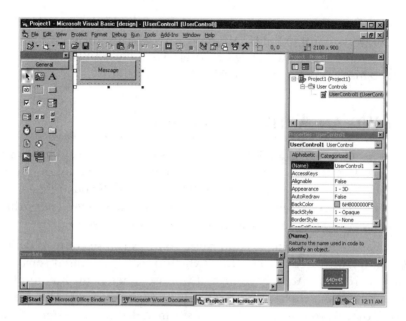

Figure 16.1 *The ActiveX control project with a single command button.*

Now we must change a couple of properties that will determine how the control will appear to other programs. Select the control itself (click on an area not occupied by the button) and change the **(Name)** property to **ctlMessage**. This **Name** property will determine one of the two parts of the final control name as it will appear when it is added to an ActiveX container environment.

If you now look in the upper-right corner of the Project window, the control in the User Controls folder will read **ctlMessage**. In the Project window, click on the project itself, which is labeled **Project1**. The Properties window will show that the project has only one property, the **(Name)** property.

When the control appears in the ActiveX control list, it will be labeled as *projectname.controlname.* Let's say that your company name is MIS. Change the project **(Name)** property to **MIS**. When we compile the control now, it will appear as **MIS.ctlMessage** to other programs.

Now that the control is configured, let's add some simple code to make it function. When users click on the button in another program, we want to display a message box. To the command button's `Click` event, add the following code:

```
Private Sub cmdMessage_Click()
    ' Display simple message box
    MsgBox "Welcome to my first ActiveX control!", vbInformation,
"ActiveX Everywhere"
End Sub
```

You've added the visual component to our control. The control can be inserted into another application, and this button will be shown. But what if you want to design a routine that does special calculations and you don't need any user interface? You need to create a public method that can be executed from the code.

Select the **Add Procedure** option from the Tools menu. When the Add Procedure window appears, type **myCalc** into the **Name** text box. We'll create a simple function that adds two numbers that are passed to it and returns the result. Because we are going to return a number, select **Function** for the procedure type. Make sure that the scope is set to **public** (so that we can access it outside the control) and click **OK**.

We want the function to accept two values and return a single value (the sum of the two values passed). You will need to add two input arguments (which we have created as inp1 and inp2). If you set the name of the function to the result of the addition of these two values, this value will be returned to the routine that calls the function. Your function should look like this:

```
Public Function myCalc(inp1 As Double, inp2 As Double)
    myCalc = inp1 + inp2
End Function
```

You've now created both a visual and a nonvisual component for the control. Now is a good time to save your project. Select **Save Project** under the File menu. Create a folder called **ActiveX** within the Proj folder. You have already named both the control and the project, so click **OK** on both Save dialog boxes to save the control and the project by their default names.

If we compile the control now, it will be available to all the programs on your system. Controls need to be registered in the OLE Registry to be accessible from other programs. Visual Basic automatically registers your control when you compile it, so no extra work is required.

Select **Make MIS.ocx** under the File menu. Change the filename from its default (**MIS.ocx**) to **ctlMessage.OCX** to make it more apparent what the control does. Then click **OK**, and Visual Basic will write the OCX to the hard disk. All done!

Now we need a container application in which to insert the control. Because it has been registered in the system, it will now appear on the palette of ActiveX container applications.

USING MICROSOFT EXCEL AS A CONTAINER

Microsoft Excel is used by a huge number of people as a complete environment for creating business applications. With its easy and familiar spreadsheet metaphor and complete implementation of Visual Basic for Applications (VBA), Excel lets you build an entire application within a spreadsheet.

Excel is an excellent container application for ActiveX controls. The controls can be placed directly on a spreadsheet or within a VBA user form. For this reason, we have chosen to use Excel as our ActiveX container.

You can close Visual Basic, because our control has been created, saved, and registered. Execute Microsoft Excel so that a blank spreadsheet is displayed. On this blank sheet we'll place our control, but first we need to display one of the hidden toolbars that allow controls to be drawn onto the sheet.

Placing the Control on the Sheet

Under the View menu, select the **Toolbars** submenu. From this menu, select the **Control Toolbox** option. The control toolbox will appear, floating over the spreadsheet, as shown in Figure 16.2. We need the control toolbox if we want use the visual component of our control.

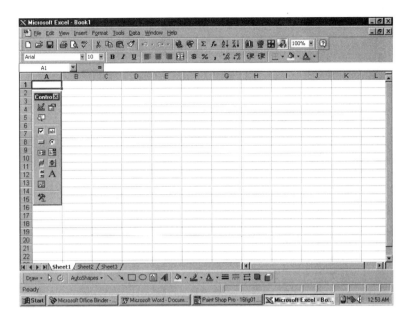

Figure 16.2 The control toolbox floating over the current spreadsheet.

At the bottom of the control toolbox you will see an icon with a crossed hammer and wrench. If you click on this icon, a menu will appear. The menu will show in alphabetical order all ActiveX controls (non-intrinsic) that are installed in the system. Scrolling down, you should be able to find your control, labeled **MIS.ctlMessage**. Click on the control.

The menu will disappear, and your cursor will turn into a crosshair that allows you to draw a control onto a spreadsheet just as Visual Basic lets you draw onto a form. Click and drag the mouse on the spreadsheet, creating a space big enough to show your control. When you release the mouse button, your control will appear on the form (as shown in Figure 16.3).

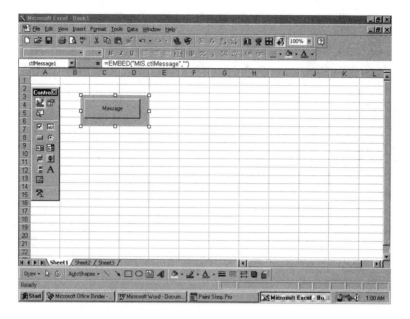

Figure 16.3 The **MIS.ctlMessage** *control inserted onto the Excel spreadsheet.*

You can't click on the button right now, because Excel is in Design mode. Notice that the very first icon on the control toolbox (the one with the ruler, angle, and pencil) now appears depressed. This icon indicates that Design mode is currently turned on. Click on the icon, and Excel will exit Design mode.

Clicking on the command button on our control will now display the message box (see Figure 16.4). This visual component demonstrates only a small part of the functionality you can build into controls. However, the true power of using a control is the passing of information between the control and the application.

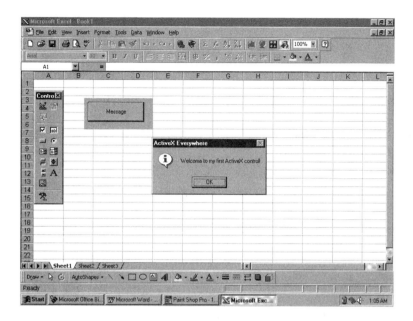

Figure 16.4 *Clicking on the **MIS.ctlMessage** control displays a message on the Excel spreadsheet.*

All the Office applications (except Outlook) provide Visual Basic for Applications, which contains the complete Visual Basic language and a subset of the development environment included with the complete Visual Basic application. VBA does not allow compilation of a stand-alone **EXE** or the creation of ActiveX controls. Any command used in Visual Basic is also available in VBA.

Using the Control from Code

Although your control might have a visible component, you might also simply want to use one of the methods of the object for calculation. In that case, the control need not appear on the spreadsheet. Recall that in Chapter 4 we discussed objects. In the metaphor given in that chapter, a class is like a blueprint, whereas the object instance is the actual house that is built from the blueprint.

When we created the ActiveX control, we created a class for the control. Using the CreateObject() function in Excel, we can create an instance of our class. Actually, when you drew the control on the form, that created an instance. This time we want to create an instance from VBA code that is not visible in the spreadsheet.

Start a new worksheet in Excel so that you can see that the control does not need to be placed on the form with the control toolbox. Do not close the toolbox, because we will need it to place a command button on the sheet to execute our code.

Click on the first icon on the control toolbox to return to Design mode. Select the command button icon on the palette and draw a command button on the sheet. Make sure that you don't draw it over cells D10 and D11. If you already have, simply move the command button out of the way by clicking and dragging it.

You now need to place code in the VBA environment. Access VBA by double-clicking on the control. The VBA Editor will appear, as shown in Figure 16.5. The VBA environment looks slightly different from the Visual Basic one we're accustomed to, but the code window functions identically.

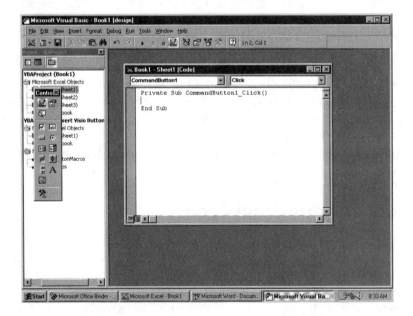

Figure 16.5 *The VBA Editor displays the Click event for the CommandButton1 control on the sheet.*

We want to add code that calls the `myCalc` method that is included in our control. The `myCalc` method must be given two numbers, and it returns their sum. We will take the numbers directly from cells on the spreadsheet and will then enter the result in another cell. Enter the following code in the `Click` event that is displayed:

```
Private Sub CommandButton1_Click()
    ' Create instance of the object ctlMessage
    Set myInstance = CreateObject("MIS.ctlMessage")
    ' Call the myCalc method of the control and obtain the
result
    result = myInstance.myCalc(Range("D10").Value,
Range("D11").Value)
    ' Place the result in the currently selected cell
    ActiveCell.Value = result
    ' Also place it in the D12 cell
    Range("D12").Value = result
End Sub
```

This procedure retrieves values from the D10 and D11 cells and writes the answer into the D12 cell. Notice that we also store the summed value to the current active cell. Storing the value in both places is simply a demonstration of the power of some of the applications you can create.

Now let's return to Excel so that we can set the cells to their proper values. Select the **Close and Return to Microsoft Excel** option on the File menu. We must exit Design mode at this point; click on the first icon (the icon with the ruler, angle, and pencil) in the control toolbox. We're finished with the control toolbox, so you can close it now.

Enter two numbers, one in the D10 cell and another one in the D11 cell. Then click on another empty cell where the result is to be placed. We chose the numbers 24 and 32 and selected the F10 cell.

Let's execute the method on our control and see it generate the sum. Click on the command button control. The sum of both numbers is placed in the D12 cell and the other cell you selected (see Figure 16.6).

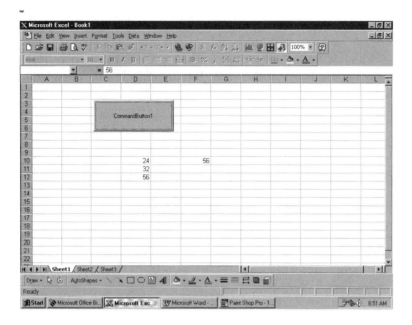

Figure 16.6 *The sum of the values in cells D10 and D11 (24 and 32) is placed in the D12 cell and the selected cell.*

Now that you know how to create a control routine, can you imagine the possibilities? You could create a control that, when given an item number, would look up the price in a database and enter it into your spreadsheet. A control could be made to calculate sales tax on an item. If the sales tax changed, you would merely change the calculation value in the control, and all the projects that use it would be updated automatically. A physics problem could be created in a control as a method. You could even display a customized graph based on information from your spreadsheet.

And these examples apply only to Excel. How about an automatically updated graph of sales inserted into a PowerPoint presentation? Or a table showing your particular stock values inserted and automatically updated in a Word document? Or even a metric-to-English conversion control added to your Access database?

Are you beginning to see some of the possibilities? Great—because we are going to expand your horizons even farther. We'll help you place your ActiveX control on the World Wide Web! Anyone from around the world who is using an ActiveX-compatible browser will be able to use your control.

ACTIVEX CONTROLS AND THE INTERNET

To use our ActiveX control on the World Wide Web, we must create a Web page file to contain the control. To create this file, we'll use the Notepad program that is included with Windows.

Execute Notepad from the Start menu, followed by **Programs**, **Accessories**, **Notepad**. An empty text window will appear. Enter the following code:

```
<HTML>
<HEAD>
<TITLE>ActiveX Sample Page</TITLE>
</HEAD>
<BODY>
<H1>Here is the Sample ActiveX control</H1>
This HTML page is a sample of inserting an ActiveX control
created in Visual Basic. Click on the button.
<P>
<CENTER>
<OBJECT ID="ctlMessage1" WIDTH=140 HEIGHT=60
 CLASSID="CLSID:002F10B9-A6FF-11D0-943A-444553540000">
    <PARAM NAME="_ExtentX" VALUE="3704">
    <PARAM NAME="_ExtentY" VALUE="1588">
</OBJECT>
</CENTER>
</BODY>
</HTML>
```

If you don't know how to make a Web page (by programming in HTML code), don't worry. Many people are using programs such as Microsoft FrontPage or NetObjects Fusion to construct Web sites. These programs do all the coding for you. If you want to do your own coding, we suggest downloading the ActiveX Control Pad from the Microsoft Web site. It's free, and it will automatically insert the code needed to place an ActiveX control on your page.

After you have entered this code, save the file as **message.htm**. We will load this file into Internet Explorer for display. To keep everything together, save the file in the ActiveX folder in the Proj folder where you originally created the ActiveX control.

ACTIVEX SUPPORT IN BROWSERS

With the release of version 3.0 of Internet Explorer, all versions natively support ActiveX controls. This means that most Internet Explorer users will be able to use your ActiveX control. However, Netscape Navigator 3.0 users require a Netscape plug-in to use ActiveX controls. This plug-in is available on Netscape's Web site (*www.netscape.com*).

With version 4.0 of Navigator and Netscape Communicator, ActiveX controls are supported natively. If the users of your control will have any of these supported browsers, they will have no problems running your ActiveX component.

Now execute Internet Explorer or another ActiveX-capable browser. With Internet Explorer, select the **Open** option under the File menu. When the Open dialog box appears, click **Browse**. This button will show a traditional Open file dialog box. Select **message.htm**, the file we just created.

When you open the file, you will get a warning that this control is not secure. An ActiveX control from an unknown source, if written with malicious intent, has the potential to infect your hard disk with a virus or to delete files. Therefore, be very careful of which ActiveX controls you accept over the Web.

In this case, we just created the control, so we know we can trust it. Click **OK**, and the Web page will be displayed. There is your control! Click on the **Message** button, and our dialog box will appear (see Figure 16.7). Although this control worked on you computer, if you placed these files on your Web site, it would not work directly.

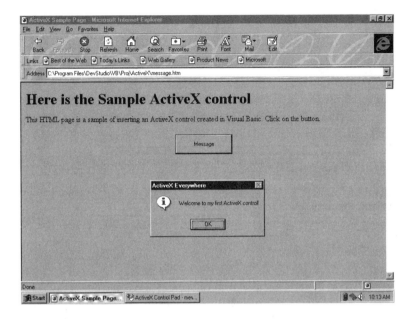

Figure 16.7 A Web page displaying the ActiveX control and its message window.

Creating a CAB File

We said that an ActiveX control must be registered with the system. If someone else accessed this Web page, his or her system would not have your ActiveX control installed. In Chapter 15, we used the Application Setup Wizard to create installation disks for the Address Book application. This time, we'll use it to package the ActiveX control for distribution on the Internet. The cabinet (**CAB**) file format is Microsoft's standard Internet format for automatic distribution of ActiveX controls.

N O T E

Cabinet files (files with the **CAB** extension) are compressed files that can contain one or more files. In the case of your ActiveX control, a **CAB** file will hold the control and all the controls that it references. Users who access your Web page need download only a single compressed file rather than several at the same time.

Execute the Application Setup Wizard. On the second screen, select the ActiveX project. In the Options frame, select **Create Internet Download Setup** (see Figure 16.8).

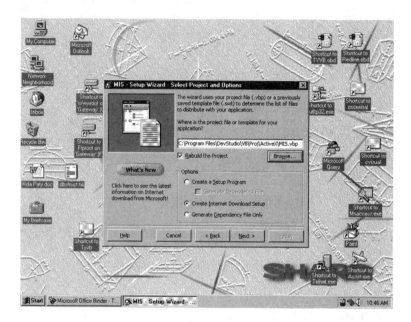

Figure 16.8 *The Application Setup Wizard selected to create an Internet download setup.*

Now follow the Setup Wizard through the other steps, selecting **Next** at each screen. Notice that the file will be placed in the \WINDOWS\TEMP\SWSETUP directory. You will need to retrieve the file from this directory for placement on the Web site. The Setup Wizard will search for any ActiveX controls used by your control. Because we used only intrinsic controls, no other controls will be needed.

The File Summary portion of the wizard will list the files that you need to use the control. In addition to your control, **VBRUN500.DLL** is included. This file is the core Visual Basic system, which includes the run time and all the intrinsic controls. If the people who will use your control will already have this file installed, there is no need to include it in the cabinet. However, for this example, we will include it.

Click **Finish** when you have reached the last step. In the SWSetup folder, you will have a file named **ctlMessage.CAB**. You must include this file with your HTML file when you place it on your Web site.

You now have an ActiveX control that can be used on individual machines and across the Internet. The possible uses of ActiveX controls are almost unlimited. We hope to see your controls on the Web!

RELATED TOOLS

The Internet is one of the best sources of information about Visual Basic development. You can get up-to-the-minute information about what is happening in the world of Visual Basic. Thousands of lines of sample code is available, as are free ActiveX controls, information and samples of commercial controls, and numerous other resources.

- Microsoft's Visual Basic site (*http://www.microsoft.com/vbasic*). Contains all the latest information on Visual Basic along with white papers that detail specific Visual Basic techniques and a tip of the week. You might also check out the VBScript (*www.microsoft.com/vbscript*) and the Microsoft Developer Network (*www.microsoft.com/msdn*) portions of the site.

- Visual Basic Frequently Asked Questions (FAQ) (*http://home.sol.no/jansh/vb*). The Visual Basic FAQ is a fantastic source of solutions to problems often encountered by Visual Basic programmers, beginning through advanced.

- Carl and Gary's Visual Basic site (*http://www.apexsc.com/vb*). One of the best sources on the Web for information about current development in Visual Basic, including sample files. You can find information, sample controls, commercial controls, and general tips in this site.

- Client/Server Central (*www.coherentdata.com/cscentral*). This is our Web site, and it is dedicated to advanced system implementation. Information and free ActiveX controls are available on our site. Come visit!

SUMMARY

The book is complete, and you have mastered many of the core Visual Basic concepts. There is much to learn about Visual Basic, and we hope you don't stop here. You have already learned a staggering amount, and we congratulate you for sticking with it. We support advanced Visual Basic development at Client/Server Central (*www.coherentdata.com/cscentral*), so please stop by. To continue your education, there are many intermediate and advanced books on Visual Basic. You might also extend your skills to the sister Visual Basic products such as Visual Basic for Applications and VBScript (for Internet and Microsoft Outlook scripting). Good luck!

The following is what you've learned in this chapter:

- ActiveX and OLE controls. There is very little difference between OLE controls (OCXs) and ActiveX controls. ActiveX controls are an extension of the OLE specification. You can be confident that these terms will be used interchangeably.

- Creating an ActiveX control. Visual Basic is an outstanding development environment for ActiveX controls. You can use the skills you've acquired learning Visual Basic to create Internet solutions.

- Using an ActiveX control. You have used the ActiveX control you created in Excel. Not only did you insert the control onto the spreadsheet using the control toolbox, but you also accessed it with the `CreateObject()` method. Creating an instance of your object allowed you to call one of the methods you created in the control.

- Creating **CAB** files. Using the Application Setup Wizard, you created a cabinet file for distribution over the Internet. Your control and all the controls that it uses can be contained within the **CAB** file.

Using Commercial Components

- Evaluating the maker of the control
- Where to get recommendations
- Royalty fees
- Two types of OCX controls

One reason that Visual Basic is popular in the developer community is the wide variety of commercially available ActiveX controls. Controls are available to do 3-D object rendering, accounting, source code control, real-time data acquisition, user interface effects, multimedia design, modem communication, and functions for a slew of other fields. Purchasing and using controls is one of the simplest and most effective ways of expanding the abilities of your programs.

Although using controls may seem as simple as buying the ones with the features you want, you should invest considerable thought into a control before making it a cornerstone of your application. What if the vendor goes out of business? What if the control has a bug? These problems and others should be considered before the purchase. We have included a number of guidelines to help you decide which controls to buy, and we recommend that you review them before you buy a component.

THINK ABOUT THE COMPANY BEFORE YOU BUY

The company that supplies the control will be your lifeline to its promised capabilities. When you write your own code, you can control any problems that arise by fixing the problem. When you purchase commercial components, much of this control is out of your hands.

For this reason, make sure you consider the maker of the control before you purchase it. How long has the company been in business? Does it have one or a number of products? Is it responsive to users' problems? Does it subject its products to substantial testing before releasing them?

The more of these questions you can answer before purchase, the better off you will be. It isn't that answers to these questions must make or break your decision to purchase. Use common sense. How critical is the control to your project? If you have problems, will the vendor fix them in a timely manner? If the vendor does not provide the support you need, is there a control with similar features that you could switch to?

We don't want to scare you away from using controls. In fact, we don't believe you can undertake a project of significant scope without using vendor controls. You cannot possibly program and debug the number of features available from a commercial control without using excessive resources and time. By using commercial controls, you can give your program functionality that approaches that of applications created by large companies at a cost of hundreds of thousands of dollars.

We simply recommend that you minimize your risk in using commercial components by first analyzing which factors aren't within your power to control. The best way to make sure you get good controls is to obtain recommendations from others who have created applications with them. There are several places to get such advice.

GET RECOMMENDATIONS FROM OTHER USERS

Recommendations are the best way to select a control. Find someone who has used a control in the feature area that you need. Quite possibly, he or she will have tried a few controls before settling on one and can tell you the benefits and drawbacks of the controls.

Inevitably, no control will have all the features you desire. Experienced users of the control can tell you what it lacks and how they worked around it. Other users can explain novel ways to stretch the capabilities of some components.

The other vital resource is sample source code. Learning to use a new control can often be a lengthy and frustrating experience. Any sample code that demonstrates the functions of the control is extremely useful in showing its potential and its limitations.

There are two primary places where you can conveniently meet your peers and obtain advice: user groups and Usenet news. The Web is also an excellent resource, but it is typically one-way. It's easy to obtain formatted information but difficult to ask your exact question.

Visit User Groups

Most cities have active user groups of Visual Basic programmers. User groups exchange information, provide a community for programmers, and often present examples of techniques and products. This interaction is invaluable to the beginning programmer. When you have trouble with something, user groups provide a forum in which to ask your question and likely have it answered by experienced users.

Questions may apply directly to a specific control. Whether you need a recommendation for a control that has a particular feature or are using a popular control, there will often be someone who knows the answer or knows where to find it.

Ask the Question on Usenet Newsgroups

The Internet has a form of online forums or user groups known as Usenet newsgroups. Both Netscape Navigator and Internet Explorer provide newsgroup readers that allow you to access Usenet through your Internet service provider.

The Visual Basic forums on Usenet are extremely active. If you have a question about a control, you can usually ask it here. You might post a message such as, "Can someone recommend the best ActiveX control for scientific calculation?" and within a day or two get a slew of responses.

CHECK FOR ROYALTIES OR LICENSING FEES

With most mainstream ActiveX controls, you simply purchase them and plug them into your project. You are free to ship the control itself, but there is often a design piece of the control (such as a license file) that you cannot ship with your application. This arrangement allows a user of your application to execute your program but not to load Visual Basic or another environment and use the control without purchasing it.

Other companies charge royalty fees for each copy that you distribute. They might also charge for every user machine that the program is installed on (called a *per seat* charge). For example, to allow 10 users to use a program that contains a certain control, you might have to purchase a 10-seat license.

Often, the controls that require these redistribution fees are worth the price. They usually are complex enough that it would take you thousands of hours to duplicate the functionality, assuming that you could duplicate it. There may also be a lesser charge for personal use compared with corporate deployment.

Check the licensing of a control before you purchase it. You don't want to build a product around a control that is too expensive to install where you want to. License fees may will also affect how a company can expand the use of the product. If a product were to cost a great deal per seat, it might seriously limit how quickly a company could grow.

ARE THE CONTROLS 16-BIT OR 32-BIT?

Before Windows 95 and Windows NT, all Microsoft operating systems were 16-bit. This includes Windows 3.1, Windows for Workgroups, and DOS. Windows 95 and Windows NT are true 32-bit operating systems. This means that they can use and process data faster on the current 32-bit microprocessors.

Visual Basic 4.0 was the last version of Visual Basic to allow you to create 16-bit applications. Therefore, all the programs you write in Visual Basic 5 will require at least Windows 95 or Windows NT. If you need to create applications for 16-bit operating systems, you will need to use version 4.0 or earlier versions of Visual Basic.

VBX controls, the original Visual Basic controls, are available only in 16-bit format. Therefore, VBXs cannot be used within Visual Basic 5. OCX controls come in either 16-bit or 32-bit versions. ActiveX controls are the same as 32-bit OCX controls. Visual Basic 5 cannot use the 16-bit OCX controls. Before you purchase a control, make sure it is available as a 32-bit OCX or ActiveX control.

Using the Debugger

- Setting breakpoints
- Adding watches to variables
- Using conditional stops

In the first few chapters, you used the Immediate window to test the values of particular variables. Using the Immediate window is the most rudimentary form of debugging your program. Most programming involves the process of trying something, executing it, looking for the reason it didn't work as planned, making a change, and testing again. Using trial-and-error methods in programming allows you to have fast failures and quickly find solutions to complex problems. This method works very effectively if you can diagnose the source of errors that occur.

If you were a doctor, diagnosing an illness would be difficult without the proper tools. Doctors have stethoscopes, MRIs, X rays, and other devices to track down a problem. Programmers need to examine variable values, set places where execution will halt so that pieces of the program can be examined, and run tests on the execution sequence of a program.

Visual Basic provides powerful debugging features that make finding errors fairly convenient (especially when compared with other programming systems). The best way to demonstrate the use of the debugger is to use it. To begin examining the debugging features included in Visual Basic, create a new project and place a command button on the form.

Insert the following code into the Click event of the command button:

```
Private Sub Command1_Click()
    ' Set up variable
    Dim i As Integer

    ' Cycle through loop and display a message box each time
    For i = 1 To 6
        MsgBox "The loop has been running for " & i & " time(s).",
vbInformation, "Number of cycles"
    Next i
End Sub
```

SETTING BREAKPOINTS

The most common way to analyze a problem routine is to watch the steps it takes during execution. Let's step through the loop we've just created to see it execute. First, we need to set a point where execution will stop. To do this, make the code window visible, showing the Click event for the command button. Notice the gray bar that runs along the left side of the window. Clicking in this area at the same horizontal level as a code line will set a breakpoint there.

Let's set a breakpoint so that we can examine execution of this routine. Click in the gray area at the same level as the For...Next line of our code. The line will immediately turn red, and a red circle will appear in the gray area, as shown in Figure B.1. Now when the code executes, the program halts at this point in the code. With the program execution halted, variables can be examined or even changed.

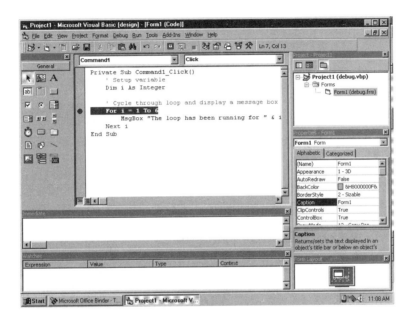

Figure B.1 *A breakpoint set at the For...Next line of the loop.*

Let's try running it now. Execute the program by pressing **F5**. Click on the command button. Program execution will halt, and you will be returned to the code window automatically. A yellow arrow will appear in the gray area to indicate where the current stop has occurred. We can now step through the code line by line. The Debug menu provides all the debugging commands that you need to manipulate the debugging environment. Most of them have shortcut access keys.

We will now step through the program to demonstrate individual line execution. Press the **F8** (**Step Into**) key. You will see the yellow arrow and the yellow line highlighting advance to the next line. Using the step commands, you can execute your program code a single line at a time.

As the program executes, functions are run and variables are modified. Let's take a look at one of the variables and observe how it changes as execution progresses. Type the following code into the Immediate window:

```
Print i
1
|
```

You can see that the variable I is currently set to 1. Press **F8** again to make another step, and the message box will be displayed. Click **OK** and press **F8** once again. The yellow arrow will return to the message box line for the second cycle in the loop. If you print the value of the variable i, you'll find that it is now set to 2. If you have more than one variable or you need to step through a loop many times, using the **Print** command can quickly become tedious. Rather than print the variables each time, there is an easier way.

ADDING WATCHES TO VARIABLES

We can use the Immediate window to examine values of a variables. However, what if you need to check the values of several variables every time a cycle is made through the loop? You can use the Watch window, where the values of selected variables are displayed automatically.

Select the **Watch Window** option under the View menu. The Watch window will appear directly under the Immediate window. We already have a program executing, so let's add a variable watch to the current variable. To do this, select the variable i anywhere in the code window. Under the Debug menu, select **Add Watch**.

The Watch dialog box will appear. All the options that we want are automatically set, so click **OK**. You will now see the variable i in the Watch window along with its current value and context (as shown in Figure B.2). Try using the **F8** key to step through the loop a couple of times. You will see the value of the variable increase with each execution.

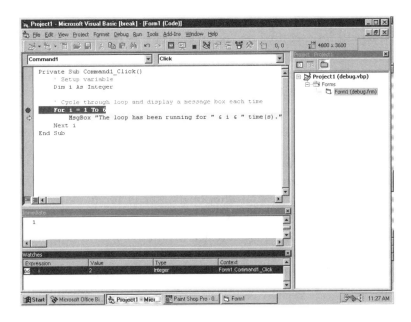

Figure B.2 *The variable* i *has been added to the Watch window and currently displays the value 2.*

You can add numerous variables to the Watch window to check their values every time a breakpoint occurs. Often, this is the easiest way to spot execution errors. Stepping through the code is a method you will use often, but there are many times when you need to execute to a certain point and then halt.

Using Conditional Stops

Not only can you examine variables individually, but you also can halt the execution of the program when a variable reaches a certain value. For example, if the program typically has problems after it has executed 5000 cycles through a loop that has 10,000 total cycles, watching the loop by hand would be tedious or impossible. In Visual Basic, you can set the program to break when a variable reaches a particular value.

Let's stop the program that is currently executing. Select **End** from the Run menu. The code window of the event is once again displayed. To remove the breakpoint we set previously, click on the red circle in the gray column. The circle and the red highlighting of the line will disappear.

Now we want to set a conditional breakpoint based on the value of a variable. In this case, let's set the breakpoint to occur when the variable i reaches a value of 3. Select the **Add Watch** option on the Debug menu. This time we will enter an expression rather than a variable name. Type the following into the expression text box:

```
i = 3
```

For the **Watch Type** option, select **Break When Value is True**. This will halt execution when the expression is set to True. Click **OK** to accept the watch command. You will notice that another line has been added to the Watch window showing the conditional stop we've just created.

Execute the program using **F5**. Click on the command button to begin execution of the code. After you have dismissed two of the message boxes, program execution will halt. You can see in the Watch window that the value of i is indeed set to 3. With execution stopped, you could examine other variables or begin stepping through the application.

You should now have a good idea of how to use the debugger to find errors. When an actual execution error occurs, you are automatically taken to the line where the error occurred. You can use the debugger to examine how your program is executing in order to make sure it is executing the functions you need.

GLOSSARY

Programming Terms

API

Application Programming Interface. Microsoft Windows has a number of subroutines and functions that you can call from within your Visual Basic programs by using `Declare` to define the calls. These functions and subroutines are often called API calls. You can use calls to API functions and subroutines to extend your Visual Basic programs. Chapter 15 of this book contains some examples of using APIs.

Argument

A value or special keyword used to supply information to a command or event handler. Arguments for event handlers can have three parts: the argument name, followed by the keyword `AS`, followed by a variable type.

Arrays

A collection of controls or variables that share the same name. You refer to a specific control or variable within an array by providing an index in parentheses, such as lines(10). For control arrays, the index must match the index number you assigned to an element in the array. For variable arrays, the index is the "number" of the variable, starting with 1 for the first element (unless you use the To keyword to set a lower and upper limit for the index values). You use the Dim or Global keyword to define variable arrays.

ASCII

A standard that defines how numeric values are assigned to characters inside a computer. The ASCII standard defines which numbers will be assigned to all the characters on a U.S. keyboard and assigns the numbers 32 through 127 to these characters. Other characters, such as ü are assigned numbers in the extended ASCII set (above 127 or below 32).

Assignment operator

The equal sign is an assignment operator. It is used to assign a value to a variable.

Boolean

A number that has only two values: True or False, where False is 0, and True is 1 or any other number other than 0. Boolean expressions always return a 0 or 1, but commands such as If..Then..Else that use Boolean expressions treat all numbers except 0 as True and treat 0 as False. Boolean expressions always return an Integer value.

Boolean operators

Boolean expressions use Boolean operators: equal to, not equal, less than, greater than, less than or equal to, greater than or equal to, not, or, Xor, equivalent, implication.

Boundary conditions	Special cases that may require you to handle a programming situation differently. For example, you may have code that erases a previous object from a form, but you won't want to call that code the first time you open the form because there will be nothing there to erase.
Break mode	One of three modes in Visual Basic. The other modes are Run and Design. In Break mode, you've temporarily halted a program you're running inside Visual Basic by pressing **Ctrl+Break** or selecting the **Break** from the Run menu. Whenever you're in Break mode, you can use the Immediate window either to run commands or to see the values assigned to variables.
Breakpoint	A line of code that you mark to tell Visual Basic to stop running your program (and enter break mode) whenever it tries to run the specified line (i.e., reaches the breakpoint). You can designate multiple breakpoints. Useful for debugging.
Bug	Some type of failure in a computer program. If your program is not doing what it's supposed to do, it has a bug. Debugging is the process of locating and solving the problem.
Code window	The window where you place your Basic code. Double-click on a form or object to bring up the corresponding code window.
Combo Box	A standard Windows control, usually a text box with a down-pointing arrow on the right side. When you click on this arrow, you can select from the list of choices that appears.

Command	Visual Basic has a number of built-in commands, such as **Beep**, that you can use in your programs to tell Visual Basic which function to perform. *See also:* statement. The words *command, statement, instruction,* and *code* are sometimes used interchangeably by programmers.
Condition	Another word for a Boolean expression, which returns a True (1) or False (0) as an number. The term *condition* is generally used when you have a Boolean expression in an If..Then statement. Conditions always return an Integer value.
Control	A special type of object that appears inside a form (even if the control is not visible at run-time). The toolbox window contains icons representing the available control types.
Control array	Multiple controls with the same name, distinguished by an index number that follows the control name in parentheses.
Currency	A type of number that is useful for currency values. Visual Basic defines five different types of numbers: Integer, Long, Single, Double, and Currency. The Currency type provides highly accurate calculations for larger currency numbers, and has a range of $-922,337,203,685,447.5808$ to $922,337,203,685,447.5807$ (almost 1000 trillion). Each Currency value uses eight bytes of memory.
Debug (Immediate) window	A Visual Basic window that allows you to run individual commands immediately by typing in the command and pressing **Enter**. This is useful for checking code, determining values of a variable, and other debugging activities.

Design mode

One of three modes in Visual Basic. The other modes are Run and Break. You'll use Design mode to create programs. The other two modes appear when you run a program you created in Design mode.

Design time

Some properties are available only when you're in Design mode, writing your program. For example, the Name property is available only in Design mode. In other words, you can't obtain the Name of a control while your program is running. There are also properties that are available only at run time.

DLL

Dynamic Link Library. Microsoft Windows allows you to write subroutines and functions in many programming languages that you can use directly from Visual Basic or other programming languages. These code modules are loaded into memory whenever they're needed. As it turns out, most of Windows itself is built from DLLs. You can use calls to DLL functions and subroutines to extend you Visual Basic programs. Using DLL calls is explained in Chapter 15.

Double

A type of number that can represent numbers with decimal points. Visual Basic defines five different types of numbers: Integer, Long, Single, Double, and Currency. The Double type uses *floating-point* calculations, which are slower than Integer or Long calculations. But Double values can be any numbers between -1.8×10^{308} and 1.8×10^{308}. They can also represent very small fractions, as small as 4.9×10^{-324}. Each Double value uses eight bytes of memory.

dpi	Dots Per Inch. dpi refers to the density of dots on your screen or printer. Many laser printers print images at 300 dpi (although some newer laser printers use 600 dpi), whereas a VGA screen is defined to have 96 dpi. The lower the dot density, the coarser the image will be. This is why printed output tends to look much better than what you see on your screen.
Dynamic array	One that can change size while your program is running. Instead of declaring the array size with the `DIM` statement, the size is omitted. Later you set the size using a `REDIM` statement.
Element	A single item or instance in an array.
Event	Windows defines a number of events that Visual Basic supports, including `Click`, `DblClick`, `MouseMove`, and `KeyPress`. You can write code to handle any of these events using event handlers.
Event handler	A subroutine that handles a type of Windows event. Controls and forms can handle a number of events, such as mouse clicks, mouse moves, and key presses. *See also* subroutine, function.
Extended ASCII characters	Special characters such as the paragraph mark (¶) and foreign-language characters such as ü are defined as extended ASCII characters. They are represented by numbers outside the standard range of 32 and 127. *See also* ASCII.
False	A number, 0, returned by a Boolean expression (condition). Any condition expression you write, such as 1=0, returns either True (1) or False (0).

Flag	A variable that is used as a Boolean value (either true or false) is often called a flag. Because the flag can be either True or False, you can think of it as being either raised (True) or lowered (False).
Floating-point numbers	Any number with something after the decimal point. For example, 1.1 and 3.14159 are floating-point numbers.
Focus	Refers to which control has the keyboard's focus of attention. The control object that is current or active is the one that has the focus. In a window full of text boxes, it would be the box where the cursor was. The focus can be moved with the **Tab** key (in most Windows programs) as well as with the mouse.
Form	According to Microsoft, "a window or dialog box that you create with Visual Basic."
Form variables	Any variable defined in the (**General**) area of a form and available throughout the form.
Function	A piece of code, such as a subroutine, that returns a value, such as a number or a string. Functions start with `Function Name As Type` and end with `End Function`. You can create a new function using the **Add Procedure** menu item in the Tools menu when you have a code window active. *See also* event handler, subroutine.
Handler	*See* event handler.
Instruction	A command or statement that you write in Basic. The words *instruction, statement, command,* and *code* are sometimes used interchangeably by programmers.

Integer

A type of number that can hold only whole numbers. Visual Basic defines five different types of numbers: Integer, Long, Single, Double, and Currency. The Integer type is the smallest and fastest type of number to work with and has a range of –32,768 to 32,767. Each Integer value uses two bytes of memory.

Long

A type of number that can hold only whole numbers. Visual Basic defines five different types of numbers: Integer, Long, Single, Double, and Currency. The Long type is a little larger than an Integer, and calculations using Longs are slower than those using Integers. But Longs allow you to work with whole numbers larger than Integers, with a range of –2,147,483,648 to 2,147,483,647. Each Long value uses four bytes of memory.

Method

An action that can be performed on an object. For example, the code `myCombo.AddItem "Red"` uses the `AddItem` method to add an item called "`Red`" to the `myCombo` object.

Modal form

A form that always stays in front of the main window until you click on one of its buttons to indicate an action. Any attempt to perform an action outside a modal form (such as click on a different window) will be refused. Modal forms do not have resizable borders, minimize or maximize buttons, or control menus.

Modular design

The modular approach to designing programs involves dividing the code into logical, self-contained modules, with connections to other modules that are as simple as possible.

Module	A file that contains nothing but code. You can include one or more modules in a project.
Modulo	A mathematical operation that calculates the remainder of a division.
Passing by reference	Passing a reference to a variable rather than a copy of the variable's data. If a subroutine alters a variable that was passed by reference, the actual variable's value will be changed.
Passing by value	Sending a copy of a variable to a subroutine so that when the subroutine alters that variable, the original variable is not changed; only the copy contains the change. Requires use of the `ByVal` keyword.
Project	A project file is a special file (with the **.VBP** extension) that tells Visual Basic which forms (**.FRM** files), modules (**.BAS** files), and custom controls (**.OCX** files) belong to a program you're working on. You work with projects using the project window in Visual Basic.
Project window	The window providing access to the forms, modules, and custom control files that are associated with a project.
Properties window	A window containing the properties of a form or control object. You select the form or control and then press **F4** to bring the Properties window to the front. With the exception of those properties that can be set only at run time, you can use this window to set the values for all other properties.

Property	A special type of Visual Basic variable that describes an appearance or behavioral characteristic of an object . When you click on an object in Design mode, that object's properties are shown in the Properties window.
Pseudocode	Code-like wording to indicate programming logic that will be used. Pseudocode is not meant to be syntactically correct and often omits the actual keywords, opting instead for standard verbs.
Random access	A technique for reading and writing disk files that allows you to treat the file as if it contained an array of records.
Record	Each item in a random-access data file. A record is similar in idea to the elements of an array. One record, for example, could be a single name and address (along with phone numbers).
Run mode	One of three modes in Visual Basic. The other modes are Design and Break. Visual Basic displays [run] in its caption whenever your Visual Basic program is running. You can enter Design mode by pressing **Ctrl+Break**, which allows you to display the values currently assigned to variables. Pressing **F5** while in Break mode will take you back to run mode.
Run time	Some properties are available only when you're running your program (in Run mode). For example, the CurrentX and CurrentY properties are available only while your program is running. In other words, you can't set the CurrentX and CurrentY properties when you're designing your programs. Other properties are available only at design time.

Single	A type of number that can represent numbers with decimal points. Visual Basic defines five different types of numbers: Integer, Long, Single, Double, and Currency. The Single type uses *floating-point* calculations, which are slower than Integer or Long calculations. But Single values can be any numbers between -3.4×10^{38} and 3.4×10^{38}. They can also represent very small fractions, such as 1.4×10^{-45}. Each Single value uses four bytes of memory.
Statement	A single line in a Visual Basic program. Statements may include commands, such as **Beep**, or they may provide information to Visual Basic, such as the `End Sub` statement in a subroutine. The words *statement, instruction, command,* and *code* are sometimes used interchangeably by programmers.
Step, stepping through	Running your program one line at a time. Useful for debugging.
Strings	Characters that you work with in Basic. You can use any character inside a string, but the string must be enclosed between quotation marks. If you wish to use a quotation mark as part of a string, type the quotation mark character twice.
Subroutine	A piece of code that has a name and can be run from other parts of a program. All subroutines start with `Sub Name` and end with `End Sub`. Visual Basic provides event handlers, which are predefined subroutines, and you can also create your own using the **Add Procedure** menu item in the Tools menu when you have a code window active. *See also* function, event handler.

Toolbox	The name of a window that contains the available controls. There are 23 controls in the standard edition of Visual Basic 5. When you incorporate controls from third-party vendors, they, too, will appear in the toolbox window.
True	A number, 1, returned by a Boolean expression (condition). Any condition expression you write, such as 1=0, returns either True (1) or False (0).
Twip	A unit of measurement created by Microsoft. It means "twentieth of a point." A point measures 1/72 of an inch, so a twip is equal to 1/1440 inch.
User-defined type	A compound variable that you define using the `Type` command. *Compound* refers to the combination of multiple variables of different types into a single variable.
Values able.	The actual numbers or strings in a vari-
Variables	A place where you can store numbers or strings of characters. Variables are stored in memory. Variable names must begin with a letter and can be as many as 40 characters long.
Variable array	A group of variables with the same name, distinguished from one another by an index number that follows the variable name in parentheses. Each individual variable in the array is called an *element*.

INDEX

... (ellipsis), 14

' (apostrophe), *See* Comments

! (exclamation field access), 271

!, 130

#, 130

$, 129-130

%, 130

%, 47-48

& (ampersand character), 130

() (parentheses), 20

* (multiplication operator) , 16, 19

* (SQL wildcard character), *See* Wildcard character

+ (addition operator) , 16, 19

- (subtraction operator), 16, 19

. (dot command), *see* Dot command

/ (division operator) , 16, 19

: (colon), 140

; (semicolon), 270

= (equal sign), 40

= command, 41

? (print command), 176

@, 130

[] (brackets), 13

\ (integer division operator) , 16, 19

^ (exponentiation operator) , 16, 19

{} (braces), 13

16-bit Access files, *See* Access 2.0 files

32-bit controls, *See* Windows Common Controls

Multiple commands on a line, *See* : (colon)

A

Access 2.0 files, 311

Access 97 format, 218

Access format Version 3.0, 224

ActiveSheet property, 73, 314

ActiveX Container environment, 326

ActiveX Control Pad, 335

ActiveX controls, 316, 341-345

  32-bit OCX, 345

  Creating, 323-340

  Distribution, *See* CAB file

  Inserting on a form, 280

  Installation, *See* Installation, Disks

  Internet, using, 335-336

  List Box,

  Objects, 67

  Royalties and licensing fees, 344

  Toolbox, *See* Toolbox

ActiveX folder, 327

Add Index dialog box

Add method, 307

Add Procedure command, 327, 359, 363

Add Procedure, 261

Add User Control command, 162, 277

Add Watch command, 350

Adding fields to a database, 226-228

Adding items to a grid, *See* Grid control

Adding menu code, 111-113

AddItem method, 246-247

  Grid, 301

additive colors

AddNew method, 251

Add-ons, 78

Address Book

  Adding Clock user control, *See* Clock user control

  Data, viewing, 299

  Feature list, 208-209

  Field list, 223-224

  Installation, *See* Installation, Disks

  MDB installation, 312

  searching, *See* Searching a database

Address.MDB, 224, 234, 300

Addresses table, 223-224

Alert box, 7-8

Algebra, 18

Alpha testing, 211-213

Alphabetic properties, 238

API, 353

Appearance property, 37, 180

Application Programming Interface, *See* API

Application Setup Wizard, CAB file, *See* CAB file

Application Setup Wizard, *See* Installation, Disks

Application, 24

Argument, 353

Arguments, 11-12, 14-15, 116-117

  Passing by reference, 361

Passing by value, 361

Array
  Bounds, 154
  Control, 114-115
  Dynamic, 154
  Element, 128, 358
  Erasing, 154
  Index, 127-129
  Lower index, 154
  Saving, 125-153
  Slots, 127
  Storage, *See* Files, Random Access
  Variables, 127-130, 354, 364

As keyword, 116, 353

ASCII, 354
  Extended ASCII characters, 358

Assignment operator, 354

Assignment operator (=), 42

AT command, 297

Attention, modem, *See* AT command

AutoIncrement field, 226, *See* UniqueID field

Automatic additions of controls, 38

Automatic DragMode, 281

Automatic saving of project, 248

Automation, OLE, *See* OLE Automation

Available Fields, in Data Form Designer, 234

B

Background Color, 35-36

BAS, *See* Module

Basic, 10

Beep command, 7, 33, 37, 55-58, 172, 264, 363

Beta testing, 211-213

Blank menu lines, 113

Blueprint, *See* Class, object

BMP files, 291

BOF method, 251-252

Bookmark property, 266

Bookmark, database 264

Boole, George, 97

Boolean operators, 354, 356

Boolean, 95-100, 354, 356, 358, 364

BorderStyle property, 259

Bound controls, 238-240

Boundary conditions, 190-191, 355

Bounds of arrays, *See* Array bounds

Break command, 5

Break mode, 9, 355

Break When Value is True, 352

Breakpoint, 355

Breakpoints, *See* Debugging

Browser, object, 78, *See* Object browser

Browsers, Web, 336

Bug, 355

Bug, origin of, 212-213

Building a form from a database, 235-237

Building the table, 227

Building with objects, *See* Objects, building

Button property, 88, 90

Button.vbp, 70

Bytes, 51

ByVal, 318-319, 361

   See Arguments, Passing

C

C Data types, 318

C/C++, 4

CAB file, 337-339

Cabinet file, *See* CAB file

Calculator functions, 16-17

Call command, 57

Calling a procedure, 57

CancelError property, 273

Caption property, 29-30

Caption, changing, 168

Carl and Gary's Web site, 339

Carriage return, to modem, 297-298

Cartesian coordinates, 181

Case sensitivity, 7

Categorized properties, 238

CBool command, 59

CByte command, 59

CCur command, 58

CDate command, 59

CDbl command, 58

Cells, setting values, 332-333

Change event, 283

Chart control, 294-296

Charttype property, 295

Checked property, 117-120

Checking menu items, *See* Menu items, check/uncheck

Choosing a control, 342

Choosing an event, *See* Event selection

CInt command, 58, 97

Class ID, object, 335

Class, object, 68-69

Clear method, 301

Clear screen, *See* Cls command

Clearing arrays, *See* Arrays, erasing

Click event handler, 35, 82, 117

Client/Server Central, 339, 340

CLng command, 58

Clock control, 159-196, 325

  CTX and CTL, 276

  ICO, 180

  Modifying, 277-279

  User control, 275-284

Clock, system, reading, 168-169

Close and Return to Microsoft Excel, 333

Cls command, 112-113, 184

Code modules, *See* DLL

Code window, 355

Code, 4, 55, 356
  Module, *See* Module
Code, menu, 111
Code-as-you-go design, 200-201
CollatingOrder property, 220-221
Collections, objects, *See* Object collections
Color combination, 187-188
Color drawing, 184-185
Color palette common dialog, 291
Color property, 292
Color, 35-36
Column in database, *See* Field
ColumnCount property, 295
ColumnLabel property, 295
COM1 port, 297
Combining strings, *See* Concatenation, strings
Combo box control, 244-248, *See* Controls, Combo Box
Combo boxes, on code window, 131-132
COMDLG32.OCX, 311
Comm control, 297-298
Comma, 12
Command button control, 26-30
Command button, Excel, 330
Command, 4, 356
Comment, 34, 119
Common Controls, *See* Windows Common Controls

Common Dialog control, 269, 291-294
Common Dialog control, missing feature, 259
Common Dialog, install, 311
CommPort property, 297
Companies, ActiveX, 342
Compiling options, 150
Compiling Sketch, 150
Compiling, *See* Run time
Completed specification design, 200-201
Complex equations, 18-20
Components menu item, 316
Components window, 292
Components, 288, *See* ActiveX controls
Compound, *See* Type command
Compressed file, *See* CAB file
Compression, installation, *See* Installation
Concatenation, strings, 46
Condition, 95-98, 356
Connect property, 220,222
Consistency in program design, 204-205
Const keyword, 183
Container application, 328
Context menus, *See* Menus, Pop-up
Control array, 114-115, 119, 245-248, 282-283, 354, 356
Control focus, *See* Focus

Control modification, 166

Control names, 109

Control Pad, *See* ActiveX Control Pad

Control properties, *See* Window, Properties

Control Toolbox, Excel, 328

ControlBox property, 254, 259

Controlling an application, *See* OLE Automation

Controls folder, 276

Controls, 25-26, 356

Accessing from code, 331

Combo Box, 355

Objects, 65

Converting data types, *See* Data Types, converting

Copies, installation, *See* Installation, Disk images

Copy, files, 276

Copying user interface elements, 203-204

Cos command, 183, 193, 195, 197

Cosine, *See* Cos command

Counter field, *See* UniqueID field

Create New Folder, 94

CreateObject command, 313, 331, 340

Creating a new database, 224-229

Creating a new table 226-227

Creating an instance, 70-73

Creating installation disks, *See* Installation, Disks

Criteria, search, 265

CSgn command, 58

CStr command, 59

Ctrl+Break, 43

Ctrl+E keys, *See* Menu Editor

CurDateTime user property, 278-279

Currency, *See* Data Types, Currency

CurrentX property, 92-93, 102, 138

CurrentY property, 92-93, 102, 138

Cursor focus, *See* Focus

Custom controls, *See* ActiveX controls

Custom properties, 304

Cut, Copy, Paste code, 252-253

Cvar command, 59

Cycles, 350

D

DAO, 220

Installation, 310

Data Access Objects, *See* DAO

Data aware control, *See* Bound controls

Data bound grid, *See* Grid control

Data control, 218, 237-239

Data Form Designer, 234-237

Data Manager, *See* Visual Data Manager

Data property, 296

Data storage, *See* Files

Data Types
  Boolean, 50, *See* Boolean
  Byte, 50
  Checking, 60
  Converting, 58-59
  Currency, 50, 356
  Date, 50
  Double, 50, 356, 357
  Integer, 50, 51-53, 356, 360
  Long, 50, 356, 360
  Object, 50
  Single, 50, 356, 363
  Strings, 50, 59, 363
  Translating between C and VB, 318-319
Data1, 239-240, 300
Database control buttons, 230
Database file, 217-222
Database security, 224-225
Database structure, 219
Databasename property, 239, 300
DataField property, 239-240, 248
DataSource property, 239-240, 248, 300
Date$ command, 197
DateSerial command, 197
DateValue command, 197
Day command, 197
DBase file format, 218
Debugging, 347-352
  Break command, 5

Breakpoints, 348
  Conditional, 351
  Stepping into, 363
  Variable Watches, Adding, 350
  Window, *See* Immediate Window
Declarations, general, *See* General declarations
Declare command, 317-320, 320, 353
Decompression, installation, *See* Installation
Delimiters, 12
Design mode, 8-9, 357
Design mode, Excel, 330
Design of Everyday Things, 214
Design time, 357
Designing Icon Clock, 160-167
Detail specification design, 200-201
Development environment, *See* IDE
Diagnosing, errors, *See* Debugging
Dialog, modal, *See* Modal form
Dim command, 128, 131-133
Dim command, 358
Disk images, installation, *See* Installation
Display routines, *See* Windows API
Displaying
  Numbers and strings, *See* Print command
Division by zero error, 54
DLL, 316-320, 357
DoEvents command, 298, 305
DOS, 345

Dot (.) command, 66, 68, 73, 119

Dots-per-inch, *See* DPI

Double, *See* Data Types, Double

Double-clicking, 37

DPI, 358

Drag and drop support, 280-284

Drag method, 281

DragDrop event, 283

DragIcon property, 283

DragMode property, 280-281

Drawing in color, 184-185

Drawing the clock hands, 180-186

DrawMode property, 185-190

DrawWidth property, 117-118, 149

Drive list, 290

DriveListBox, 288, 290-291

Drop support, *See* Drag and Drop

Drop-down list, *See* Combo Box control

Dynamic Array, *See* Dim command, *See* Arrays, dynamic

Dynamic Link Library, *See* DLL

E

E+12, *See* Scientific notation

Edit method, 283

Editing menus, *See* Menu Editor

Element, Array, 358, 364

Elements of array, *See* Array elements

Else keyword, 98-99

Embedding an ActiveX control in HTML, 335

End button, 32

End command, 8-9, 42, 351

EndDoc command, 149, 272

English language, 13

Entering data, 229-230

EOF marker, 229

EOF method, 250-252

Equal, 42

Equivalent, 354

Erase menu item, 112

Erasing arrays, *See* Arrays, erasing

Erector set, 64

Errors, 7-8

Event code, writing, 88-90

Event handler, 32-37, 82-84, 358, 359

Event model, 84

Event selection, 87-88

Event, 358

  Click, 35, 117

  KeyPress, 84

  MouseDown, 101-102, 133-135

  MouseMove, 87-88, 133-135

  MouseUp, 121

Event-driven programs, 84-85

Evolutionary program design, 201-202

Excel automation, *See* OLE Automation

Excel container application, 328

Excel object model, 315

EXE program, 24, 150, *See* Installation, Disks

Executing Visual Basic, 2

Existing tab, 277

Exit
Command, 204
Current program, 8-9, 42, 351
Menu item, 109-111
Visual Basic, 3

Exp command, 22

Exponentation, 18, *See* Exp command

Exposing a property, *See* Public variable

Exposing user controls in project, 278

Expression, 13-15

Extended ASCII characters, *See* ASCII

F

F2 key, *See* Browser, object

F4 key, *See* Properties window

F5 key, *See* Start button

False command, 95-100,m354, 356, 358

FAQ, Visual Basic, 339

Feature list, program, 207-209

Fees, *See* ActiveX controls

Field object, 221

Fields and records view of database, 220

Fields, 219

File dialog, 290

File formats, CAB, *See* CAB file

File lists, 290

File Summary screen, installation, 311

File Summary, for installation, 338

FileListBox, 288, 290-291

Filename property, 293

Files
Random Access, *See* Random Access Record, 362

Filter property, 229, 293-294

FindFirst method, 266

FindNext method, 265-266

Fix command, 59

FixedCols property, 301

FixedRows property, 301

Flag, 359

Flags property, 294

Flexgrid, *See* Grid control

Floating Point numbers, 359
Double, *See* Data Types, Double
Single, *See* Data Types, Single

Floating-point numbers, 49

Floppy disk, installation, *See* Installation, Disks

Focus, 243, 359

Font command button, 303

Font common dialog, 291, 293

Font error, 294

Font object, 35, 254

Fonts, multiple, *See* RichTextBox control

FontSize property, 293

For...Next command, 137, 139-141, 154, 247

Foreign characters, *See* ASCII, Extended

Form Layout, 37

Form variables, 359

Form, 3, 359

Form, removal, 237

Format$ command, 175-176, 196

Format, Format$ command, 21

FormatString method, 301

Form-level variables, 133, 192

FORTRAN, 140

FoxPro DBF, installation, 310

Frame control, 288-290

FRM file type, 94

FRM, *See* Form

FromPage property, 270

FrontPage, Microsoft, 335

Function, 55, 57, 359

G

General declarations, 131-132, 262

GetString command, 261, 263

Girders, 64

Gold master, 212

Good user interface design, 213

Graphing, *See* Chart control

Grid control
  Data bound grid, 299-300
  Flexgrid control, 300-301

Grouping controls, 288, *See* Tabbed Dialog control

H

Handler, *See* Event Handler

Handles, 28, 163

Height property, 242

Help common dialog, 291, 293

Help, 135

HelpCommand property, 293

HelpFile property, 293

Hierarchical display, *See* TreeView control

Homogenous grid, 301

Hour command, 175

House, as object, *See* Class, object

HTML code, 335

I

I Variable, 140

Icon, application, 179-180

IDE, 3, 24

If...Then statement, 134

If...Then commands, 90-91, 95-97

ImageList control, *See* Windows Common Controls

Immediate window, 4-10, 40, 95-98, 347, 356

Immediate window, displaying time, 175

Immediate window, setting a caption, 168

InBufferCount property, 298

Included Fields, in Data Form Designer, 234

Index property, 114-115, 283

Index, adding, 228

Indexed array, 356

Indexed fields, 228

Indexes, 222-223

Information Hiding, 68, 75-76

Inhouse testing, *See* Alpha testing

Initialize event handler, 192

InputLen property, 297

Inserting an ActiveX control, 280

Inserting menu items, *See* Menu items, inserting

Installation template, *See* Template, install

Installation
  Compression, 312
  Decompression, 312
  Disk images, 312

Installation
  Disks, 309, 310-312
  Visual Basic, 2

Instances, 68-69
  Creating, 70-73

Multiple, 161,166-167
  of Clock, 280

Instantiation, 69

InStr$ command,59

Instruction, 4, 356, 359

Int command, 59

Integer division operator, 17

Integer, 58, *See* Data Types

Integrated Develop Environment, *See* IDE

Internal pointer, for index, 222

Internet control, *See* ActiveX controls

Internet Download Setup, 338

Internet Explorer, 336

Interpretor, *See* Run Time

Interval property, 172

Intrinsic controls, 288, 325

Inverting screen dots, 185-186

Invisible controls, Timer, 171

IsArray command, 60

IsDate command, 60

IsEmpty command, 60

IsError command, 60

IsMissing command, 60

IsNull command, 60

IsNumeric command, 60

IsObject command, 60

J

Jet 2.x, installation, 311

K

Key values, 307

Key values, *See* ASCII

KeyPress event handler, 84

Keyword, 13

L

Laser printers, 149

LCase$ command, 59

Left property, 242

Left$ command, 59

Legend, for chart control, *See* ShowLegend property

Len command, 59

Libraries, Dynamic Link, *See* DLL

Libraries, object, 315

Licensing fees, *See* ActiveX controls

Like SQL keyword, 261, 263

Line command, 86, 89-90, 184, 193, 316

Line thickness, *See* Line width

Line width, 115-117, 146-147, 149

Lines, menu, 113

List Box control, drag and drop, 281

List Box, *See* Controls, List Box

ListCount method, 253

ListView control, *See* Windows Common Controls

Load event, 247, 260, 263

LoadPicture command, 291

Loop, 154-156

Do...Loop, 155

For...Next, 139-141, 154, *See* For...Next

While...Wend, 155-156

LTrim$ command, 59

M

Macro submenu, 315

Main window caption, *See* Modes

Make EXE options, 150

Making an EXE, Sketch, 150

Managing program development, 201

Masks, draw mode, 187-188

Matching Parentheses, *See* Parentheses

Max property, 305

MDIForm, 83

Me keyword, 36

Member of collection, *See* Object collections

Members of a class, 315

Memory
    Variables, *See* Variables

Menu code, 250-253

Menu control arrays, 114-115

Menu Editor, 106-110

Menu Editor, saving work, 110

Menu items, check/uncheck, 117-120

Menu lines, 113

Menubar, 105

Menubar, creating, 249-253

Menus items, inserting, 113

Menus, Pop-up, 120-122

Merge, draw mode, 187

Message Box, *See* MsgBox

Message.htm, 335-336

Method, 55, 66-68, 360

  Public, 327

Microsoft design, 214

Mid$ command, 59

Millisecond, timing, 172

Min property, 305

MinButton property, 254

Minimize button, 136, 167

Minimize operation steps, *See*
  Process flow

Minute command, 175,182

Mnemonic access, 107-108

Mod command, 17-18

Modal form, 258-260, 360

Modem application, *See* Comm control

Modes, *See* Break mode, *See* Design
  mode, *See* Run mode

Modular design, 360

Module, 361

Module-level variables, 133

Modulo operation, 18, 361

Month command, 197

MouseDown event handler, 101-102,
  133-135

MouseMove event handler, 87-88,
  133-135

MousePointer property, 266, 313

MouseUp event handler, 121

MoveFirst method, 270, 272

MoveNext method, 251, 257, 272

MovePrevious method, 251, 257

MsgBox command, 33, 82, 306

Multiple font editing, *See*
  RichTextBox control

Multiple instances, *See* Instances,
  multiple

Multiple variables, *See* Type command

Multiplication, large numbers, 53-5

N

N variable, 41

Name property, 28-29, 92

Naming a control, *See* Control names

Naming variables, *See* Variable, naming

Netscape Navigator, 336

Network install, *See* Installation,
  Disks

Network protocols, *See* Windows API

New database, 224-229

New folder, 31, 94, 276

New Form command, 70-72

New keyword, 71-72

New Project, Sketch, 86

New table, 226-227

News groups, *See* Usenet news

No Fonts Installed, 294

Node data type, 307

Nodes, *See* TreeView control

NoMatch property, 266

Non-intrinsic controls, Excel, 329

Non-visual controls, *See* ActiveX controls

Norman, Donald A., 214

Not command, 97-98, 354

Notepad, creating HTML file, 335

Notes field, 242, 273, 276, 280, 282-284

Nothing keyword, 77

Now command, 174-178, 279

Null pointer, 319

O

Object
Browser, 78, 315

Building, 74-75

Collections, 73-74

Definition, 64

Hierarchy, 65-66

Market for, 74

Model, 315

Programming, 63-77

Referencing 66-67, *See* Set command

Wrapper, 77

Object Oriented Programming, *See* OOP

OCX
16 and 32 bit, 345

See ActiveX controls

OK modem response, 298

OLE Automation 312-316
Server, 313

OLE Custom Control, *See* OCX

OLE Registry, 327

Online Help, *See* Help

OOP, 77

Open common dialog, 291

Open Project, 95, 106

Opening an HTML file, 336

Operator precedence, 18-20

Operators, 16

Option buttons, 288-290

Option tabs, *See* Tabbed Dialog control

Or, 354

Organizing information, *See* TreeView control

Origin of bug, 212-213

Output property, 298

Outputting, *See* Printing

P

Paint event handler, 135-136

Palette, color, *See* Color palette common dialog

Palette, *See* Toolbox

Paradox file format, 218

Parentheses, 20-21

  Counting, 20-21

Pascal, 106

Passing arguments, *See* Arguments, Passing

Paste, files, 276

Pasting controls, 245

Path list, 290

PathListBox, 288, 290-291

Pattern search comparison, 264-265

Pattern, search, 264

Pen mode, *See* DrawMode property

Pi value, 183

Picture property, 180, 291

Pixel, 364

Pixel, *See* PSet command

Pixels, menu items, 114-115

Pixels, *See* ScaleMode property

Placing the Clock on a form, 165-167

Planning a database, 223-224

Planning an application, *See* User Interface design

Point method, 68, 364

Polyline API command, 317-318

Pop-up menus, *See* Menus, Pop-up

PopupMenu command, 121

PortOpen property, 297

Precedence, *See* Operator precedence

Preference tabs, *See* Tabbed Dialog control

Preliminary design, 207

Primary key, 228

Print and Print Setup dialogs, 269

Print command, 9-15, 40-45, 96, 270-272, 350

Print command, alternate, 176

Print common dialog, 291, 294

Print formatting, 11-12

Print Setup common dialog, 291, 294

Print, Format, *See* Format command

Printer object, 147-149, 270-272

Printer routines, *See* Windows API

Printing a database, 269-273

Printing, the Sketch drawing, 147-149

Private keyword, 56, 83, 128, 131-133, 192

Procedure

  Function, *See* Function

Procedures, 55

Process flow, 205-206

Program Testing, *See* Testing, Alpha and Beta

Program, 24

Program, installation, *See* Installation, Disks

Programming environment, *See* IDE

Programming, 4

Progress bars, 205

ProgressBar control, 305-306, *See* Windows Common Controls

PROJ folder, 276

Project window, 25

Project window, 361

Project, 25

Project, 361

Project, opening, 95

Properties window shortcuts, 242

Properties window, 91, 361

Properties, 66-68

Properties, Alphabetic or Categorized, 238

Property, 362

Prototype, *See* Pseudocode

Prototyping a form or screen, 210-211

Prototyping an application, 203

PSet command, 102, 138, 146

Pseudocode, 190-191, 362

Public keyword, 56, 83, 128, 131-133, 278-279, 327

Q

Quotient, 17

R

Random access, 362

RandomFill property, 295

Readme.txt, install, 311

Recent tab, 106, 277

Records, 219

Recordset object, 250, 257, 266, 271-272, 283-284

RecordSource property, 239, 267-269, 300

Redesign, 213

Redim command, 358

Redrawing forms, 135-140

Reference, passing, *See* Arguments, Passing

Referencing methods and properties, 66

Referencing objects, *See* Set command

Refresh database view, 268

Registry, OLE, *See* OLE Registry

REM, *See* Comments

Remainder, 17, 47

Remarks, *See* Comments

RemoveItem method, 76, 246, 253

Removing a form, 237

Resizing a control, 28, 163

Resources, *See* User groups

Reusable component, 67, 162

RGB command, 184-185

RichTextBox control, 302-303

Right mouse button, 134

Right$ command, 59

Right-click, Visual Data Manager, 229

Rounding, numbers, 52

Row and column data display, *See* Grid control

Row in database, *See* Record

RowCount property, 295

Rows method, 301

Royalties, *See* ActiveX controls

RTrim$ command, 59

Run command, 37

Run mode, 8, 355, 362

Run time, 362, *See* Run mode

Running a program, 4

S

Save Before Run, 248

Save common dialog, 291

Save option, Clock control, 279

Save Project, 91

Save Project, button.vbp, 31, 36

Saving Project, Clock, 164

Save Project, Sketch, 94

Saving lines in an array, 125-153

Saving the installation template, *See* Template, install

Saving the project automatically, 248

Scale command, 181-182

ScaleHeight command, 197

ScaleLeft command, 197

ScaleMode property, 36

ScaleTop command, 197

ScaleWidth command, 197

Scientific notation, 54

Scope of variables, *See* Variable scope

Screen object, 266, 313

Screen space, maximizing, *See* Tabbed Dialog control

Searching a database, 258-267

Searching criteria, 265

Searching, object model, 316

Second command, 175,182

Security, ActiveX, 336

Seek command, 229

SelBold property, 303

Select Case command, 103

SELECT SQL clause, 267

Selecting an event, *See* Event selection

Self-contained, 64

SelFontName property, 303

SelFontSize property, 303

Self-taught programmers, 201

SelItalic property, 303

SelLength method, 263

Selling objects, *See* Object, Market for

SelStart method, 263

Semicolon, 12

SendKeys command, 252-253

Set command, 71, 77

SetFocus method, 303

Setting breakpoints, *See* Debugging

Setting the application icon, 179-180

Setting the DrawMode, *See* DrawMode property

Settings property, 297

Setup Wizard, *See* Installation, Disks

Setup

Visual Basic, 2

Setup.EXE, 312

Shift property, 88

Shipping your program, *See* Installation, Disks

Show method, 260

ShowColor method, 292

ShowFont method, 293

ShowHelp method, 293

Showing

Form,

Immediate window, 4

ShowLegend property, 295

ShowOpen method, 293

ShowPrinter method, 270, 272-273, 294

Sin command, 183, 193, 195, 197

Sine, *See* Sin command

Single, *See* Data Types

Size property, 35

Sizing a control, 163

Sketch drawing, printing, 147-149

Sketch program, building, 85-86

Sketch program, code, 151-153

Sketch, saving a drawing, 125-153

Sketch, standalone EXE, 150

Slider control, *See* Windows Common Controls

Software design, 200-203

Drawing a screen, 210-211

Feature list, 207-209

Sorting a database, 267-269

Sorting, database, *See* Indexes

Source property, 284

Space, 12

Speaker, *See* Beep command

Specifications, detailed, 201

Spreadsheet data view, *See* Grid control

Spreadsheet, blank, 328

SQL, 267-268

Standalone application, *See* Installation, Disks

Standalone application, Sketch, 150

Standalone program, 24

Standard EXE, 3

Standards, time, 169

Start button, 32

Start, menu option, 5

Starting Visual Basic, 2

Startup object property, 237

Statement, 4, 356, 359, 363

Status, program, 205

Statusbar control, *See* Windows Common Controls

Step Into command, 349

Stepping into code, 363, *See* Debugging

Stepwise refinement, 126

Stop command, 37

Storing numbers and characters, *See* Variables

Str command, 59, 284

String command, 129

Strings, 44-46

Strings, *See* Data Types, Strings

Structured Query Language, *See* SQL

Structures, variable, *See* Type command

Styles, fonts, *See* RichTextBox control

Sub keyword, 56-58

Subroutine, 55, *See* Procedure

Subroutine-level variables, 133

SWSetup folder, 310, 338-339

Syntax, 11

System clock, reading, 168-169

T

Tab function, 21

Tab key, indenting, 89

Tab key, *See* Focus

Tab order, 243-244, *See* Process flow

Tab stops, 21

Tabbed Dialog control, 303-304

TabIndex property, 243-244, 260

TableDef object, 221

TableDefs collection, 221

Tables, 219

TabStop property, 254

TabStrip control, *See* Windows Common Controls

Telecommunications, *See* Comm control

Telephone, modem, *See* Comm control

Template, install, 312

Testing, Alpha and Beta, 211-213

Text property, 284

Time functions, 174-178

Time$ function, 168-169

Timer command, 298

Timer control, 169-173

  Setting, 171-173

Timer control, 297

Timer event handler, 169

Timer interval, 173

Timer updates of variable, 279

TimeSerial command, 196

TimeValue command, 196

Toolbar control, *See* Windows Common Controls

Toolbars, submenu, Excel, 328

Toolbox, 364

Toolbox, Excel, *See* Control Toolbox, Excel

Toolbox, using, 170

Top property, 242

ToPage property, 270

Tracking program development, 201

Transactions property, 220

TreeView control, 306-307, *See* Windows Common Controls

Trigonometric functions, 197

Trigonometry, for clock hands, 181-183

True command, 354, 356, 364

True, 95-100

Trusted controls, 336

Twip, 36, 364

Type command, 364

Type mismatch error, 48

Types, variables, *See* Variables, types

Typing

  Into the Immediate window, 6

  Programs, 13-16

U

UCase$ command, 59

Unique field values, 228

UniqueID field, 226,230, 235

Unload command, 252

Unload command, 263

Updatable property, 220

Update method, 248

Update method, 283

Usenet news, 343-344

User Control icon, 162

User groups, 343-344

User interface design, 202-215

User interface, progress, 205

User interface, progress, *See* ProgressBar control

User testing, *See* Beta testing

User-defined Type, *See* Type command

V

Val command, 59

Valid variables, 60

Value property, 306

Value property, Option control, 289

Values, 364

Variable array, *See* Array

Variable scope, 132-133

Variable structures, *See* Type command

Variable values, 44-51

Variable, naming, 43-44

Variables, 39, 364

Variables, array, *See* Array variables

Variables, Types, 47-51

Variables, watching, *See* Debugging

VB Script, 325

VB Script, Web site, 339

VBA Editor, 332

VBA, 313

VBP (Visual Basic Project), 31, *See* Project

VBRUN500.DLL, 338

VBX, 324, 345

Vendors, control, 342

VGA, 358

View menu, 5

Visible objects, 65

Visible property, 122, 299

Visual Basic Add-ons, 78

Visual Basic Extension (VBX), *See* VBX

Visual Basic FAQ, 339

Visual Basic for Applications, *See* VBA

Visual Basic Web site, 339

Visual Basic

Boot screen, 3

Installation, 2

Program group, 2

Setup, 2

Visual controls, *See* ActiveX controls

Visual Data Manager, 218, 224-230, 234

W

Watch Type option, 352

Watch Window, 350-352

Watches, variable, *See* Debugging

Web browsers, *See* Browsers, web

Weekday command, 197

Where SQL clause, 265

Width property, 242

Wildcard SQL keyword, 264, 267-268

Win32API.txt, 318, 319

Window, 3

Code window, 355

Project window, 361

Properties window, 361

Window, Project, 25

Windows 3.1, 345

Windows 95 controls, , *See* Windows Common Controls

Windows 95, NT, 345

Windows API, 316

Windows Common Controls, 304-307

Windows Explorer, 276, *See* TreeView control

Windows for Workgroups, 345

Windows functions, *See* DLL

Wizard, database form creator, *See* Data Form Designer

Wizard, install, *See* Installation

Word Processor, mini, *See* RichTextBox control

Workbooks, Excel, 314

Wrapper, *See* Object wrapper

X

X property, 88

Xor, 185, 354

Y

Y property, 88

Year command, 197

About This Disk

The disk included with this book contains all of the source code and project files for all of the examples. The code is well documented with Visual Basic comments. All of the examples use the same project, control, and folder names as those shown in the book.

Included on this disk:

- Clock user control
- Address Book application and accompanying database
- Clock shared control
- Chapter 14 ActiveX control examples
- Debug project
- Sketch application
- Microsoft Excel OLE Automation project and spreadsheet

All of the code can be loaded using Visual Basic 5.0. The folder should be copied into the Visual Basic folder on your C: drive. The path of the VB application should be:

```
C:\Program Files\DevStudio\VB
```

To install the examples, simply drag the Proj folder on the disk into the VB folder on your hard disk.

For more resource information on the book and additional free sample source code, check out the teach yourself Visual Basic Web site at:

```
www.coherentdata.com/tyvb
```

Be sure to check the README.TXT file on the disk for your official registration number to access the special TYVB owner's section on the Web site.